WITHDRAWN

D1376972

The Culture of Teenage Mothers

THE CULTURE OF TEENAGE MOTHERS

Joanna Gregson

SUNY PRESS

Cover design by Zachary Pfriem

Published by State University of New York Press, Albany

© 2009 State University of New York

For information, contact State University of New York Press, Albany, NY
www.sunypress.edu

Production by Diane Ganeles
Marketing by Fran Keneston

Library of Congress Cataloging-in-Publication Data

Gregson, Joanna, 1971-
  The culture of teenage mothers / Joanna Gregson.
    p. cm.
  Includes bibliographical references and index.
  ISBN 978-1-4384-2885-7 (hbk. : alk. paper)
    1. Teenage mothers—United States. I. Title.
  HQ759.4.G745 2009
  306.874'320973—dc22

                                            2009005419

10 9 8 7 6 5 4 3 2 1

This book is dedicated to Patti and Peter Adler, for everything.

CONTENTS

Acknowledgments ix

ONE Introduction 1

TWO Methods and Setting 15

THREE Getting Pregnant 39

FOUR Keeping the Baby 57

FIVE Competitive Parenting 75

SIX Teen Mothers' Conceptions of Fatherhood 89

SEVEN Defining, Excusing, and Justifying Deviance:
Teen Mothers' Accounts for Statutory Rape 105

EIGHT The Stigma of Teenage Parenting 127

NINE Transformed Selves, Transformed Relationships:
The Consequences of Teenage Parenting 139

TEN Conclusion 159

References 177

Index 191

Acknowledgments

I discovered sociology the way most undergraduates do: I took an introductory-level course to fulfill a university requirement and quickly abandoned my previous plans to study business. I am forever grateful to my professors at Western Washington University for showing me the light. John Richardson, Kris Bulcroft, Rick Bulcroft, Dianne Carmody, and especially Carl Simpson were key figures in my formative years as a budding sociologist.

At the University of Colorado, I was fortunate once again to be surrounded by encouraging professors who gave me the tools I needed to carry out this research. Many thanks to Dan Cress (who had something logical and insightful to say about every phase of my writing and research), Kirk Williams, Janet Jacobs, Joanne Belknap, and Jim Downton.

My graduate school peers held me accountable and kept me laughing while I carried out this research. I am especially grateful for the friendship of Jen Lois, Alice Fothergill, Dana Johnson, and Jen Owen Walsh. We read each other's papers, held regular meetings to discuss our respective research projects and prepare for qualifying exams, and somehow made time to go running, play tennis, and watch reruns of *90210*. In my post-graduate school years, I have been fortunate to become even closer with the rest of the "Adlerians," especially Katy Irwin, Adina Nack, and Lori Peek.

The people I have been privileged to know at Pacific Lutheran University make it a pleasure to come to work every day. I am especially grateful for the support of my colleagues in sociology—Arturo Biblarz, Teresa Ciabattari, Dick Jobst, Anna Leon-Guerrero, Kate Luther, Kay

McDade, Dan Renfrow, and Alicia Suarez—and for the former students whose energy and inquisitiveness continue to inspire me: Aislinn Addington, Allison Hicks, Corrie Hulse, Kari Keller, Jen Shutt Walsh, and Kristian Wiles.

My deepest gratitude also goes to Kristen Allen-Bentsen, for coming up with words when I was stumped and encouragement when I hit a wall. I thank Chris Higginson and the Higginson family for their support, companionship, and good humor throughout my college and graduate school years.

I am incredibly lucky to have the support of my family in all that I do. My mom, Janell Gregson, instilled in me an appreciation for research and for reading, and my dad, John Gregson, sincerely believes that I have the potential to do anything I set my mind to. My siblings and siblings-in-law, John and Alyssa Gregson and Jill and Paul Zawatski, keep me grounded, amused, and well fed, and I am deeply grateful for their support. My cats, Emma and Daniel, have provided the kind of companionship only animal lovers understand; I can't imagine completing this book without one (or both) of them on my lap.

To the young women at the Teen Center, whose stories are at the heart of this book, I am forever in your debt. Your honesty and candor made this research possible, and your friendship made it that much more meaningful. I am grateful, too, for the generosity shown to me by the staff at the Teen Center; thank you for letting me into the center, and for letting me be the "least adult" person in the room.

And I owe a huge debt of gratitude to the folks at SUNY Press who brought this project to fruition. My editor, Nancy Ellegate, should earn a medal for the patience she demonstrated during this process. Senior production editor Diane Ganeles was an efficient and a kind taskmaster, and copy editor Michele Lansing found typos that dozens of other pairs of eyes had missed.

Most of all, I am grateful for the unwavering support, wisdom, and encouragement of Patti and Peter Adler, my graduate school mentors, role models, and lifelong friends. It was Patti who jokingly suggested that I study adolescents because of my youthful appearance, and it was she who read—and critiqued—every word I wrote. I benefited tremendously from the "two-for-one" combo of Patti and Peter Adler. They not only taught me about ethnographic methods, they also taught me about being a professional sociologist and a grown-up woman. I lovingly dedicate this book to them.

Portions of earlier versions of chapters 1, 2, 5, and 10 have appeared as Joanna Gregson Higginson. 1998. "Competitive Parenting: The Culture of Teenage Mothers." *Journal of Marriage and the Family* 60:

135–49. I am grateful to Blackwell Publishing for granting State University of New York (SUNY) Press permission to use this material. Portions of chapters 1, 7, and 10 have appeared as Joanna Gregson Higginson. 2001. "Defining, Excusing, and Justifying Deviance: Teen Mothers' Accounts for Statutory Rape." *Symbolic Interaction* 22(1): 25–44. I am grateful to University of California Press for granting SUNY Press permission to use this material.

ONE

INTRODUCTION

In the 1990s, pregnancy rates and birthrates among American teenagers declined significantly, a trend that continued through 2005, when birthrates for teens began to climb again (Henshaw 1998; Santelli et al. 2004; Hamilton, Martin, and Ventura 2007). While birthrates have, for the most part, declined over the past few decades, rates of abortion and adoption for teens also dropped (Barth 1987; Henshaw 1997; Jones et al. 2008). What this means is that while fewer teenagers became pregnant in the 1990s and early 2000s, those who did get pregnant were increasingly likely to carry the child to term and raise it themselves (Henshaw 1998; Jones et al. 2008). Indeed, research suggests that over 90 percent of adolescents in the United States who give birth keep their children (Chandra et al. 1999).

Teenage pregnancy and childbearing are at the forefront of our collective consciousness, with adolescent women and their sexuality being objects of national concern (Nathanson 1991). Luker (1996) described Americans as being convinced that we are experiencing an "epidemic" of teenage pregnancy, despite data revealing an opposite trend. Writing in the early 1990s, Nathanson (1991) remarked that the "Newspaper headlines, television screens, and magazine covers that bombard us with evidence of how frequently these norms [of sex before marriage and childbearing before adulthood] are violated" have given this problem "remarkable staying-power" (4–5). References to teenage parenting abound in mainstream culture ten years later, including the blockbuster film *Juno*, the well-publicized pregnancy of teenage celebrity Jamie-Lynn Spears, and the national furor over Republican vice-presidential candidate Sarah Palin's pregnant adolescent daughter. Meanwhile, public opinion polls show that the majority of Americans think something should be done about this behavior, that it is, in short, a social problem (Luker 1996; Albert 2007; Monmouth University/Gannett New Jersey Poll 2008). As the numbers creep upward again, it seems likely that the alarm bells will continue to sound.

However, as Adams, Adams-Taylor, and Pittman (1989) suggested in the late 1980s, "Adolescent pregnancy is *not* an epidemic and our [public] concern is not due to the size of the problem" (223, emphasis in original). Instead, teenage pregnancy and parenting have been construed as social problems because of the negative consequences we have come to associate with early childbearing. Furstenberg (1991) noted that, like other social problems, our interest and concern over teenage parenting have waxed and waned as the societal view of teenage pregnancy has shifted from individual pathology to social illness.

In recent years, researchers have debated whether teenage parenting is really the social problem it has been made out to be—that is, whether the negative outcomes discussed with such alarm even exist. Reflecting on his longitudinal research on teenage mothers—a project spanning more than forty years—Furstenberg (2007b) noted that "the consequences of early childbearing are not as great as most of us initially thought," and that "many apparent consequences of early childbearing are really due to . . . preexisting differences" (79). Nevertheless, the framing of teenage pregnancy and parenthood as social problems continues, with the problems being couched in one of three domains: costs to teenage mothers, costs to the children of teenage mothers, and costs to the greater society.

TEEN PREGNANCY AS A SOCIAL PROBLEM

Perhaps the most intensely contested area among contemporary researchers is the extent of the direct costs incurred by teenage mothers, themselves. Much of the scholarship in this area has focused on the decreased life chances that come with an adolescent birth. For example, a number of researchers have focused on the relationship between early childbearing and educational attainment, exploring whether having a child cuts short a teen parent's schooling. Given their age as adolescents, a time when one would expect them to be in school, and given the important influence of education in determining future economic status and employment opportunities, examining the effect that child rearing has on schooling makes intuitive sense. Early research on this question suggested that adolescent childbearing results in a truncated high school education for the teenage mother (Hofferth and Moore 1979; Marini 1984), as have several studies of teen parents born in the 1950s and 1960s (Astone and Upchurch 1994; Hoffman, Foster, and Furstenberg 1993). Other studies, especially those using more recent generations of teen parents, claim that adolescents who become pregnant while still enrolled in school earn diplomas at the same rate as their peers without children (Upchurch and McCarthy 1990). Numerous studies have revealed that a large proportion of teenage mothers get pregnant after dropping out of school (see, e.g., Fergusson and Woodward 2000; Manlove 1998; Upchurch and McCarthy 1990). However, those teens who drop out and then become pregnant are not as likely to complete their high school education (Rindfuss, Bumpass, and St. John 1980; Upchurch and McCarthy 1990). One explanation for this discrepancy is that earlier generations of teenage parents did not have the opportunity to remain in school, for it was not until the early 1970s that Title IX legislation first took effect, prohibiting schools from barring pregnant and parenting teens (Luker 1996). Thus early studies may not accurately reflect today's adolescent parents, who not only have the legal right to remain in school, but who also benefit from the school-based programs that have come about in an effort to assist parenting teens in graduating. At the same time that programs such as Title IX have made completion of high school more accessible for teenage mothers, the most current cohorts of teenage mothers are constrained in their ability to attain postsecondary education by an altogether different public policy: the shift from Aid to Temporary Families with Children (AFDC) to Temporary Aid to Needy Families (TANF) has meant that teen mothers who have graduated high school must be employed at least twenty hours to receive public assistance, a contingency that makes enrollment in college difficult (Hofferth, Reid, and Mott 2001).

The tremendous concern with teenage parents' ability to complete school is rooted in the assumption that insufficient schooling will lead to restricted employment opportunities and, consequently, poverty. In their follow-up study of adolescent mothers, Furstenberg, Brooks-Gunn, and Morgan (1987a) found that adolescent motherhood does not guarantee long-term welfare dependency. Indeed, the majority of participants in their study were employed and economically self-sufficient. Nevertheless, in Teti and Lamb's (1989) comparison of teenage and mature mothers, teenage mothers were found to experience the poorest socioeconomic outcomes. Luker (1996) added a new twist to this controversy, arguing that adolescent pregnancy is a symptom rather than a cause of poverty. She says, "Many young mothers would be poor (and would have children who grew up to be poor) no matter how old they were when they gave birth" (111), because the social and economic structures with which they are confronted would be the same regardless of their age. Thus blocked opportunities because of race, class, or gender would not disappear simply because a teenage woman aged; she would encounter the same obstacles as an adult. Put another way, Jaffee (2002) argues that adolescent parenting only exacerbates inequalities that already exist.

The costs for the children of teenage parents are also perceived as negative consequences of teenage parenting. Although some researchers have gone to great lengths to explain that it is not teen parents' age that leads to negative outcomes for their children but, rather, the disadvantaged backgrounds from which they come (Luker 1996; Nathanson 1991; SmithBattle 2007), the abundance of studies remarking on these negative consequences cannot be ignored. The children of teenage parents have been reported to be more likely than other children to die as infants (Geronimous 1987), have low birth weight (Chedraui 2008), grow up in poverty (Geronimous and Korenman 1992), get into trouble at school, drop out of school (Dangal 2006; Furstenberg, Brooks-Gunn, and Morgan 1987a), be overweight or obese (Lemay et al. 2008), become criminals if they are boys, and become adolescent parents themselves if they are girls (Maynard 1996). At minimum, the fact that these topics continue to be studied reveals the role researchers play in constructing a phenomenon as a social problem.

A final category of negative outcomes resulting from teenage childbearing relates to social costs. The dollar amounts spent on teenage pregnancy and parenting are staggering. It has been estimated that between 1991 and 2004, teenage childbearing cost U.S. taxpayers over $161 billion (Hoffman 2006). Teen mothers account for a large proportion of recipients of some government programs; for example, in the 1980s, 59 percent of women receiving AFDC payments were teenagers when they gave birth to their first child (Moore 1990), and, historically, about 50 percent of adult welfare recipients have been teenage parents (Kisker, Eliason, Maynard, Rangarajan, and Boller 1998).

A social cost that has only recently been linked to the teenage pregnancy problem is the exploitation of young women by older men in the form of statutory rape. It is estimated that over 60 percent of the fathers of babies born to teenage mothers are not teenagers themselves but adult men (Oberman 1994; Phoenix 1991). People concerned with reducing the fiscal costs of teenage pregnancy have often been concerned with the role of the fathers (or absent fathers) and their financial contributions to their offspring (Maynard 1996). Studies revealing the relatively older age of the fathers are appealing because they essentially criminalize the vast majority of teenage pregnancies. Because they see criminalization as a deterrent to future teenage pregnancies, some groups have argued that the laws should be enforced with more regularity (Lauer 1981; Odem 1995). Others want the laws to be enforced not because of their potential to deter teenage pregnancy or reduce taxpayer burden but because of what they perceive to be the tremendous social costs of statutory rape: the victimization and exploitation of young women by older men (Lauer 1981; Odem 1995). In this way, the relationships from which many teenage pregnancies result have also been cast as problematic.

Of course, for some groups, one of the most significant social costs of teenage parenthood is a perceived erosion of public morality. As Rhode (1993–1994) argues in her work tracing the history of public policy and teenage pregnancy, the reason many conservative groups, especially, define teenage pregnancy and parenthood as social problems is because their presence is perceived to reflect "cultural permissiveness, a decline in parental authority, and a weakening of community sanctions against illegitimacy" (651). The public outcry over adolescent pregnancy reflects patriarchal control over women's sexuality, and the fact that teenage pregnancy contradicts ideologies of childhood sexual innocence and marriage-only sexual activity (Nathanson 1991).

A final theme contributing to the idea that teenage parenthood is a social problem is the idea that motherhood for all marginalized groups has been defined by society as problematic. Our standards for "good" mothering are based on white, heterosexual, middle-class norms (Garcia-Coll, Surrey, and Weingarten 1998). Women who are "living on welfare, divorced or unmarried, aged under 20, lesbian, drug-users, or who have committed criminal offenses are all marginalized in relation to the category of 'good mother'" (Rolfe 2008, 300). The fact that teenage mothers are disproportionately likely to be black, Latina, or American Indian (Hamilton et al. 2007), poor (Jaffee 2002), and unmarried (Martin et al. 2007) makes teenage mothers socially marginalized to begin with, before age of entry into parenthood is even considered (Rolfe 2008). An affiliation with any of these groups, let alone all of them, is marginalizing.

Taken together, the popular and scholarly focus on teenage parenting as a social problem leaves little doubt about the stigma associated with teenage parenting. Teen mothers are, as Kaplan (1997) asserts, marked as deviant. The very language we use to describe this phenomenon—from distinguishing between "teen mothers" and other (over age twenty) mothers, to using phrases such as "babies having babies"—perpetuates the idea that childbearing before age twenty is nonnormative (Fields 2005). But we know little about how teen mothers experience the deviant label—whether they notice it, and how it affects their parenting, their self-concept, their relations with significant others, or even their decisions to become parents in the first place.

Responses to the Problem

Given the negative tone of the public's conception of teenage pregnancy and parenting, it is not surprising that a number of intervention programs have been introduced to ameliorate the costs and consequences of what has been construed as a significant social problem. According to Roosa (1991), the 1980s witnessed a tremendous growth in the number of federal government, local government, private foundation, community hospital, and school district funded programs designed to prevent adolescent pregnancy and reduce the negative consequences of teenage parenting. The solutions that have been introduced to prevent teenage pregnancy range from financial incentives paid to young women for not becoming pregnant while they are still of school age to mentorship programs designed to give young women role models in education and industry.

Another group of programs has been designed to prevent the negative outcomes associated with early childbearing. These include mentorship programs for pregnant and parenting teens, wherein teens are paired with positive parenting role models (Wharton 1991) and school-based teenage parenting programs. School-based programs are by far the most common type of intervention program, with most large school districts and many smaller districts offering teenage parents some combination of counseling, parenting classes, and, in some cases, child care (Roosa 1986). These programs aim to reduce subsequent pregnancies, train young mothers in parenting and life skills, and, most importantly, help young mothers complete their high school educations (Roosa 1991).

Studies of school-based intervention programs have almost always focused on program evaluation (Hoyt and Broom 2002). Thus if the goal of the program was to improve graduation rates for teenage mothers, the number of dropouts and graduates were compared (see, e.g., Sung and Rothrock 1980; Kisker et al. 1998). Other studies have evaluated whether programs have successfully taught young mothers to be economically self-sufficient (see, e.g., Polit 1989; Kisker et al. 1998; Sangalang 2006), or whether they have influenced the mother's attitudes about parenthood and knowledge of human reproduction (Roosa 1986). Taken together, these quantitative studies have yielded fairly positive results with respect to the influence of school-based programs. Evaluative studies have revealed that mothers who attend school-based programs have higher average educational levels than teen mothers who do not participate in such programs and greater knowledge regarding human reproduction. At the same time, however, school-based programs have been found to have little long-term impact on parental attitudes or children's development (Roosa 1986).

Qualitative research with teenage mothers involved in intervention programs has also been conducted, although the focus has not been on evaluation as much as on exploring the dynamics at play within the program. For example, Wharton (1991) focused on the relationships between teenage mothers and volunteers in a program designed to prevent child abuse, Kelly (1998) studied the teachers at a high school with a school-based teenage parenting program, and Horowitz (1995) examined the relationships between program staff and teenage mothers participating in a program for the teens to earn their general equivalency diplomas (GEDs). Although these studies were based in adolescent parenting settings, both had as their focal point the adults who interacted with the teen mothers. Wharton (1991) examined the characteristics of adult volunteers who were able to forge the most intimate relationships with teenage mothers, Kelly (1998) examined the discourse used by teachers to describe teenage parenting, and Horowitz (1995) analyzed whether staff members who interacted with teen mothers as "arbiters" or "mediators" were considered by the young women to be better mentors. The qualitative piece to the puzzle that is still missing is an examination into the lives of the young mothers enrolled in a school-based program. In short, the question that needs to be addressed is how participation in a child-rearing culture affects teen mothers' parenting—whether the culture buffers them from the stigma of the larger society, shapes their identities, or influences their relationships with significant others, including their children.

THE CULTURE OF TEEN PARENTING

Although the question of how teen parenting affects schooling has received a great deal of attention in the quantitative tradition, the question of how schooling affects adolescent parenting has not been addressed in either qualitative or quantitative studies. The question of whether being in school and surrounded by peers (both parenting and nonparenting) influences the values, beliefs, practices, and identities of teenage mothers has not been answered. Large-scale quantitative studies are useful in identifying trends facing a large population of teen mothers and their children, but in-depth, smaller-scale studies are necessary to understand how adolescent mothers experience and perceive the world. Furstenberg, Brooks-Gunn, and Morgan (1987b) noted that teen mothers feel proud of the job they are doing as parents and put a tremendous amount of energy into their parenting, but we know little about what good parenting means to adolescents, or what their motivation is for practicing it. These questions lend themselves to qualitative methodology—becoming a part of the everyday lives of teen parents to understand their perceptions and experiences. Specifically, I am interested in what constitutes good parenting to teen mothers, how these mothers' beliefs about parenting may have been shaped by the pervasive negative public sentiment toward teenage parenthood, how they view the consequences of early parenting for themselves and their children, what they think about the contributions of their babies' fathers, and how all of these conceptions are influenced by participation in the child-rearing culture of a school-based parenting program. Above all, I am interested in how stigma affects young women's experiences as mothers in each of these areas.

Culture will serve as a conceptual framework throughout this book. I rely on Swidler's (1986) conceptualization of the term, defining culture as "symbolic vehicles of meaning" (273). Swidler's perspective allows for culture to be seen as a "'toolkit' of symbols, stories, rituals, and worldviews, which people may use in varying configuration to solve different kinds of problems" (1986, 273). In this case, the problems are the challenges presented by teenage motherhood; the toolkit provides a host of possible ideas and actions the teens can draw upon as they navigate their way through these challenges.

The theoretical perspective that best addresses these questions of culture is symbolic interactionism. Herbert Blumer, one of the seminal thinkers in this tradition, posited the following as the fundamental assertions of symbolic interactionist theories: "that human beings act toward things on the basis of the meanings that the things have for them . . . and that the meaning of such things is derived from, or arises out of, the social interaction that one has with one's fellows" (1969, 2). According to Blumer and other symbolic interactionists, it is through interaction with other people that we learn what meanings have been assigned to other objects—including ourselves.

The symbolic interaction perspective is ideally suited for an inquiry into the shared culture of teenage mothers. This framework lays the foundation for a study that makes its focus the meanings that belong to setting members and the ways in which these meanings are transmitted. For example, the way in which young women describe their paths to motherhood and their feelings about pregnancy resolution options conveys a great deal about the way their culture defines motherhood, pregnancy, abortion, and adoption. These definitions—these meanings—

have profound implications for how the teens chose to resolve their pregnancies and how they learned to view themselves as a result.

The methodological implications of this theoretical framework are straightforward: to study the meanings of a social world, the researcher must gain an intimate familiarity with that world. As Blumer (1969) says:

> To study [human beings] intelligently, one has to know these worlds, and to know these worlds, one has to examine them closely. No theorizing, however ingenious, and no observance of scientific protocol, however meticulous, are substitutes for developing a familiarity with what is actually going on in the sphere of life under study. (38–39)

These are the principles that guided my research questions and my methods for studying the culture of teen parenting.

STUDYING THE TEEN CENTER

I collected data during a four-year participant-observation study of the Teen Center, a schoolbased teenage parenting program located inside Lakeside High School (pseudonyms used throughout). As a staff member, intern, mentor, and friend, I interacted with the Teen Center participants in a variety of different contexts, both inside the school setting and out. To understand their culture, I became a part of their world. The next chapter describes in detail the different roles I assumed in the setting, the nature of my relationship with setting members, my techniques for gathering data, and the unique problems that arose during my research.

The Teen Center at Lakeside High School served pregnant and parenting teens from the local school district's junior and senior high schools. Lakeside is located in a university town, fewer than five miles away from a major research university. The surrounding community is well educated (more than one-fourth of the city's residents hold graduate degrees), affluent, and predominantly white (nearly 90 percent). The Teen Center had been in existence for fifteen years when I began my research, and in that time had served over 500 teens. Through the center, the young parents (mothers and fathers) receive free child care during the school day, busing to and from school, the opportunity to take special classes on parenting and child development, and daily access to both a nurse and a social worker. The Teen Center's location inside Lakeside High School allowed the teen parents to complete their high school classes and spend time with their children by earning class credit for volunteering in the center's nurseries.

The Teen Center served between forty-five and sixty young parents and their children at a time. At the beginning of this study, there were fifty teen mothers and three teen fathers participating in the program, ranging from age fourteen to twenty-one and from grades 8–12. The teen parents' racial and ethnic backgrounds closely paralleled the composition of the school district itself. The majority of teen parents at the center were white, but there were eight Latinas, two African Americans, and one Asian American. Of the teen fathers participating in the program, two were white, and one was Chicano. This predominantly white sample of teen mothers does not reflect the image most Americans have of teenage mothers (Furstenberg 2007a), but it does resemble the reality. Although black and Hispanic teens have children at a disproportionately higher rate than teens from other racial backgrounds, white teens account for the largest percentage of adolescent mothers (Hamilton, Martin, and Ventura 2007).

The teens were similar to one another with respect to their socioeconomic backgrounds; the majority came from lower-middle or working-class families. The center boasts a graduation rate (including GED completion) of 88 percent, which is substantially higher than the national average of around 54 percent for teen parents (Hofferth, Reid, and Mott 2001; Hoffman, Foster, and Furstenberg 1993; Upchurch and McCarthy 1990). Like other teen mothers across the country, many of the adolescent parents at the center became pregnant *after* dropping out of school (Fergusson and Woodward 2000; Manlove 1998; Upchurch and McCarthy 1990); when they eventually returned to school, it was to the Teen Center.

PORTRAITS OF TEEN CENTER MOTHERS

The teenage mothers whose lives I became a part of entered the Teen Center through different paths and at various points in their lives. Some of the young women joined the center when they were pregnant at the recommendation of their social service caseworkers. An example of this type of teen is Sunshine, a white, seventeen-year-old girl who grew up in the South. Her parents divorced when she and her brother were very young, and her father relinquished custody to the mother after she threatened to report his alcoholism to child protective services. Sunshine's grandparents were devout Jehovah's Witness group members, and they expected Sunshine and her younger brother to obey the rules of their religion—attending services five days a week, reading the Bible every day, and associating only with members of the church. When they were not at church, Sunshine and her brother were either studying the Bible, doing chores around the house, or being physically abused. The abuse came without notice and became progressively worse as Sunshine and her brother grew older. To escape the oppressive household, Sunshine turned to her grandfather's secret stash of alcohol. By the time she was in seventh grade, she was showing up to school drunk. When she was sixteen years old, Sunshine's aunt invited her and her brother to move in with her in another state. Sunshine enrolled in a local high school and for the first time in her life found herself with a circle of friends. Old habits die hard, though, and it did not take long for her drinking and pot-smoking habits to land her with a tough crowd at school. She dropped out of school after her junior year in high school to join a group of traveling hippies. Twelve months later, after a year of casual sex with dozens of partners and heavy consumption of drugs and alcohol, Sunshine found herself in Lakeside—homeless, starving, and pregnant. She arrived at the Teen Center five months' pregnant and weighing less than ninety pounds. The birth of her son provided the impetus for yet another major life change: she finished high school and earned a certificate in veterinary assistance at the local community college. The year after she graduated from high school she had a job with a veterinarian, her own apartment, and, most importantly, a son who was the light of her life.

Eighteen-year-old Kristina grew up in the city of Lakeside. Her family was white, upper-middle class, and well known in the community. The youngest child of four, Kristina felt like an outcast in her own family: she was neither academically inclined like her older brother, socially competent like her middle brother, nor deserving of special attention like her mentally challenged sister. A shy girl, Kristina's only friends were the friends her older brothers brought home with them. One of these friends, a sixteen-year-old boy from their neighborhood, became her first boyfriend when she was twelve. After a short courtship, he convinced her that they should have sex, and, if she wanted, to try to have a baby. Kristina was thrilled at the chance to become a mother, something she had looked forward to being since she was a little girl. Thus despite the fact that her boyfriend only wanted to have sex in the context of rape (with objects, with force), Kristina knew that it would be an unpleasant means to a desirable end. She had four miscarriages in the next four years. Her parents had her institutionalized for depression; there, she met Kyle, the man who became her husband. Kristina became pregnant with her new husband's child the day after their wedding, when they were both seventeen. She dropped out of school so she could devote all of her energy toward working and saving for her baby. When her baby was six months old, Kristina returned to school with a new plan: she would graduate from high school and get a scholarship so she could go on to college and become a teacher. Three years later, Kristina was in the process of divorcing Kyle so she could marry her older brother's college roommate. She was also a sophomore in college with a 4.0 grade point average.

Seventeen-year-old Blair was a Latina from a lower-middle-class family. Like many of the Latina members of the Teen Center, her attendance and participation in the program were sporadic. Blair grew up in Texas with her parents and two brothers. She was popular, played sports, and always had a boyfriend. When she was in junior high school, her parents divorced, and she moved to Lakeside with her mother. She had a difficult time adjusting to her new life—being so far away from her father and her old friends was hard, and it was difficult living with her stepfather too. Blair took a job at a fast-food restaurant to occupy some of her now-abundant free time, and there she met John. A sixteen-year-old Latino, John was everything Blair wanted in a boyfriend—he was kind and affectionate, he wanted to get married someday, and he loved children. After dating for six months, Blair and John decided to have a baby. Blair joined the Teen Center when she was newly pregnant, at her mother's behest. She went on maternity leave for two months, then returned with her newborn son. She attended semiregularly for two months, then dropped out of school, telling her friends at the Teen Center that she just wanted to be home with her baby and her fiancé. Two years later, when she was nineteen and her son was two years old, she came back. Blair was no longer wearing her engagement ring—she and John had broken up when the baby was six months old, and they had not seen each other since. This time, she stayed three days. The center had an open-enrollment policy, which meant new members could join whenever they chose, rather than waiting for the beginning of a new semester, and Blair took advantage of this policy. Every two months or so, she and her son came back to the center, met with the program director, and laid out a plan that would enable her to graduate as quickly as possible. A few days later, without fail, Blair would phone in and say she was not coming back. She had no interest in being a student: all she wanted to do was be a mother.

In the chapters that follow, I weave together anecdotes and quotes from Sunshine, Kristina, Blair, and a number of their peers from the Teen Center. Together, their stories paint a picture of young women whose lives have been transformed as a result of their early motherhood. Contrary to the public conception of teenage childbearing as replete with costs, the young women at the Teen Center come to view their early motherhood as the best thing that ever happened to them. I explore the sociodemographic and cultural factors that explain how they came to view motherhood in this way, and I examine how these feelings manifest themselves in their aggressive efforts to defend their decisions to become mothers, the way they parent, and the kinds of relationships they have with their boyfriends.

TWO

METHODS AND SETTING

It is my contention that the clearest and most comprehensive understanding of any social group can be achieved through participation in and observation of group members' daily lives. These are the methods advocated by the qualitative research paradigm, which calls for the study of social life within its natural setting. The primary goal of qualitative research is to uncover the shared meanings and social processes among persons in a social setting, with an emphasis on understanding the world from the point of view of the people being studied (Emerson 1988). To understand what parenting means to teen mothers, to learn how they describe their relationships with their children, boyfriends, and family, and to study how they perceive and manage the stigma cast upon them for being young, unmarried parents, a qualitative approach was necessary. In short, I knew that to understand the world of teen mothers, I had to become a part of it.

The qualitative paradigm maintains that the perception of reality is relative to the groups and settings being studied; these realities are viewed as shared meanings that are not "true" in an absolute sense as much as they are valid for the specific time, place, and situation in which they are observed (Guba and Lincoln 1994). Qualitative methods are designed to tap into these subjective constructions of reality "through interaction between and among investigator and respondents" (Guba and Lincoln 1994, 111). The qualitative researcher seeks to gain an understanding of the people being studied and their social reality by experiencing their world and interacting with setting members in as intimate a manner as possible—through "active, empathetic participation in the rounds and structures of life and meaning of those being studied" (Emerson 1988, 2). Although quantitative methods have been effectively used to gain numerical information about teen mothers at one point in time, longitudinal qualitative methods are best for understanding why things occur over time (Denzin and Lincoln 1994). A qualitative approach is therefore ideal for an exploration into such topics as how the relationship between a teen mother and her baby's father changes over time, how she copes with the competing demands of family and school on a daily basis, and how the transition from pregnant to parenting teen influences her perception of self. I knew that through prolonged, intimate contact a clear portrait of teen mothers' reality would eventually emerge. To achieve this understanding, I became a member of their setting for four years, from 1994 to 1998.

GETTING IN

My entry into the Teen Center and its culture arose through a serendipitous set of circumstances. In the fall of 1994, I enrolled in a graduate seminar on field research. Students were required to find settings they could study for at least the two-year duration of the course, taking into consideration their sociological interests, connections in the nearby community, and personal attributes. My interests in sociology were deviance, criminology, and family. I was also interested in adolescence, and since I was only twenty-three at the time—and was regularly mistaken for a teenager because of my youthful appearance—I thought an adolescent setting where I could focus on deviance and family issues would be ideal. Because I had no local connections to adolescent groups, I began to phone local middle schools with the hope that a friendly teacher or two might let me sit in on their classes; I envisioned observing students in the classroom and chatting with them at lunch and between classes. My requests to do research were unceremoniously denied at all of the middle schools and most of the high schools I called. I soon realized that the word "research" conjured up images of quantitative measures—tests, surveys, and other invasive procedures—that made administrators wary of letting me into their schools. As a last-ditch effort to make this project work, I phoned a local high school and inquired about doing an internship. The vice principal of Lakeside High School immediately invited me in to discuss my interests and goals. Once my foot was in the door, I elaborated on the details of my plan to use my "internship" as a basis for a paper in a research methods course and potential dissertation topic. He soon realized that my methods—basically hanging out with students—

were not only harmless but could also provide the school with some interesting information and much-needed volunteer help. He took me on a tour of the high school, pointing out various cliques of students with whom he thought I might want to spend time (e.g., the kids smoking cigarettes behind the cafeteria). We ended the tour in the basement, where he told me the district's program for pregnant and parenting teens was housed. He introduced me to the program coordinator, a petite white woman in her fifties named Helen, who invited me to volunteer in the program nurseries that afternoon. I was pressed for time, but I told her I would be back.

The next day I returned to Lakeside for a follow-up meeting I had scheduled with the vice principal, only to find he had been called out of the building on an administrative emergency. With nothing else to do at the high school, I wandered down to the Teen Center to see if Helen was still interested in my doing some volunteer work. She sent me to the toddler nursery, where I introduced myself to the two staff members and asked what I might do to help. They were loading up the children to go play in the school gym and asked me to push a stroller. As we were leaving the room, two teens rushed in, dropped their backpacks on the floor, and took a child by the hand to walk up to the gym. Within five minutes of our arrival in the gym, I was approached by one of the teens, fifteen-year-old Michelle, who wanted to talk: her boyfriend was spanking her two-year-old son against her wishes, and she did not know what to do because she did not want to lose him. Her foster parents threatened to kick her out of their home if she did not break up with him, and someone at the grocery store had told her she was too young to be a good parent. I was amazed at how quickly she accepted me as a trustworthy confidante. I was also intrigued by her story and thrilled that I had found myself in a place where I could study family and deviance simultaneously. I volunteered a few more days to make sure the setting was as ideal as it initially seemed. I then approached Helen about the possibility of remaining at the center indefinitely as a setting for my course project and dissertation research. She immediately consented and gave me free rein to set up my own schedule for volunteering in the nurseries.

The center was comprised of two nurseries for infants (from birth to eight months and from eight months to one year) and one for toddlers (over one year). Each nursery was staffed by three paraprofessional child-care employees; these staff members were all white women in their forties or fifties who had backgrounds in nursing, early childhood education, or previous day care experience. In addition to the paid child-care providers, the nurseries were also staffed with several volunteers from the community who came on a rotating schedule during the week, and the teenage parents who came and went throughout the day. There were two classrooms at the center; private offices for the program director, teacher, nurse, and social worker; and a lounge with a kitchenette, tables and chairs, computer workstations, and several couches where teen parents could study, eat lunch, or visit with each other.

I began going to the center three days a week, for at least four hours each day, volunteering in the different nurseries as needed. I soon learned that not all of the teens were as forthcoming in trusting me—or even talking to me—as Michelle was on that first day; in fact, I quickly realized that the burden of initiating and maintaining conversations lay entirely on my shoulders, as the young women viewed me as merely another college student volunteer. Early on, then, I did a lot of observing. I watched the teenage mothers interact with their children, with each other, and with the nursery staff, and I considered how I might present myself to them to better facilitate interaction. I knew I did not want to act like Helen or the nursery staff, because these women had too much authority over the teens and were often regarded as meddlesome; at the same time, I found the existing role of a college student volunteer quite limited, as this often implied that the volunteer was a stuck-up do-gooder who came and went without notice. As I pondered my role options, Helen approached me about the possibility of carrying out a follow-up study of former program participants, something that had never been done in the program's fifteen years of existence. I realized a project of that magnitude—attempting to reach 400 former participants by mail and phone in a three-month period—would justify my spending more time at the center, would give me an excuse for initiating conversations with the teens (Helen wanted me to practice the instrument on them), and would provide me with the unique role for which I was searching. From that moment on, I became known as the center's resident researcher, and I slowly saw my role evolve from observer-as-participant (Gold 1969) to that of a peripheral member of the group (Adler and Adler 1987). Like Horowitz (1986), in her study of Chicano gangs, I had to invent a research identity, because there was no single existing role that would allow me to get close to the teen mothers or afford me entree into the different facets of their lives.

My peripheral membership role was multifaceted and expanded over time. Shortly after I was enlisted to do the research project, the nursery staff started recruiting me to cover their shifts when they were ill, giving me the additional title of nursery substitute. At least once a week I worked as a paid staff member in one of the nurseries. On these days I performed all of the duties the other nursery staff members did: I fixed meals and bottles for the babies, fed them, played with them, changed

their diapers, and rocked them to sleep. An important difference that separated me from the regular staff was that I also interacted with the
mothers as much as I could while I was in the caretaker role, striking up
conversations with them when they were in the room and including them
in our adult conversations. I also made a point to include them in
decisions that affected the children, asking their advice for what meals I
should prepare or whether a crying baby sounded tired, hungry, or upset.
The rest of the staff made those decisions themselves and typically
consulted only the other adults in the room with matters concerning the
children. Unlike the existing staff member role, which called for the
adults to be somewhat distant from the teens in order to devote their full
attention to their primary duty of tending to the children, I interacted
with the teens as if we were equals and seized the opportunity of being in
the same room with the mothers to introduce myself to them and get to
know them.

My time in the nursery also allowed me to forge close relationships
with the women who worked in them. The nursery staff members were in
their forties and fifties; I was the age of their grown children. With my
own family miles away in another state, the women welcomed me into
what they called their "Teen Center Family." They made me homemade
Christmas gifts and invited me to their summer barbecues. I became
especially close to the program nurse, Katie, who was in her early thirties.
I babysat Katie's children when I was free on Saturday nights and became
so close to her seven-year-old daughter that she selected me as the topic
for her second-grade "Biography" assignment (while her classmates chose
women and men with significant historical importance). There was very
little turnover among the center's staff; the child-care providers made
more at the center than they would have in a private day care center
because they belonged to the teacher's union and received regular raises,
and the school setting meant they had spring break, long winter recesses,
and summer vacations. Only one staff member left the setting in the four
years I was there. Thus although the teen mothers graduated, transferred
schools, or dropped out, the staff remained essentially the same. As a
result, they became valuable research companions for me, serving as
independent sources of information to cross-check the teens' stories and
giving me updates on the young women's lives when I was absent from
the setting for any length of time.

In addition to my roles as researcher and nursery substitute, I was
also occasionally referred to as "the intern," "the mentor," and "the
graduate student," and I was given projects that were deemed appropriate
for these roles. On days when I was needed as an intern, I did everything
from writing grants for additional program funding to interviewing

prospective program participants—giving them a tour of the facilities, finding out about their educational and family backgrounds, helping them fill out necessary forms, and introducing them to the other program participants. As a mentor, I helped teens with homework and assisted them in everything from filling out welfare applications to searching for part-time jobs in the newspaper. Because I had done a rudimentary statistical analysis of the follow-up study findings, the program staff considered me a math expert, and my mentorship role often entailed helping young women with their algebra. In fact, whenever anyone in the program had a math question, they were directed to find me at the center or call me at home. In one instance, Helen asked me to intervene with a math teacher on behalf of a teen mother who had missed so many classes that she was in jeopardy of failing the course. Helen decided that the young mother should take the rest of the semester through independent study and thought the math teacher would be more willing to accept me, a PhD student, as the supervisor of her work than any of the other program staff. I met with Amanda every Monday, Wednesday, and Friday for one hour, and on several weekends as well. We also talked on the phone almost every night, working through math problems together.

For most of my four years in the setting, my role was a unique combination of responsibilities that changed on a daily basis. On some days, I spent all of my time in the nurseries helping watch children; on others, I accompanied teens to appointments at social services or simply floated from room to room, helping the young mothers with homework, chatting with them in the center's lounge, or visiting with them while we watched their children play. As my time in the setting increased, and as I became more intimate with the teens, I began to carry my role outside the confines of the school setting.

RELATIONS WITH SETTING MEMBERS

The first school year I spent in the setting I was primarily an observer, although the added role of "researcher" did help me become a recognizable fixture in the program. My role as a more active participant in the teens' lives was the result of a shift in our relations from virtual stranger to close friend, a shift made possible by my presence at an important school function. When the second school year began, I had the opportunity to get to know the center participants from the first day of school. Helen asked me to organize and cohost the welcome-back picnic the day before school started, and I learned that being in the setting on the first day was ideal for getting to know the teens. Many of the young women were new to the program and the high school, so they were happy to have me pay attention to them, and I was delighted to have people seek me out as well. One of the teens I met at my first picnic, Kristina, became my key informant for the school year. She was new to the school and apprehensive about leaving her daughter for the first time in the program nursery. I sat with her at the picnic, and when she arrived at school the next day, I welcomed her and her daughter by name and told her I would be working in the nursery where her daughter would be placed. As it turned out, I was in that nursery every day for the first two weeks of school because one of the nursery workers was ill, and Kristina warmed to me immediately. She brought her six-month-old daughter Lea to me to hold when she unpacked her backpack, talked to me about her day while we waited for Lea to wake up from her nap, and even waited for me after school so we could walk to our cars together. She later told me that she liked me immediately because I remembered her daughter's name and because I took an interest in how they were both adjusting to being in school (Kristina had been out of school for over a year); she told me that when she went home from school on the first day, she told her mom all about me.

When I sensed that we were becoming closer, I worked to speed the pace of our developing friendship: I started to ask Kristina about more personal events in her life—and I reciprocated by telling her things about myself—and mustered up the courage to call her at home, which was the turning point in our friendship. After I called her at home (to tell her something cute Lea had done in the nursery that day) she knew that I was interested in being friends with her, and we became more and more intimate. She ate lunch with me whenever I was at Lakeside for the day and called me several times each week. If I was not home when she called, she left messages on my answering machine addressed to "Lea's second mom" or "Lea's best friend." In December, I decided it was time to invite Kristina to do something outside of school. She had told me over the phone how much she loved the Christmas season, so I called one day and asked if she would come over and help me decorate a Christmas tree. We went to Target together to buy ornaments and a tree and then spent the afternoon at my apartment talking and decorating. When we returned to school on Monday and told other teens what we had done, I could see that many of the teen mothers looked at me differently—I was not a strange adult, I was a potential peer. As Kristina, a senior, became immersed in the center's culture, she became one of the most popular participants: she was nice to everyone, pretty, and widely regarded as the "best" mother there. My association with her enhanced my status at the center—in effect, she de facto sponsored me by vouching for my "coolness" and trustworthiness to the other teen mothers simply by being seen talking to me. By the time school ended for winter break in my second year at the setting, I found myself immersed in the teen parenting culture.

From my early connections with Kristina, I soon became friendly with the rest of the young women in the program, and I learned what I had to do to establish rapport. I found that I had to approach the teens myself, ask them their names, tell them my name (and repeat it the first few times I saw them), and that gradually they would—and did—accept me. It just took time. Like the volunteers in Wharton's (1991) study of a teen parenting program, I was initially intimidated by the prospect of having to "win over" the teen mothers; like the successful volunteers, I learned that an informal approach where I played up our similarities (e.g., in popular culture, in liking children) and downplayed our differences was key to gaining their acceptance. Every school year I had a key informant like Kristina—someone I spent a great deal of time getting to know in the beginning of the school year—who worked as a "gatekeeper" into the rest of the teen parenting culture. In the third school year that person was Sunshine, a seventeen-year-old mother who was, like Kristina, new to the school, and who instantly became the most popular teen in the program. Sunshine arrived at the center in the middle of the semester, and she was immediately the center of attention: she was only about four and a half feet tall and weighed ninety pounds. She wore funky, secondhand clothes (plaid shirts with checkered skirts, neon tights, velvet hats) and dyed her blonde hair red. She was a true Southerner—she spoke with an accent and used regional phrases that made the other moms laugh ("It's fixin' to rain")—she was funny, she was smart, and she had an adorable son. The day she arrived at school, I happened to be working in my intern role, and it was my responsibility to get her registered for classes, show her around the school, and introduce her to people. A few days later, I observed her talking to a group of young mothers in the lounge. The other teens told her how surprised they were that she fit in so well so quickly, because they had all been nervous and shy when they arrived. She told them that she knew from the first day that she would have at least one friend there, and she then pointed to me. One of the teens I did not know very well said, "But she's an adult!" Sunshine replied, "Maybe, but she's cool and she was so nice to me when I got here that I knew I would never be lonely." Because I had learned with Kristina that it would be up to me to make the first move if I wanted to pursue our friendship outside of school, I wasted no time in giving Sunshine my phone number. She had no family in town, nor did she have a car, so she took me up on my offer to help her out with transportation and called me frequently to drive her to the doctor or to the grocery store. As more and more teens witnessed

Sunshine and I together—or heard stories of things we had done together—my status increased. In fact, when she invited me to her son's first birthday party and told a group of mothers at the party that she considered me one of her closest and most dependable friends, I found myself with access to almost every clique in the program. Like it had been with Kristina, Sunshine's approval was key.

After attending Sunshine's son's birthday party, I soon found myself invited to the birthday party of every other child in the program; during one eight-week period, I attended six birthday parties. I also began receiving invitations to other significant events in the girls' lives, including weddings, baby showers, and graduation parties. I was also invited to participate in other special occasions: their rare "girls' nights out" where we went out to dinner or a movie if they could find baby-sitters and holiday dinners at their parents' homes. On a more regular basis, my extracurricular participation included going with different teens on weekly grocery shopping trips or their never-ending visits to the pediatrician. Performing these varied roles inside and outside the school setting allowed me access to different groups of teen mothers and afforded me the opportunity to observe them and participate with them in a variety of different contexts. As Jorgensen (1989) suggested, per-forming multiple roles in the setting allowed me to develop a "comprehensive and accurate picture" of the setting. My different roles afforded me the opportunity to watch the girls interact with each other, to meet their families and boyfriends, to observe their relationships with one another, to see where they lived, and to notice how they handled their interactions with strangers, who often made comments about their ages, their parenting, and their children when they took their own children out in public. It was through this extracurricular participation that I witnessed some of the most compelling and memorable events of my study: I saw seventeen-year-old Sunshine burst into tears at the gro-cery store checkout line when the clerk rolled his eyes over her food stamps and refused to process her order because she did not have the proper form with her (something she had never had to do before at that store, she told me); I learned that thirteen-year-old Lila, who was eight months' pregnant at the time, was functionally illiterate when I took her out to lunch and she asked me to read the menu to her; I watched eighteen-year-old Kristina's father berate her for "marrying a loser" and ruining her life when I joined her family for dinner one night; and I saw the father of Amanda's son act like he did not know her when we ran into him at the mall one Saturday afternoon.

At the same time that I worked to gain entree into the different friendship groups, I also cultivated relationships with some of the more marginal members of the setting. These were the teens who were not popular because they were known to be chronic liars (lying about having a boyfriend, for example), because they became involved with someone's ex-boyfriend, or because they were deemed uncaring parents. Every year at least one teen mother was the unanimous outcast—the scapegoat everybody picked on, got mad at, or made fun of. These young women were easier to connect with because they were desperate for someone to pay attention to them, and getting to know them gave me a broader perspective than just knowing the more popular teens. I had to be careful with these marginal relationships, though, because I knew that just as association with a cool teen gave me cool status, association with a marginal teen could make me marginal (Kirby and Corzine 1981). To defend myself against that potential problem, I initially contained my relationships with the marginal members to two specific situations: when other teens were not in the room or when I was in the nursery worker role (because nursery workers have to talk to everyone). As more and more teens became aware of my researcher role and my desire to observe all members of the program, and as they came to realize that I always presented myself as a neutral party who was nice to everyone, my association with the marginal members was understood. Thus when Theresa threw a birthday party for her daughter and I was the only one who showed up, several teens commended me for being kinder to her daughter than they could imagine themselves being; when a group of popular seniors saw Stephanie braiding my hair in the nursery, one of them later said to me, "I can't believe she asked to play with your hair—she's lucky you went along with it."

An important component of my after-school relationships with the teen mothers was the time we spent on the telephone. I spoke with many of the teens on the telephone for hours at a time, usually about nothing in particular, although they occasionally called when they were upset about something a boyfriend or parent had done, or if they needed help with homework. Like many other adolescents, the teens made their telephone relationships a vital element of their social lives; as a member of their peer network, I found myself a member of their phone network. I learned a lot about the young women in our phone conversations. For example, it was on the telephone that Kristina first shared details of her abusive childhood and that Brooke told me she was going to drop out of school. Talking on the telephone was an easy and a practical way to develop intimacy. Because they could rarely find babysitters, the teens' social lives were quite limited, but they were able to talk on the phone for long periods of time when their children were sleeping or playing quietly nearby. It was often the only opportunity they had to interact with someone other than their child, and they eagerly introduced new topics to prolong our conversations.

With my varied roles in the setting, I found myself walking a fine line between being an adult and being a teenager. Like Mandell (1988), I worked to fulfill the "least adult" role; that is, I tried to diminish the difference between my age and the teens' ages by acting more like a peer to the teen parents than an adult. I showed that I was a trustworthy peer—and not a meddlesome authority figure—in large measure by looking nonplussed when they did the things that other adults in the room told them not to do or gave them disapproving looks for doing: swearing, smoking, and talking about partying. I presented myself as an interested bystander, being careful not to look as if I approved of these things (I did not want the adults to ask me to stop coming to the center) and being equally cautious to avoid looking like I was hearing something shocking or new. In this way, I practiced "moral neutrality" (Jorgensen 1989), making myself as nonthreatening as possible in an effort to develop rapport and, ultimately, to receive as much information from the teens as possible (Lofland and Lofland 1995). Several situations called this tightrope walk into crisis. For example, on one occasion I was working as a nursery substitute when an argument broke out between two mothers, popular Jen and marginal Stephanie. The other nursery staff person was on a lunch break, leaving me the only adult in the room. A "regular" adult would have intervened and told Jen to leave Stephanie alone; as the "least adult," I decided to let their interaction evolve naturally, which is what they would have expected from any other peer in the program. I worried that a staff member might walk by and wonder why I was not intervening, so I provided an excuse for myself by scooping up a baby and busying myself with changing her diaper. I spent the rest of the afternoon worrying that word would get out to the other staff member that I had done nothing to diffuse the fight, and I was grateful for my good fortune when a week passed with no mention of the event. In another instance, I came across three teen mothers smoking on campus, which was illegal and punishable by detention. The adult expectation was to turn in the teens to the vice principal; the peer expectation was to act like nothing was wrong and join them. I did not want to risk being caught violating my adult responsibility by another adult, so I simply waved and rushed into the building as if I were too busy to stop and visit.

I further facilitated my least adult role through my physical appearance, blending in with the teen mothers and distinguishing myself from the professionally dressed staff by wearing the same jeans and tennis shoes they wore. I never told the young women I was a teenager. In fact, I learned early on that a great way to get them to notice me (and, hence, talk to me) was to casually mention something about my real age, which inevitably sparked a conversation about how they thought I was a teenager and how funny it was to be "so old" and look so young. Looking and acting young, while being relatively older, gave me a certain amount of status in the setting that helped tremendously in developing rapport; I was not as old as the nursery staff (all of whom were in their forties or fifties), but I was older than the teens, giving me sort of an older sister status. Punch (1994) posited that some settings require youthful researchers, and I saw early on that this adolescent group was such a setting, as older adults were treated with skepticism and guarded intimacy. As Wax (1979, 517) suggested in her discussion of age and a researcher's ability to gain entree to different settings, "like a child, the young person is relatively harmless and threatens no one." Wax also noted that educated young women are often welcomed as researchers by female setting members because they "might be regarded as someone to whom one could talk, in whom one could confide, and from whom one might get valuable information about grooming, deportment, and the arts of sociability" (519). The teens came to me when they had problems about anything that they thought I might be able to help them with, from problems with boyfriends to persuading a teacher to give them an extension on a homework assignment. The older sister role I created for myself was possible because of my age and my gender. In these ways, my ascriptive characteristics made me a perfect fit for a role that the young women accepted and understood.

I further developed rapport with the teens by helping them in ways that I, an adult with a driver's license, car, and job at a university, was in a position to offer: I drove them to the grocery store and to doctor's appointments; I occasionally loaned them change for a soda or a bus ride; I treated them to fast-food meals on special occasions; I let them sit in on my classes so they could see what college was like; and I taught them to drive. I also did other favors that were keeping in line with my role as older sister and friend: I donated blood during a school blood drive so a young mother could get extra credit for a health class; I watched their children when they were in a bind or simply needed some time to themselves; I intervened with social services and other agencies when they had questions about which they could not get straight answers; I spoke to them on the phone whenever they were lonely or needed a friendly ear. These favors were useful in a number of different ways. First, they helped me carve out a role as a reliable, trustworthy advocate, which facilitated many close relationships and aided in the data collection process as they felt comfortable telling me the truth in interviews, and I felt comfortable asking them questions. Second, through the norms of reciprocity (Jorgensen 1989), I found that the teens felt obligated to do something for me after I had done something for them—usually this meant being friendly to me if I had done something nice for them (e.g., cared for their children in the nursery; driven them to an appointment during the school day). Perhaps most importantly, the favors I did made me feel as if I was in some way paying back the young women for the rich data they provided me. When a staff member asked me why I agreed to drive a teen mother twenty miles to the bus station at 5:30 one morning to meet her boyfriend, I replied, "It was the least I could do." Rather than being upset that I had to get up early (as she had assumed I would be), I was instead flattered when the young woman told me I was the only person she knew well enough to ask such a big favor. I was happy to do these small favors for the teens.

The favors I did for the young women and the nonthreatening personae I adopted worked. Over time, I became a trustworthy friend to many of the teens. I knew I had achieved this position when they turned to me for help when they were in a bind. For example, at 7 o'clock on a Friday morning, I had a phone call from Vanessa, who was frantic because she and her daughter were at school and there were no nursery staff members there yet. Although I was not scheduled to work for anyone at the center that day, I told Vanessa I would be there in ten minutes to watch her daughter so she could go to class. The fact that she called me instead of any of the six paid nursery workers whose numbers were posted by the telephone showed me that she thought of me as a reliable friend who could be called at any time. On another occasion, I returned home from a day at the university to find a phone message from Kristina. The message simply said that she needed my help and was at the local hospital. When I arrived, I found that she had been at the doctor's office for a routine examination when the doctor discovered she was pregnant, but that the fetus had not survived. They rushed her to the hospital for emergency surgery. Kristina called me, she said, because she did not know who else to turn to. She needed emotional support, and she needed someone to watch her one-year-old daughter while the procedure was being done; she told me she did not trust anyone else to keep the pregnancy a secret from the rest of the center's participants. Other teens regularly asked for me when they were home sick from school and needed to get their homework collected, even if another adult happened to answer the phone at the center.

Because I became part of the teens' extracurricular lives, I had the opportunity to develop relationships with their families, husbands, and boyfriends. I found that their parents were usually quite eager to meet me—many parents could not believe that their daughter had befriended a twenty-something PhD student, and they were anxious to put a face to the name they had heard about at home. Once the introductions were made, they almost unanimously asked me the same questions: what had I found in my research, what caused teenage pregnancy, and whether their family was normal. For example, at the center's annual Halloween party, seventeen-year-old Whitney introduced me to her parents. As soon as Whitney was out of earshot, her mother asked me how common teenage parenting was. I gave her the statistics for the county and the nation and told her how many teens were enrolled in the program. She then asked me if I had noticed any common patterns in the relationships between the teen parents and their own parents. After I probed a little to clarify what she wanted to know, she revealed to me that she was upset that her daughter never let her be alone with her granddaughter—not even for a second—making her feel as if she did not trust her or did not want her to be a part of her granddaughter's life. I assured her that I had seen a similar thing happen in many other families and explained that adolescents are often so consumed with proving their maturity that they consider it a failure to allow anyone to help them with their children. Her mother was visibly relieved and sought me out whenever she stopped by the center to say hello. In another instance, I was eating dinner with Kristina at her parents' house; I had met them briefly at Kristina's apartment a few weeks earlier, and they were eager to encourage a friendship between us. When Kristina got up to wash dishes after dinner, her father motioned for me to step outside on the porch with him, where he asked me what caused teenage pregnancy and whether there was anything he and Kristina's mother could have done to prevent it. I felt awkward bringing up some of the antecedents of pregnancy of which I was aware— sexual abuse, low self-esteem, and so on—especially since Kristina had shared with me that her parents were never around when she was a child, and that her father was verbally and physically abusive. To avoid breaking Kristina's confidence—and feeling awkward myself—I explained that the pathways to parenthood varied, and I told him of other teens at the center who came from families similar to theirs: upper-middle-class families with professional, dual-working parents, families that were seemingly "normal." He was relieved to hear that his family was not unique, which led to many more invitations to family dinners; he also occasionally got on the phone to say hello to me when I was talking to Kristina, and he surprised me with a pair of expensive baseball tickets to thank me for being so kind to his daughter.

I had good relationships with the boyfriends and husbands I met too. I usually joked around with them or talked about sports. The young women often told me later that their boyfriends thought I was cool—and the teens loved it that they had brought someone home who was off limits romantically (because I was in a relationship) but someone of whom their boyfriends approved. When I was at Brooke and Mark's one Saturday night for a party they were having, one of Mark's friends (an eighteen-year-old high school dropout) pulled Brooke aside and asked who her cute friend was, pointing to me. Brooke was just beaming when she told him that I was her friend, and that I was working on my PhD. She was so proud that someone she brought home had impressed her boyfriend and his friends that she repeated that story several times to different people at the center the following week. I usually interacted with boyfriends in situations like this—birthday parties or other family celebrations—although they occasionally stopped by the center. Often, doing something social with one of the teen mothers meant doing something with her boyfriend as well. For example, one Saturday Kristina and I planned to go shopping; on the way to the mall, I drove Kristina's husband Kyle back to the halfway house at which he was staying as part of a deferred prison sentence. In another instance, Brooke invited me over for lunch during spring break. Her boyfriend Mark got off work early that day, arriving home just as we sat down to eat, so the three of us spent the afternoon together watching talk shows on television.

COLLECTING DATA

In the four years I spent at the center, I made formal and informal observations of the teen parents and their children. During that time, I kept field notes of these observations that I typed up every day after returning from the setting. As the research progressed and I began to see patterns emerging, I conducted in-depth interviews with several teen mothers. The interview process was designed to generate rich descriptions of the teen parent's experience in order to lay the groundwork for inductive theory construction, rather than to verify existing theory as in a deductive model. I conducted interviews with twenty-four teen mothers; I interviewed most teens once, and several as many as three times. Each interview lasted between one and two hours, and each took place in a vacant office at the center, at the park adjacent to the center, or at the teen's home, whichever she preferred. My data and analysis come not only from the twenty-four interviewees but also from my interactions with and observations of the larger group of program participants, which ranged from fifty to seventy teens over the four years. Throughout the interview and observation process, I cross-checked respondents' accounts by comparing them to accounts of the same incident given by their peers and, occasionally, the program staff.

The longitudinal nature of the study allowed me to see patterns I would have missed if the project had been cross-sectional in design (Denzin and Lincoln 1994). For example, during my second year in the setting, a new student, Blair, joined the program. She was eight months' pregnant and beaming about the fact that she and her boyfriend John had purposefully became pregnant, and that they would be getting married that summer. She dropped out of school immediately after the baby was born but returned when he was two years old. I noticed that she was not wearing her engagement ring anymore and asked her what happened with John. She told me they broke up when the baby was six months old, and that she had not seen him or his family since. Kristina, who was married when we met, graduated from high school, went to college, got divorced, graduated from community college, and got remarried in the four years that I spent in the setting. Some dramatic changes also occurred in Sunshine's life over the three years I knew her in the setting. She arrived at the center pregnant, homeless, and depressed because she did not know which of two men was her baby's father. For the first two years of her son's life, she tried unsuccessfully to track down the men, and she gradually came to accept the fact that she would be a single mother. When her son was two years old, "father possibility number 1" wrote her a letter and offered to take a paternity test. He did, and the test proved he was Jonah's father. After a year of correspondence, Sunshine and Randy rekindled their relationship, and she moved to Alabama to live with him in the house he had built for the three of them. The impressions I would have had of the young women—of Blair getting married to her baby's father, of Kristina as a high school graduate married to an incarcerated criminal, of Sunshine not knowing who her baby's father was—would have been incomplete without the long-term exposure I had to their lives.

I coded my field notes and interview transcriptions according to different conceptual categories and analyzed them for "sensitizing concepts" (Blumer 1969)—that is, concepts and meanings that originated from the teens themselves. In keeping with the principles of grounded theory (Glaser and Strauss 1967), I grouped participants' responses and my own observations around different categories and worked to integrate these categories into an analytic framework. With these emergent theories in mind, I returned to the field and asked more questions to weed out ideas that were not empirically sound or theoretically useful. I searched for a full range of possible responses in the categories that remained. In this sense, I engaged in what Glaser and

Strauss (1967) called "theoretical sampling," for I collected data with theory construction, rather than theory verification, in mind. Thus I intentionally carried out interviews with teens I thought might have experiences or viewpoints that would assist me in refining and reformulating the emerging theory. Unlike probability sampling, my goal was not to interview a large, representative sample of mothers. Rather, my objective was to tap into the full range of similarities and differences of experience through in-depth interviews with a group of purposefully selected participants. Like other qualitative researchers, my aim in this process was "depth rather than breadth" research (Ambert et al. 1995). I continued to gather data in this fashion until my observations and interviews no longer yielded new themes or forced me to reconceptualize my emerging models, a process Glaser and Strauss (1967) called "theoretical saturation." Finally, I combined ideas that proved fruitful and interesting into the theoretical frameworks described in the following chapters.

PROBLEMS AND ISSUES

Several problems arose that were unique to my setting of adolescent parents and their children. Many of these problems had their origin in the fact that these mothers were teenagers—cliques, boyfriends, and being popular or being left out were just as much a part of the teen parenting culture as they are in other adolescent school cultures (Adler and Adler 1996; Eder 1985). As a participant-observation researcher, I had to weave my way through their status hierarchy and cast myself as a neutral member, one who was accepted by all cliques and rejected by none. This would not be an easy undertaking for an adolescent, and it was even harder for an adult with no legitimate reason for wanting access to their friendship groups. I had several strategies for achieving this: I befriended people like Kristina and Sunshine, who gave me the coveted status I sought; I talked with them about soap operas, movie stars, and popular music; I wore modern, semi-trendy clothes; and I moderated my interactions with marginal members of the group. My age helped me (having an older friend was cool for these young women, just as having an older boyfriend was) and so did my personality, as being friendly to everyone gave me a degree of popularity. Because the center was located within a school setting, there was a high turnover of "cool" setting members—Kristina graduated after one year in the program, Sunshine after two—and I had to constantly work to establish relationships with the gatekeepers of the different friendship groups.

Another unique problem revolved around the fact that these young women were mothers, and that I was affiliated with their children's caregivers. There were times when the teen mothers had grievances with the nursery staff—some of which were legitimate concerns, others that were not. They often confided in me and occasionally asked me to intervene on their behalf. For example, in my second year, two teens were upset with a nursery worker who they thought was too rough with the babies. They came to me because they did not want to confront the woman themselves in case they had to leave their children with her again, but they wanted something done about it or they were going to drop out of school. I did not know if it would be appropriate for me to confront the nursery caregiver myself, as I was in many ways her peer (as a nursery substitute), so I decided to share the story with Helen, the program coordinator, at a lunch meeting we had scheduled for the following week. In the meantime, Brooke decided that she could not stand it any longer and decided to stop going to school. Because I had no plans to be at the setting and no commitments at the university, I offered to babysit Chris so Brooke could go to school, an arrangement that seemed ideal to both of us: she did not miss any class, and I had the opportunity to spend some time with her infant son, whom I adored. That evening, the center's nurse called me at home to warn me that Helen was very upset with me. Evidently Brooke had told the truth when people asked where her son was—that he was with me—and Helen overheard. Helen told the nurse that she had to "have a word with me" about proper relationships with center participants, implying that what I had done was improper. With the nurse's warning, I went to the setting the first thing the next morning to explain that I volunteered to watch Chris since I knew Brooke was on the verge of dropping out of school because of the nursery worker. I expected her to be understanding of, if not pleased by, the fact that I had intervened to make sure one of the teens did not drop out of school. I was surprised to find that Helen defended the staff member, belittled the teens' complaints, and told me that I needed to work on "defining my boundaries," a phrase I interpreted to mean that I should not be so involved with the teen mothers. She told me that Brooke would never learn to make it on her own if she always had me to fall back on. I tried to explain that the mentorship role I had carved out for myself revolved around my being someone the teens could fall back on, but Helen did not change her opinion. Although she did not ask me to leave the setting, she did say she expected that this would never happen again. In this instance, taking on the "intervener role" (Glesne and Peshkin 1992) and attempting to change something in the setting jeopardized my status with Helen, the center's ultimate gatekeeper; for several weeks I worried that she might ask me to leave the setting when she realized how much a part of the teens' lives I was, and I was careful to avoid bringing up any instances of our extracurricular socializing. We never spoke again about the matter, but the anxiety I felt made me careful to encourage the teens to air their grievances with her from then on rather than taking it upon myself to do so.

The staff members were also aware of my intimate relations with the teens and often asked me to fix some perceived problem so they would not have to come across as the meddlesome authority figure. For example, at different times I was asked to convey to a teen that she was too inconsistent with her son's discipline; tell a young mother that her perpetual negative attitude was worrisome and possibly symptomatic of a mental health problem; and find out why one of the teens was thinking of dropping out of school. Because I aligned myself with the teens, I took their requests more seriously than the staff requests, intervening only in cases where I deemed it truly necessary—situations where someone's health was a concern, or where the teen mother might find it inappropriate for me not to intervene because of the close nature of our relationship. For example, the program coordinator, counselor, and one of the nursery staff workers all approached me in the spring of my third year in the setting to see if I could do anything about Amanda. During the past school year, Amanda had alienated most of her friends and was visibly depressed. The adults were worried that her attitude was affecting her parenting (making her too harsh with her son) and her physical health, as she was so depressed that she could barely sleep. The staff members told me that I was the only adult Amanda trusted enough to discuss personal problems without it seeming like I was putting her down or telling her what to do. I agreed to take part in their "intervention," whereby the program coordinator, counselor, and I invited her into a private office and confronted her with our suspicions that she was in need of mental health support. I told her that my purpose for being in the meeting was to help her because she was a close friend of mine and I hated to see her so down all the time, and she embraced me and told me she was lucky to have a friend who noticed. I helped her make the phone call to the mental health specialist, drove her to her first appointment, and watched her three-year-old son when she was in with the doctor. Intervening in her personal life was something I knew I was in a position to do, but the anxiety of wondering how she might react—given her rude treatment of most of the other adults in the program—kept me awake all night the day before we met.

My involvement with the teen mothers and their children also took a toll on me personally, in two distinct ways. First, I did not anticipate the emotional intensity my interactions with the teens might have. On good days, I pinched myself over my good fortune of finding such a wonderful group of "younger sisters" to spend time with; we laughed together, reveled in their triumphs together, and became close friends. At the same time, however, our intimacy meant I found myself involved in their personal tragedies—when their children were seriously ill, when their boyfriends left them, and when they reflected on abusive childhoods—which left them, and often me, in tears. I usually went straight from the setting to my teaching job at the university, and several times I had to delay the beginning of class while I recomposed myself and put their sad stories out of my mind.

The second way I was affected personally was being subject to a never-ending series of childhood illnesses because the young children were in a day care setting. I was with them for enough time each week to become exposed to everything they had, but not enough to develop immunities. During my four years at the center, I had several illnesses that usually showed up exclusively in children: an ear infection (my first ever), whooping cough, and croup (which manifests itself as laryngitis in adults). My doctor was amazed every time I walked into her office showing symptoms of sicknesses she usually saw in small children. In addition to these childhood illnesses, I had several bouts of bronchitis, constant sniffles, and numerous cases of a sore throat. These illnesses took a toll on my physical health, as can be expected, and they also taxed my mental health, as I struggled to complete course work, teach classes, and show up at the center.

I was also confronted with several ethical dilemmas. One of my biggest ethical concerns when I first entered the setting was deciding how I would deal with situations shared with me in confidence. I figured that intimate relationships with teenagers would certainly involve knowledge of deviant behavior on their part, and I also worried that I might learn of physical abuse, substance abuse, or other potentially dangerous situations. Early on, I asked Helen about my obligations to report such matters. She informed me that because I was not a teacher, I was not required to report anything, although she expected that I would. Fortunately, this problem never arose. In the handful of instances where I was privy to something potentially problematic going on in a young woman's life, I was always aware that a staff member was already involved in reporting it, or that the incident had already been reported to the proper authorities. For example, in my second year, I was talking with the program teacher when we overheard two teen mothers talking in the hallway outside of her classroom. She motioned for me to be quiet and proceeded to listen to their conversation. Brooke was telling Linda that her boyfriend had been taken to jail the previous night for hitting her. In this case, I knew the police were involved and that the teacher knew what was going on, so I did not feel compelled to intervene. In another instance, I noticed a burn on a toddler's foot and pondered for a split-second about what to do. At that moment, one of the nursery workers picked up the child to change his diaper and noticed it right away; she took it upon herself to tell the nurse and eventually Helen (who reported the case to Children's Protective Services), leaving me no opportunity to intervene myself. I was also made aware of problematic situations in the course of my interviews, when many teens shared stories of abusive pasts with me. Because no one ever told me a story about ongoing abuse (or the potential for it), I never had to deal with the dilemma of breaking their confidences to ensure their safety; the stories they told me dated back to their childhoods.

There were times when I knew of teen mothers' involvement in minor forms of deviance—skipping a class, smoking on a part of campus where they should not have been—but I never once felt the need to report their transgressions. When I entered their adolescent setting, I assumed I would have to deal with "guilty knowledge" (Van Maanen 1992), because I knew from my own experiences that adolescents often break the rules. I protected their confidences and their identities when they engaged in these deviant acts, because I knew that was the only way that I, an adult, could establish and maintain trust with them, and because I personally viewed these norm violations as harmless.

Research with vulnerable populations, in this case minors, can result in other ethical dilemmas. To avoid taking advantage of their young age, I gave them consent forms outlining their rights as subjects for them to read and sign before I interviewed them. The teens under age seventeen who were not emancipated were asked to have a parent or guardian sign a similar form. The teen mothers always laughed when I explained about voluntary participation and how they had the right to refuse to be part of the study, because they wanted to be in the project. One young woman actually approached me about the prospect of doing an entire chapter on her and her baby. Participating in the project gave them a chance to share their stories to an interested person (and not just anyone, but a person who had considerable status in the setting) and made them feel like their lives were interesting. To further protect them, I changed all of their names and many identifying characteristics in my write-ups. I agree with Emerson's (1988) contention that it is not always useful to explain the purpose of research to children. Although my setting members were adolescents, I learned early on that they were not interested in anything other than the fact that I was writing a book about what it is like to be a teen mother. In fact, during an interview with a twenty-year-old girl who

I thought was old enough to understand a little more about my purpose, I ventured to explain some of my analytical hunches. She told me the next day that it was like I "became this different person," because suddenly I was talking over her head. After that incident, I stuck with the simple account that I was a college student and had to write a book about teen parenting to finish my degree.

LEAVING THE SETTING

My decision to leave the setting came during the end of my fourth school year at the center. For a great deal of the fourth school year, I felt a sense of theoretical saturation (Glaser and Strauss 1967). I was not seeing anything new, and the stories I heard from the current cohort of teenage mothers were strikingly similar to the experiences of the mothers I had known one, two, and three years earlier. As a result, I began spending less time at the setting (one or two days a week instead of three or four) and more time writing. I also invested less energy in developing rapport with the teens, as I knew my time in the setting was almost finished, and I felt my energy could be better spent writing. Because I was making great progress in writing my dissertation, I applied for a tenure-track position at a university in another state. When I was offered and accepted the position, my decision to leave the setting was final. I told the teens and program staff about the job when I first applied for it, and went to the setting right away after I accepted to tell them the news. Some of the newer teens with whom I had not forged close relations were happy for me; others I had known for several years were very sad, and it was hard for me not to break down and cry as I told them that I would not be returning in the fall. I did promise to return to the following year's graduation to watch Tracy, one of the first teens I met at the setting, walk through the ceremony. I also exchanged addresses with many of the teens so we could correspond. Because so many teens with whom I became close had already left the setting, and because those still there knew their time was limited (until they graduated), my decision to leave did not really affect the outcome of our relationships—we had known all along that our time together at the center would be short. Over the years, I had already practiced keeping in contact with the teenage women who left the setting through telephone calls, letters, wedding and baby showers, and occasional lunch dates, so I left the setting having already practiced "leaving" for four years.

Leaving the staff was another story. Like the teens, they knew that my time there was limited to my time in graduate school. But because there was such low turnover among the staff from year to year, I knew my departure would create a significant void. Two staff members took me aside privately and expressed their wish that I remain in Lakeside indefinitely so that I might eventually take over Helen's job of running the program. The nurse, with whom I became especially close, invited me to a farewell dinner with her family, and she promised to visit me in my new home. As a group, the staff took me to dinner at a fancy restaurant for a going-away party, where we exchanged addresses and reminisced about some of the funnier moments at the center. I was reluctant to engage in these farewell activities, fearful that it would make leaving that much more difficult. Months later, when I was physically and emotionally removed from the setting, I realized how important it was for me to end this chapter of my life with a formal conclusion.

THREE

GETTING PREGNANT

Adolescent mothers' non-normative entry into parenthood necessitates two distinct lines of inquiry: one relating to their sexual activity and pregnancy, and a second regarding their decisions to resolve their pregnancies by bearing and rearing their own children. I explore each of these topics in turn, with this chapter exploring pregnancy and the next chapter exploring the path to parenthood.

Pregnancy accounts were part of the culture of the Teen Center. Being pregnant was, after all, the common denominator the girls shared. In being asked (oftentimes repeatedly) to tell their pregnancy stories, new participants learned that being a teenage mother meant having to disclose intimate details about their sexual histories. Thus one of their earliest exposures to the culture of teenage parenthood typically came when they first entered the center, for it was then that they were asked to share the story of their own pregnancy and heard the stories of other teens in return.

GAMBLING WITH CONTRACEPTION

Several researchers have noted that the vast majority of teenage mothers do not get pregnant intentionally, but that they fail to use effective contraception nevertheless (Furstenberg 1991; Jacobs 1994; Trent and Crowder 1997). Although the majority of pregnant adolescents report that their pregnancies were unintentional (Coleman 2005), researchers interested in the causes of teenage pregnancy are divided when it comes to the question of intent. In her classic study of women seeking abortions, Luker (1975) posited that unwanted pregnancy is the end result of an informed decision-making process. Thus she argued that it is usually the result of a conscious decision to have sex, followed by a decision not to use protection. A series of risky behaviors—risky choices—leads to the unintended consequence of motherhood. Other researchers have presented contrasting views of the path to early motherhood, eschewing the pivotal role of individual choice. For example, Ruddick (1993) argued that teenage women have limited capacity to make choices because of the disadvantaged position in which their age, gender, and often social class have put them. Nathanson (1991) criticized many attempts to address problems of teenage pregnancy and parenting for their focus on the individual teen's choices rather than emphasizing the structural constraints that may be at play. Trent and Crowder's (1997) research into early nonmarital childbearing revealed that "an individual's social position influences their risk of early, non-marital childbearing. . . . Introducing birth intentions into these models does not appreciably change the effects of race and ethnicity, poverty, or family structure" (531). They conclude that their research provided "little evidence . . . that premeditation or rational planning prior to pregnancy helps to explain racial, economic, or family structure differentials in early, non-marital childbearing" (531).

The contraceptive patterns of most Teen Center mothers illustrate both schools of thought. As their stories reveal, the teens often weighed the pros and cons when deciding whether to use contraception, but those choices were constrained by the resources available to them. The net result was an irregular pattern of contraceptive use; they used contraception when it occurred to them, when it was readily available, and when they deemed it necessary. The rest of the time, they went without. For most of the teenage women, pregnancy—and ultimately motherhood—was the result of choosing not to use contraception rather than a failure of a contraceptive method. Perhaps more significant, though, is the fact that the language they used to frame their pregnancy stories shows an effort to deflect the stigma associated with teenage parenting by placing the blame for the pregnancy somewhere other than their personal choices.

BARRIERS TO USING CONTRACEPTION

Adolescents in general are not particularly likely to use contraception, and the younger the teen, the less likely she is to use it (Miller and Moore 1990; Phipps, Rosengard, Weitzen, Meers, and Billinkoff 2008). Indeed, Miller and Moore posit that "one of the strongest and most consistent

predictors of contraceptive use is the age of the adolescent" (1990, 1031).
At the Teen Center, younger adolescents—those who were thirteen or
fourteen when they became pregnant—often told stories suggesting that
they did not use contraception because they did not know how to access it
or did not think they needed it.

Many of the Teen Center participants did not use contraception for
the simple reason that they did not know any better. They were ignorant
about the reproductive system, unaware of their contraceptive options,
and naive when it came to judging their boyfriends' claims that they did
not need contraception. Fifteen-year-old Vanessa, a white mother from a
middle-class family, said her lack of knowledge about birth control, and
lack of access to it, kept her from using contraception when she began
having sex at age fourteen with her twenty-year-old boyfriend Marcus.
This came up in the context of a discussion we were having about her
mother, when she told me she wished her mother would have been more
open about sexuality:

> And you know, my mom never talked about sex or anything like
> that, and I think that is one of the reasons why I got pregnant.
> She just didn't talk about, like birth control or anything, so I
> didn't know what the options were, and I would have been
> embarrassed to ask her about it. I'm going to be a lot different
> with Hope. A lot different. Just being more open. I mean, I
> don't want to be like my mom, just not saying anything about
> sex. I think it needs to be brought up to your kids. That would
> have made a big difference for me.

Vanessa's feeling that a discussion with her mother may have prevented
her pregnancy is in line with what most researchers have found regarding
the relationship between communication about sexuality and contraceptive use by adolescents. According to Newcomer and Udry (1985),
teenage women whose parents discuss sexuality and contraception are
more likely to consistently use contraception than other young women.
Research by Kahn (1994) revealed that teenage women view their mothers as the most important source of information about sex, and that
mothers perceive themselves as communicating more about sex than
daughters perceive. Thus Vanessa's mother may have felt that she had
communicated contraceptive options to her daughter, while Vanessa felt
that her mother viewed these topics as inappropriate to discuss.

The fact that Vanessa knew birth control existed and that it may have
prevented pregnancy supports Luker's (1975) claim that most sexually
active women have "some" or "much" birth control knowledge, and that

it is not ignorance of the existence or availability of contraception that leads to unwanted pregnancy but rather a set of circumstances that prevents them from using these contraceptive "skills" (23). For Vanessa, these circumstances involved a relationship with her mother that was not very intimate, resulting in her being too embarrassed to bring up the topic of birth control. In Scott and Lyman's (1968) terms, Vanessa's pregnancy account includes both a scapegoat (her mother) and an appeal to defeasibility ("I didn't know what the options were").

While Vanessa and some of the other white teens cited embarrassment in talking about sex with their mothers as a barrier to their access to contraception, several of the Latina teens told me that their religion prevented them from using birth control. For example, sixteen-year-old Laura explained:

> I'm Catholic. I went to church every Sunday with my family, and I had my first communion. I had my quincinera last year—that's for Hispanic girls in the Catholic church. It means the beginning of our womanhood. And you know, Catholics say "no sex before marriage and no form of birth control." So I did one thing right! [laughs]

Research by Studer and Thornton (1987) revealed a similar pattern, with sexually active religious adolescents reporting less contraceptive use than their nonreligious peers. Although religious affiliation is also found to be associated with a decreased likelihood for engaging in sexual activity (Manlove et al. 2008), those adolescents who are sexually active put themselves at an increased risk of pregnancy in their effort to avoid doing what Laura referred to as "sinning twice." Just as Vanessa's account of her pregnancy directed blame to her mother and her own ignorance, Laura deflected it onto her culture and her religion.

Nineteen-year-old Julie, a white mother with three sons, viewed the medical aspects of obtaining contraception as formidable obstacles that prevented her from using birth control. I spoke with her when she was pregnant with her third child and asked whether she planned on having more children:

> Three is definitely the end of the line. I wanted to get my tubes tied, but they have a certain age limit I guess. You have to be twenty-one or have like five kids I think. And it's like, I'm only nineteen and I have three kids! I think I'm going to do the Depro-prevera shot. People at the clinic are like, "You can get sterile from that." And I'm like, I don't care! That's what I *want*!

That's what I was trying to get when I asked to have my tubes tied! (respondent's emphasis)

In Julie's eyes, the public health clinic's rule that patients reach a certain age or family size before they are surgically sterilized was a barrier to accessing contraception. Later, I asked whether she and her boyfriend Thomas considered using any form of contraception when she became pregnant with her third son, and she recalled another obstacle: "Well, no! Because, Thomas will even tell you it's my fault, because he kept saying, 'Go get on the pill' and I wouldn't because I can't stand doctors." Like the women in Luker's (1975) study, Julie saw the cost of seeking medical attention as outweighing the benefit of contraception. The cost of going to a doctor included paying for an appointment and for prescription pills, and also embarrassment, for going to the doctor entails admitting that one is sexually active and exposing private areas of the body. For Julie, contraception meant medical contraception; when these methods were not available or were undesirable, the decision not to use birth control was an easy one.

One of the most surprising findings of my research at the Teen Center was the frequency with which I heard stories of adolescents who did not use contraception because their boyfriends told them they were sterile. Luker (1975) noted a similar pattern in her study of women seeking abortions, as a significant number of women mentioned "trickery by men concerning their own fertility" (58) as an explanation for why they did not use contraception. At the Teen Center, these boyfriends were significantly older than the teens, all of whom were sexually inexperienced when they began relationships with them. Sixteen-year-old LaNiece, an African American teen, told me she was thirteen when she began dating her baby's father, who was twenty at the time. She explained that because of her young age, she did not think to question him when he told her they did not need to use contraception

> Well, I was only thirteen, keep that in mind, 'cause he told me, "Oh, I can't have kids, I can't have kids." And I believed him! I was like, "Oh, okay." You know, I didn't know anything about the reproductive system—I was only thirteen. So he said he couldn't get me pregnant and I believed him.

When I asked whether they used any form of birth control, she replied, "No. He told me we didn't need to. God, I was so stupid! Now that I think of that I just want to punch myself! I can't believe I didn't know!" LaNiece resembled the young African American women described in

Bralock and Koniak-Griffin's (2007) research, who were more likely to engage in risky sexual behavior when they had significantly older partners. Sixteen-year-old Kerry, a white teen from a working-class family, told me a similar story. She was fifteen when she had sex with her baby's father, nineteen-year-old Tony. Like LaNiece, she was also under the impression that her boyfriend was sterile. When I asked whether they used contraception, she told me this:

> He was on drugs. They had a study that said that being on these drugs can make a guy sterile. And we didn't know, he didn't know that his ex-girlfriend before me was on birth control. She had lied to him about that. So he thought he was sterile. Because she said that she was not on birth control and they didn't use any other protection. So he thought he was sterile. But I said, "No, you need to get a test to find out which one of you was sterile." But since I wasn't getting pregnant, we kind of assumed that it was him. He says he wants a blood test now because he still thinks he's sterile.

The teens' relatively young ages, their concomitant naiveté regarding sexuality, and their older boyfriends' successful pleas for them not to use birth control served as barriers preventing many of the youngest women at the Teen Center from using contraception.

CONTRACEPTIVE FAILURE

Given the low level of consistent contraceptive use among adolescents, it is not surprising that many sexually active teens become pregnant. It makes less sense, though, that teens who do use birth control on a regular basis could become pregnant. This was the case with several Teen Center participants who told me they did not want to get pregnant, and who they thought they were taking sufficient precautions to avoid pregnancy.

The three adolescent mothers who told me they used contraception every time they had sex were white teenagers from middle-class families. They were college-bound students who had always done well in school. For example, seventeen-year-old Jessica and her boyfriend, seventeen-year-old Patrick, both honors students, used condoms every time they had sex. Jessica told me they "tested" the condoms before they used them by stretching them out and looking for holes. According to Jessica, the pregnancy resulted from a condom that "exploded." Tim and Jen were similar to Jessica and Patrick in that they were college-bound honors students who identified themselves as regular contraception users. When they found out Jen was pregnant, they were juniors enrolled in advanced-placement and college-level classes at Lakeside. Jen told me they never had sex without a condom, and she blamed her pregnancy on its failure. Like adolescents in general (Miller and Moore 1990), the Teen Center mothers like Jessica and Jen who reported consistent contraceptive use had high expectations for themselves in terms of educational attainment, school success, and career opportunities. There are different explanations for these patterns: some say it reflects a higher motivation to prevent pregnancy (because of concrete educational or career plans), while others argue that these teens may have a better understanding of how to use contraception (Miller and Moore 1990).

However, something else may explain Jessica's and Jen's reported use of contraception: they may have given me what they deemed an appropriate answer. I learned that, often, using contraception at some point in their relationships made teens feel justified in answering the question "Did you use protection?" in the affirmative. It was only after I probed for more details that I learned a "yes" answer meant that they had used contraception at least once, but not necessarily—and not usually—every time they had sex. The teens knew that the right thing to say was that they did use contraception (to prevent early pregnancy, to prevent nonmarital pregnancy, and to prevent sexually transmitted infections), so that was the first answer they gave. Luker (1975) also found that her respondents gave "somewhat inflated" reports of their contraceptive use, telling doctors they used it more regularly than they really did. She posits that this may come as a result of a "desire to provide a socially appropriate presentation of self" (24). In light of their identity as "contraceptive users," many teens considered their pregnancies the result of contraceptive failure, when in reality it was the result of a failure to *use* contraception. Thus despite low clinical failure rates for condoms (about 2 percent) and oral contraceptives (about .1 percent) (Trussell and Kost 1987), the most common forms of contraception used by adolescents, about one-fourth of pregnant adolescents report that they were using contraception at the time of conception (Swenson et al. 1989).

Two Teen Center mothers gave accounts that illustrate this pattern. Twenty-year-old Amanda explained to me that she and her baby's father, Robby, used contraception every time they had sex. Later, she added the detail, "This was when we first started dating." She said she was adamant about using birth control in the beginning of their relationship because she feared getting AIDS. Once he convinced her that he had never been with another woman, she relaxed and they began using contraception when it was convenient. Even though they did not always use contraception, she considered her pregnancy a result of contraceptive failure because she did at least use it occasionally, and she said she had "no way of knowing" if the pregnancy was the result of protected or unprotected intercourse. I noticed when she told the story of her pregnancy to other people—to the students in my class at the university when she came to speak about teen parenting, and to the newspaper reporter who came to the Teen Center—that she always said she had used protection but it failed.

Nineteen-year-old Julie, the mother of three sons, considered her third son the result of contraceptive failure. Like Amanda, she was not actually using any contraception, but because she *thought* about using something, she felt she could justifiably call the pregnancy the result of failed contraception. When I asked whether she and her boyfriend Thomas had been using protection, she replied, "Well, no! [laughs] Which is really bad, but I mean, none of the three pregnancies have been *planned*!"

A DESIRE FOR CHILDREN

Unlike the adolescents who did not use contraception because they did not know any better or had difficulties accessing it, another group of teens told me they did not use contraception because they either wanted to get pregnant or they would not mind getting pregnant. The prospect of getting pregnant was exciting for many of the teens, particularly those who had been dating the baby's father for an extended period of time. Thompson (1995) found a similar pattern, noting that many of the adolescent mothers in her study had children as teenagers because "they had dreamed all their lives of falling in love and becoming mothers" (117). For many teens, pregnancy and motherhood were linked in a romantic script, where falling in love meant having a baby.

Nineteen-year-old Kristina, a white teen from a middle-class family, tried to get pregnant from the time she was fourteen. At age twelve, she began seriously dating her sixteen-year-old next-door neighbor, who was also her brother's best friend. When she was fourteen they stopped using condoms so she could get pregnant. She became pregnant immediately but miscarried during her first trimester. At age fifteen, she met Kyle, the man who would become her husband, and she had three more miscarriages over a three-year period. At age eighteen, and just one day after she married Kyle, Kristina got pregnant again, and this time she carried the baby to term. She explained to me her conscious decision to become a parent at a young age, and thus her decision not to use birth control:

> I've always wanted to be a mother. . . . My parents have these [video] tapes of when I was in first grade, and what does it say on it? I want to be a mom at age ten. Because I thought I'd be old enough at age ten. And I love it. This is the only thing I wanted to become in life. Even if I was a street rat, I'd still want to do it. This is the only thing I really wanted to become in life that meant a whole lot to me—becoming a parent. Once I met Kyle, I knew it was time.

Kristina went on to tell me that becoming a parent at that point in her life was the "natural" thing for her and Kyle to do, since they were so much in love with each other.

Seventeen-year-old Blair, a Latina from a middle-class family, also got pregnant intentionally because she and her boyfriend, seventeen-year-old John, felt ready to become parents:

> Actually, I always felt like I was ready. I've been feeling that since I was about sixteen, like a year ago. And John kind of felt like he was ready, so we planned it. It was planned. We'd been using condoms and then we stopped when we decided to have a baby.

Like Kristina, Blair's plans to have a child were intertwined with her feelings for her boyfriend. Research by de Anda, Becerra, and Fielder (1988) showed that Mexican American teens are more likely to get pregnant in the context of a long-term relationship than white teens. Blair, a Chicana, went to great lengths to tell people at the Teen Center that she and John were planning on getting married *before* they became pregnant to prove to everyone that they truly loved each other. Her wedding—which, incidentally, never happened because they broke up after the baby was born—was her favorite topic of conversation, followed by comments about John's enthusiasm for fatherhood. In Rubin and East's (2008) research, Hispanic teens and teens who were married were more likely than other adolescents to report that they became pregnant because they wanted a baby.

Fourteen-year-old Angelica, a Latina from a working-class family, had been married a few months to twenty-year-old Arturo when they decided it was time to have a child. She explained to me that when she was younger, "like in sixth and seventh grade," she did not like children and had no plans to have one of her own. In eighth grade, she got married and changed her mind. She was proud of her choice and said most teens she knew got pregnant intentionally, and not because of peer pressure, a notion that made her laugh:

> Well with teenage pregnancy, mostly they say it's because of peer pressure, that you're having sex because your peers are. I don't really believe that. I mean, they do it because they want to. And they get pregnant because they don't do anything to *not* get pregnant, which means they must want it, right?

Several teen mothers told me they did not try to get pregnant, but they did not use contraception either, because they "didn't mind" the prospect of getting pregnant. This notion of "not minding" pregnancy is not unique to Teen Center participants; Miller and Moore (1990) posited that 1 in 10 white teens and 1 in 5 black teens "either didn't think about pregnancy or they didn't care whether a pregnancy occurred" (1030), and Luker (1996) suggested that many teens get pregnant "because they believe pregnancy is not such a bad thing" (151). Seventeen-year-old Andrea, a white teen from a working-class family, exemplified this pattern. She did not set out to get pregnant, but it was not wholly unexpected. She explained to me why she and her boyfriend of three weeks, nineteen-year-old Charlie, had not used contraception:

> It wasn't like we planned to have Gary, but it was like, we didn't use anything and afterwards we talked about it and we were like, "Oh well, if it happens it happens." So when it happened, it wasn't a shock. It was like, this is what we get! But it wasn't bad for either one of us.

Two months before she got pregnant, Andrea dropped out of tenth grade because, as she said, "I'm just, I don't know, not the school type. I don't know why. I mean, there's certain subjects in school that I like but not many, and you know, I just don't like going to school." Not coincidentally, she dropped out when her younger sister gave birth to a baby girl, whom Andrea adored. Brooke, one of Andrea's best friends, took me aside after my interview with Andrea and told me that no matter what Andrea may have told me, she had told Brooke that she set out to get pregnant because she was jealous of the attention her sister was getting.

Eighteen-year-old Brooke also claimed that she did not mind getting pregnant. Although she explicitly told me she did not intentionally get pregnant, it became clear as our conversation progressed that there was little doubt in her mind that she would get pregnant, and that she would welcome a baby:

> We weren't using protection, so of course we knew it was gonna happen *eventually*. And we lived together and we had already planned on getting married, you know, before we found out that I was pregnant. And we had wanted a baby, only because we weren't on any government assistance and we were on our own, and we had our own place, and we were in love with each other.

The remarks by Teen Center mothers like Brooke suggest that the distinction between intentional and unintentional births may be a false dichotomy. An unintentional birth may not be an "accident"—a failure of contraception or a failure to use contraception—as much as it is something that was not necessarily planned in advance with great detail. Thus Brooke considered her pregnancy unintentional because she and Mark had not planned a specific date for getting pregnant, nor had they publicly announced to anyone that they wanted to have a child. In this way, they framed their contraceptive decisions as a gamble; they knew they would get pregnant "eventually," but the uncertainty of when it would occur led her to think of the birth as unintentional. This fuzzy interpretation of "unintentional" illustrates the measurement problem described by Luker (1996) and Zabin, Astone, and Emerson (1993), who pointed out that the terms intentional and unintentional are ambiguous and context-dependent and do not effectively distinguish one group of mothers from another. The frequency with which their pregnancies were referred to as unintentional (when in most instances nothing had been done to prevent it) suggests that this explanation had become part of their culture. The teens drew from their cultural toolkit (Swidler 1986) to frame their early pregnancies for themselves and others in a way that kept them from being deviant.

DISCOVERING THE PREGNANCY

Upon learning of their pregnancies, the emotions experienced by Teen Center mothers ranged from absolute joy to utter despair. The initial reactions varied depending on the individual teen's circumstances. Their age, the nature of their relationship with their baby's father, their future plans, and whether they had even considered the possibility of pregnancy all played a part in how they dealt with the news.

Shock and Despair

About half of the teenage mothers with whom I spoke reported being devastated when they first learned of their pregnancies. This was especially true for the younger teens who had no idea that they were putting themselves at risk of pregnancy by having unprotected sexual intercourse. For example, African American LaNiece, who attended a special school for gifted children before she had her baby, was thirteen when she became pregnant. She was shocked, to put it mildly, because her twenty-year-old boyfriend had told her that he was infertile. When I asked whether her boyfriend was also surprised when she told him the news, she said: "He knew before I knew. I don't know how, but he did. He just felt it. I was like, having all these pains and I knew something was wrong and he said 'Are you pregnant?' And I said 'No, of course not!'"

LaNiece went on to tell me that she did not even consider pregnancy a possibility because her boyfriend had convinced her that they did not need to use contraception. When she found out she really was pregnant, she was so upset that she tried to force a miscarriage:

> I like jumped around and tried to roll over on my stomach, tried to throw myself down the stairs. And I took all these aspirins, but all it did was make me go to sleep. It didn't work. Then I tried to deny it. And see, my closest friend, we were like friends since kindergarten, she was like the really promiscuous one and she didn't get pregnant, and I was the quiet, ugly, fat one in the gifted program, and I was the one who ended up pregnant. It just didn't seem right.

Fifteen-year-old Kerry was also shocked, and for the same reason as LaNiece: her boyfriend had also convinced her that he was sterile. She thought she had the flu or an ulcer and went to the hospital for tests when the symptoms did not subside. Because pregnancy did not even enter her mind, she sent her mother to the hospital to pick up the test results:

> Well behind my back my mom had asked for a pregnancy test, without even telling me. And my mom went down to the hospital and got the results to the pregnancy test. They can do that when you're under eighteen at a hospital, they can tell the parent first. So she found out before I did. And it was terrible.

Kerry went on to explain that her mother had gone to the hospital to pick up the test results at the exact same time that her boyfriend was at her house breaking up with her:

> So five hours after we broke up she closes the door to the family room and says, "I want to talk to you about the results of your urine sample." I said, "OK." So she said, "Well let's go upstairs." And I said, "Why, is it bad?" She goes, "No, let's just go upstairs." Because, see, my dad was downstairs. And my dad flipped out when he found out my sister was pregnant, he didn't talk to her at all. So we go upstairs and she says, "You're pregnant." And I flipped out. I was crying and crying. I almost hit her so many times, 'cause I was crying and I just wanted to hit something so bad. I just wanted to make it go away.

Linda, a popular cheerleader who had been dating the captain of the football team for two years, was devastated when she became pregnant at age sixteen. She realized she was pregnant shortly after breaking up with the boy (after finding him in bed with two girls she knew from school):

> After I broke up with him he called me like every day, and I thought, well maybe I can get back together with him. But I was like, "Did you sleep with someone here?" when we were in his car, and he said, "Well, not *here* [in the front seat]; in the back seat." And I was like, that's it. So January 20 we broke up. And I found out I was pregnant on Valentine's Day. He gave me chocolates and I ate one of them and had to go outside and throw up because I was having morning sickness. And it was horrible, horrible. I didn't want to be pregnant. But my friend's mom took me to get a test and it came back that I was pregnant and I was like, "Oh God." And I just cried and cried.

The teens like Linda who were the most upset about their pregnancies had several things in common: the thought of becoming pregnant had not even entered their minds, and they were no longer dating the baby's father when they learned of their pregnancies. Perhaps most significantly, they all knew that the news of their pregnancy would be a shock to their parents, and they were scared to think that they would have to face them. As Marci said, her first reaction to her pregnancy was "Oh God. I'm going to have to tell my mom. And my dad." Just as Schofield (1994) found in her study of teen mothers, teens' reactions to their pregnancies are dominated by the anticipated reactions of others, especially their parents.

A DREAM COME TRUE

Unlike Fischman's (1975) study, where a majority of the pregnant adolescents were happy when they discovered they were pregnant, only a minority of Teen Center participants told me they felt this way initially. The only teens who reported positive feelings from the outset were those who purposefully did not use contraception because they wanted to get pregnant. These young women were delighted when it actually happened. For example, seventeen-year-old Blair, who stopped using contraception at age sixteen when she and her boyfriend decided they were ready to become parents, told me it took two months for her to get pregnant. When she found out she was definitely pregnant, she was ecstatic:

> I didn't find out for sure until I was four and a half months because I'm irregular so I didn't really notice. But I was playing softball and I wanted to be careful so I stopped playing at four and a half months and went to the doctor to find out for sure. And sure enough, I really was pregnant—and so, so happy!

Nineteen-year-old Julie had just run away from home to escape an abusive stepfather when she became pregnant the first time. The pregnancy was a welcome event in her life:

> Me and my friend were on the run for about, I don't know, a week or two and then I got pregnant with Alex. I think I was pretty happy. I mean, I know everybody else is always like, "I just started crying when I found out I was pregnant," but I think, I think with Alex I was very, very happy.

Andrea, who had just turned seventeen when she became pregnant, was thrilled to find out she was pregnant. She and Charlie, who had said, "Oh well, if it happens, it happens," discovered that they both secretly wanted to have a baby. She explained her feelings about her pregnancy:

> So I knew when I missed my period and there was other signs that my sister had told me about. I didn't even need to go get a test I'm just like, "OK, this is it." I just knew. But I went in for a throat culture and I was like, well I might as well get this done

while I'm here. And the nurse told me and she's like, "There's these options, . . . " but I was just like, "Whatever!" I was kind of ignoring her because I was just thinking, "I'm so happy!"

Andrea resembles the vast majority of teen mothers in that she became pregnant after she dropped out of school (Fergusson and Woodward 2000; Manlove 1998; Upchurch and McCarthy, 1990). Rindfuss, Bumpass, and St. John (1980) posited that "the direction of causality might run from education to fertility," meaning that school failure might lead adolescents to choose early parenthood as an alternative means of success, rather than the oft-cited converse, that early parenthood leads to school failure (441). Andrea was thrilled about becoming a parent for many reasons but, above all, her impending motherhood meant she would soon have a visible symbol of achievement, something she had not experienced at school, in her social life, or at home.

Eighteen-year-old Kristina also had difficulties in school, where her learning disability made academic success difficult and her shy personality prevented her from having much of a social life. She explained to me her reaction to her fifth pregnancy, which followed four miscarriages:

I was very happy and excited but I was mostly scared of being able to have her. I was so scared. Like I said, she was my fifth pregnancy. We thought we weren't gonna be able to have kids. And all I did my first three months was talk to her, and pray to her. Talk and pray to my stomach and say, "Please come into this world." And that's all I'd say when I was pregnant. I wanted a baby more than anything in the world.

Like Andrea, Kristina had always wanted to be good at something, and she told me she had known from a young age ("since I was in first grade") that she would be a good mother. Motherhood was not only a welcome event, it was the *only* achievement she could conceive of for herself.

MIXED FEELINGS

Several of the teens told me they were ambivalent about their pregnancies. The prospect of motherhood was exciting, but they also realized that their young age would make it difficult on many levels. Seventeen-year-old Marci, who wanted to get pregnant since she was fourteen, started thinking at sixteen that maybe she should wait until she was older. She told me, "By the time I was sixteen I had one more scare and I started thinking, you know, how am I going to pursue my career and everything else? And I got to the point where I was like, you know, I don't really want a, you know, I don't want a baby now." She had mixed feelings when she finally did get pregnant at sixteen. On the one hand, she was thrilled about finally getting pregnant, and glad to tell her boyfriend that she really *was* pregnant (because he did not believe her when she told him she thought she was), but at the same time, she was worried about how her family would react:

> Once I actually was pregnant I could tell right away, like within the first week, because I was so exhausted I knew it had been like a sudden change. I was kind of scared at that point because I'd had so many negative pregnancy tests. And when I was fourteen every time I'd get a test and it would be negative it was really upsetting because I wanted it to happen. And my best friend didn't even believe me anymore when I told her that I thought I was pregnant, she was like "OK, whatever, Marci." When it came back positive and I was alone in the room with the nurse and, you know, she showed me the stick but I couldn't really read it. So she was like, "Yeah, you are." And I was like "Oh!" And I kind of laughed. My first reaction was laughter! But I think it was more like, you know, shock. And then I got in the car on the way home, and that's when it hit me—that's when it hit me that I'd have to tell my parents.

Seventeen-year-old Jessica also had mixed feelings. An honors student with lofty educational plans for herself, having a baby at a young age was never part of her master plan. Thus on the one hand, she felt a sense of dismay at what having a child might mean for her future. On the other hand, the thought of actually having a baby to love and care for was exciting, and she was puzzled at the amazing sense of calm she experienced when she was pregnant. She told me the feeling began when she realized the condom "exploded":

> I kind of felt something and I thought, "Oh great, I know it. I know I'm pregnant." So I kind of knew the second it happened. And this was like a week after we started having sex! It was within the first week. And I just kind of . . . stayed on an even keel. My hormones were already changing but in a weird way. Because I was so calm about everything. No problems. I mean, I could deal with everything—nothing bothered me. It's hard to put into words how I felt. I was just kind of—neutral.

Jessica went on to explain that she was surprised to feel so "neutral" about the pregnancy because she had always told herself that it would be a big deal if she became pregnant before she graduated. She tried to convince herself to feel unhappy about the pregnancy, or to at least feel ambivalent, but the reality was that she was happy about the prospect of becoming a mother.

FOUR

KEEPING THE BABY

For the most part, Teen Center mothers became parents because they deemed it the only suitable resolution for a pregnancy. Like the teenage women in Thompson's (1995) study of adolescent mothers, many of the teens I spoke with did not view pregnancy resolution as involving choice; if they became pregnant, the only option was motherhood. Of course, this was especially true for teens such as Kristina and Blair, who intentionally became pregnant, but it also held true for the teens who were shocked and upset by their unplanned pregnancies, many of whom did not even contemplate other options.

TELLING THE FAMILY

Most of the teen mothers told me the thing they feared most about their pregnancy was the fact that they would have to tell their parents. Regardless of whether they were happy about the pregnancy or upset about it, they were practically unanimous in their fear of telling their parents. Farber (1991) noted a similar pattern in her study of adolescent mothers, commenting, "Fear was a common reaction both before and especially after confirmation of their pregnancy, often because of the anticipated response of their parents to the news" (703). Many of the young women at the Teen Center, like the women in Schofield's (1994) study of teen mothers, were so scared about the prospect of telling their parents that they put off telling them for several months. Given the tremendous influence parents, especially mothers, have on adolescents' decisions regarding pregnancy resolution, the reactions of their parents were crucial in shaping their choices to carry their pregnancies to term and to raise their babies themselves (Brazzell and Acock 1988; Kahn 1994; Schofield 1994).

Initial Shock, Eventual Acceptance

Thompson (1995) explained that the general sequence of events among the teens in her study who told their parents they were pregnant was "family drama," followed by shock, back-and-forth debates about how she should resolve the issue, and, ultimately, some degree of tolerance, acceptance, or support. Farber (1991) recounted similar stories of the young mothers in her study and noted that although most white and black pregnant teens anticipated anger as their parents' first reaction, the white teens were more likely to be met with parental concern, unhappiness, or disappointment than anger. These sentiments resemble descriptions given by white Teen Center participants as well. For example, nineteen-year-old Julie told me that her mother and sister were both shocked when she became pregnant the first time at age sixteen, despite the fact that her older sister had two children as a teenager. By the time she became pregnant for the third time, they were less than pleased:

> I mean, with this one, my mom, instead of saying "Congratulations!" she said "Well I'm sorry to hear you're pregnant again." My mom only had two kids and she's had abortions every time after that. And my sister, well, she didn't say, "I'm sorry." She asked what I was going to do and I told her I was going to keep him. And she was like, "Oh, OK. As long as you know what you want to do." But I could tell that she thought I was making a mistake.

By the time Julie was in her second trimester, however, both her mother and sister had come around; her mother gave Julie a car so she and her sons could get to school easier when the baby arrived, and her sister volunteered to babysit the three boys if Julie ever wanted to leave them at home.

Seventeen-year-old Andrea, who became pregnant after dating her boyfriend for three weeks, had to face telling her grandmother, who had raised her since she was three years old. After Andrea's younger sister's pregnancy, her grandmother put tremendous pressure on Andrea to finish high school and to go to college before starting a family, and she was disappointed when Andrea also became pregnant. Andrea told me her grandmother initially asked her to move out of the house, but added that her anger did not last long: when Andrea had complications early in her second trimester, it was her grandmother who took her to the hospital and cared for her when she returned home.

Fifteen-year-old Vanessa was so afraid of telling her parents about her pregnancy that she kept it a secret from them until she was five months along:

> I was scared to tell my mom. Really scared. And when I did finally tell her, she got really upset. She went through her denial thing, you know, saying it couldn't be true 'cause I was too young and everything. But after a while she started to accept it, and now she loves the baby. My stepdad was furious. He made my mom send me to live with my dad in Texas during my pregnancy because he didn't want me around embarrassing him or whatever. And my dad, oh, he was so mad! But he came around after I was out there with him, and I guess my stepdad is okay with it now that I'm living with them again, but I don't really ever talk to him because I hate him so much.

Like Andrea's grandmother and Julie's mother and sister, Vanessa's parents were disappointed in her and let her know it, but the disappointment gave way to acceptance once the baby was born.

Many of the teens told me they received different reactions from their mothers and fathers. Bracken, Klerman, and Bracken (1978) posited that pregnant teens often turn first to people they think will be supportive and avoid "authority figures" they think will be angry with them or disagree with their decisions for resolution. At the Teen Center, the supportive person was usually the adolescent's mother, and the authority figure was her father. The teens were unanimous in telling me that their mothers were more supportive about the pregnancy than their fathers and, perhaps anticipating this support, they usually told their mothers first.

Twenty-year-old Amanda told her mother before she told her father because her mother broached the subject with her:

> One night my mom was at the computer and she goes, "You're pregnant, aren't you?" This was still before I had gone to the doctor but I had gone to Planned Parenthood and they said I definitely was pregnant. So she looked at me and said, "You're pregnant, aren't you?" So I lied and said, "I don't know. I went to Planned Parenthood and I have to call." Even though I had already known for sure for like a week. So I called some random

number—'cause they were closed—and I hung up and I came back crying. Then we went to her room and we were crying. And she made me go out and tell my dad and it was *so* hard. I was sitting there crying so he was like worried, and I was like [crying sounds]. And I'm like, "I'm pregnant." And he just sat there and didn't say anything and then he and my mom went for a ride. But they were both happy the next day. We all went [to] garage [sales] the next day, and we bought baby clothes. And that was it. They were ready to be grandparents.

Linda, the popular sixteen-year-old girl, was afraid to tell her parents about her pregnancy because she knew they would be disappointed. Her parents were well educated—her stepfather had a PhD in economics—and expected her to coast through high school and go on to a prestigious college. She was so fearful of their reaction that she avoided telling most of her friends, because she worried that the news would get back to her parents eventually:

My friend Jill knew I was pregnant because she went with me to get the test, but I told her that I had miscarried, so really nobody knew. I only gained, I think maybe ten pounds. The people around me, my close friends would say, "God you're getting fat." So I'd just go along with it and say, "Yeah, I haven't been exercising much," or whatever.

Finally, her mother confronted her:

When I was eight months' pregnant, my mom asked me. She said, "Have you noticed that you're gaining weight? Do you think that maybe you could be pregnant?" And I just burst out with "Yes, I am!" And I started bawling. And she said, "How far are you, around five months?" So I told her, "No. Eight." And then she started crying too. Then she took me out to dinner and we ate a bunch of chocolate together.

From that moment on, her mother supported her pregnancy. Like the other teens, Linda was most fearful of explaining her pregnancy to her father. In fact, she was so afraid of telling her dad, whom she saw only a few times a year, that she waited until her baby was three months old:

Actually, his dad was in the hospital dying, so I guess it was sort of a weak point to tell him, but he didn't react at all. He was just like numb to everything. So in a way, it worked out better for me to tell him that way. And now he plays with her and he tells her to call him "Gammpies." But I was really scared about how he might have reacted, that's why I waited so long to tell him.

Only one teen with whom I spoke thought her parents would be supportive of her pregnancy, and it turned out she was wrong. Fourteen-year-old Angelica, who intentionally became pregnant, said she figured her parents had no choice but to be supportive:

I mean, they couldn't really be mad because I was already married. My mom, she didn't talk to me, or she ignored me, for about a week. But we're best friends now. My dad was mean though. 'Cause the stupid thing he did is told my mom, "It's either Angelica and the baby or me." 'Cause he thought him and my mom should disown me for getting pregnant. And my mom said, "Well, I guess you gotta leave." Because, see, my friend had just had a baby—she's the one who introduced me to my husband—and my dad was like, "Oh, are you going to go and copy her?" I'm like, "You don't go copy someone to go get pregnant." But that's what he thought I did. And he gave my mom this, "Either choose me or choose her," and my mom said, "My kids always come first." So he didn't like that very much, and he left.

Whereas Angelica's decision to marry at an early age was enthusiastically supported by her Latino mother and father who, she told me later, expected all of their daughters to marry before they were twenty, her parents did not subscribe to the cultural norm for young married women to begin child rearing as soon as possible. This stance may have been a result of their location in a well-educated, affluent, university community. In Lakeside, education was clearly the path to success, and Angelica's parents may have seen having a child as interfering with her chance for achieving the success they wanted for her.

IMMEDIATE ACCEPTANCE

In Schofield's (1994) study of teen mothers, several of the adolescents' mothers were described as being excited about the pregnancy from the moment they learned of it. Although this was not as common at the Teen Center, a few young women recounted similar stories. For example, seventeen-year-old Sunshine told me her mother was thrilled when she learned the news: "My mom, she was like totally excited because she was going to have her first grandbaby." Sunshine had not seen nor heard from her mother from the time she was three years old until she was thirteen because her father's parents raised her and her brother after her parents divorced. Sunshine explained to me that she and her mom "weren't like mother-daughter," but more like friends because of the long time they had been apart, and she thought that might have explained why her mother took the news better than the mothers of some of her Teen Center friends.

LaNiece's mother also responded to the news of her thirteen-year-old daughter's pregnancy with immediate enthusiasm. Before LaNiece herself knew she was pregnant, her mother suspected it. LaNiece had mentioned to an older girlfriend that she was not feeling well; the friend became suspicious that she might be pregnant and told her own mother, and the friend's mother called LaNiece's mother. LaNiece explained:

> Well, my mom knew early on. And she kept asking me, "Are you pregnant?" And I'd always say, "No." And then one day I came home and I had this really bad fever but then it went away, like, within the hour. And she said, "Aha! You're pregnant." And I was like, "No I'm not." I didn't show until I was eight months, and Shawn told me he couldn't have kids, so I didn't think I was pregnant.

Her mother made an appointment for her to see a doctor and sat with her while they waited for the test results. She explained her mother's reaction: "My mom, she was like totally happy. She was so excited. She was like, 'When you have the baby I want to be close to it!'"

Unlike LaNiece's and Sunshine's mothers, who immediately accepted the idea that their daughters would carry their babies to term and raise them, Tracy's mother was accepting of the situation and supportive of *any* resolution option that Tracy chose. Tracy, who became pregnant two days after her fourteenth birthday, was on vacation with her mother in California when her mother confronted her with her suspicions that Tracy was pregnant. Tracy did not think it could be possible, since Eddie had told her he was sterile, but she went to Planned Parenthood with her mother anyway. She said her mom was supportive of her and told her she would stand by her no matter how she chose to resolve the pregnancy: "She said that we'd do—that we'd be—that she'd help me with anything I chose." Tracy's and LaNiece's stories were similar in two ways: their mothers were both supportive from the outset, and their mothers both recognized that their daughters were pregnant before the daughters themselves knew it. It could be that the reason they were supportive was that they had time to come to terms with the pregnancy while they were paying attention to the symptoms. For them, the pregnancy was not as much of a shock as it was for the parents who did not notice any of the signs and whose daughters dropped a bombshell on them.

A significant number of the teens told me they did not expect their families to be as supportive of their pregnancies as they were. Twenty-year-old Brooke was afraid to tell her parents that she and her boyfriend were expecting a baby. In fact, she hid in the bathroom with the door locked while her boyfriend broke the news to her parents. She told me she was pleasantly surprised when "they were supportive from day one." Perhaps because they belonged to the Church of Jesus Christ of Latter-day Saints, the idea of Brooke beginning her family at a young age was not as terrible as she thought it might be, especially since she and her boyfriend were engaged. Similarly, seventeen-year-old Jessica told me her mother was thrilled about the baby, and she too thought it might have been her mother's religious background that softened the blow:

> I told my mom right away when I thought I was pregnant. She's the one who made the appointment actually. She was really excited about it, really excited because she thought it was a sign from God. Especially when she found out it was a boy because you see I have four sisters and you know, some religious people think they need to have a son for some reason. My mother is different. She's really religious—she's a religious zealot. She started kind of getting under the impression that this was a child that was going to be sent to her through me from God.

Jessica was one of the few teens who told her mother she might be pregnant before she knew for sure herself. Most of the other teens told me they took pregnancy tests first, then told their mothers. I asked Jessica how she came to tell her mom first:

> My mother and I at that point were a lot more like friends. I had never really been a daughter. And so I just told her and thought either she'd accept it or she wouldn't. I think it's because she's always needed a friend. I used to be a lot more mature than my age when I was growing up, so she was—she just thinks of me as a friend.

PROLONGED ANGER

A small number of teens told me the initial shock and anger expressed by their parents never wore off, that their relationships had been irreparably damaged by their pregnancies. In every case, the fathers were the ones who showed continual disappointment in their daughters, or expressed unwavering anger toward the men who had done this to their daughters. Mothers may have expressed these feelings initially, but by the time the baby was born, they had forgiven their daughters.

LaNiece's story is a good example of this difference in how family members reacted to the pregnancy. Her mother was excited about the prospect of becoming a grandmother from the moment she found out about her daughter's pregnancy, her two brothers were disappointed but supportive, and her father was angry:

> My dad was mad. He was always shooting at him, at my son's dad. You know, he'd take out his gun and whenever Shawn would come by he'd *shoot* at him to scare him off! And my brothers, oh my gosh, my brothers were so mad and they beat him up so bad. Shawn was like two or three years older than my big brother, and a lot of times my brother used to be scared of him because he was older, but my god, he just beat him up. But they weren't mad at me, which was weird. My brothers were supportive. They would always try to touch my stomach or feel him kicking. They, I don't know, they felt kind of bad, my older brother would say, "Oh you messed up your life, you'll never do anything." But my dad, he didn't want to talk about it then, and now it's almost three years later, and he still barely talks to me.

Seventeen-year-old Sunshine's father did not go as far as shooting at his grandson's father, but he let Sunshine know he was disappointed with her through the first comment he made to her after she told him she was having a baby. Because she was so afraid of his reaction, she waited until the month before the baby was born to call and tell him she was pregnant: "When I first told my dad, I was like eight months' pregnant. And his reaction was—he wasn't shocked. He said he was wondering when it was going to happen, which kind of pissed me off but I didn't let him know that." She went on to tell me that this was his way of saying that nothing she could do would surprise him, because she had already disappointed him so much.

Tracy, who had just turned fourteen when she found out she was pregnant, also got a different reaction from her father than she did from her supportive mother. Her parents were divorced, and she lived some distance from her dad, so she told him over the phone:

> My dad was a different story. I didn't tell him 'til I was four months along 'cause I was so young we didn't know if the pregnancy was going to last. When I told him it was complete shock. He was quiet on the phone for five minutes and then I got this, "How the *fuck* did this happen?" He said the only way that he'd accept it was if he saw the baby—otherwise, he wouldn't believe it. Nobody believed it, actually. I was Little Miss Virgin and Little Miss Goody-Two-Shoes that nobody thought that would ever happen to. And Eddie was my first, and he's still the only one I've ever been with.

Two years later, I attended Tracy's son's birthday party and noticed she did not interact very much with her father. After the party ended, I asked her about their relationship, and she explained to me that he never forgave her for getting pregnant, and that she and her son rarely saw him. In fact, she told me she was surprised he even attended the birthday party.

The young women at the Teen Center whose fathers expressed continual disappointment in them resembled the teenage mothers of past generations described by Solinger (1992). In her historical analysis of nonmarital pregnancy, Solinger provided anecdotes of several fathers from the 1940s and 1950s who threatened to kill their unmarried, pregnant daughters and others who planned to ship their pregnant daughters off to another part of the country and tell everyone that she had died. Most fathers did not go to those extremes, of course, but Solinger reported that it was not uncommon for the fathers of pregnant teenagers to react to their daughters' pregnancies by denying their existence.

CHOOSING MOTHERHOOD

Most of the young women at the Teen Center felt that abortion and adoption were unsuitable choices for all women, a perception held by adolescent mothers in other studies as well (Bracken, Klerman, and Bracken 1978; Farber 1991). Barth (1987) posited that "The unsympathetic attitude of most adolescents toward adoption is shown in their increasing disregard and even disdain for this option" (323). Abortion is often viewed as an even less desirable alternative, as many adolescents have internalized the discourse of the anti-choice movement and have come to view abortion as selfishly ending an unborn child's life, and not as an opportunity to delay parenthood to work toward goals of their own. As Thompson (1995) argued, "Anti-abortion rhetoric and regulations undermined girls' sense that they were important in themselves by stigmatizing and limiting their right to put their own futures first in deciding what to do about a pregnancy" (112). She added that anti-abortion rhetoric "valorized motherhood, communicating that far from being something to be ashamed of, maternity was heroic" (1995, 112). Indeed, not just teenage mothers feel this way; adolescents in general share the sentiment that abortion is an irresponsible cop-out, and they refer to anti-abortion catchphrases, such as the notion of "abortion being used as birth control" to describe their feelings about abortion, reflecting the powerful influence of the anti-choice movement (Stone and Waszak 1992, 56).

Rejecting the Alternatives

In the adolescent culture of the Teen Center, having an abortion or relinquishing a child for adoption was deemed an irresponsible choice. The responsible thing to do was to raise the child, regardless of whether the pregnancy was planned or unplanned, and regardless of one's personal circumstances. Anything else was a cop-out—an easy solution.

Several teens faced pressure from family members and other significant adults to consider abortion or adoption, but they did not change their minds. Vanessa, who became pregnant at age fourteen by her twenty-year-old boyfriend, explained how she arrived at the decision to keep her baby:

> My mom, man, did she pressure me. She wanted me to give her up for adoption but I told her no way. 'Cause I think that's even worse than abortion. I was actually thinking about adoption at one time, but then I thought about it more and I just said "no." Like, I've had friends who've been adopted and it's just so hard for them not to know their real parents. And they have these other people pretending to be their parents and they just hate it. And there's no way I could have an abortion. No way.

Marci, the young woman who tried to get pregnant beginning at age fourteen, felt pressure from her mother to get an abortion. She thought her mother was supportive of her decision to raise the child herself, until one telling incident occurred:

> It started really turning into a lot of passive-aggressive stuff you know, like I remember there was like a week of time until it was

too late to have an abortion and we were somewhere and I said, "Well, it's too late to have an abortion anyway" and she said "Well, it's *not* too late, you know, we have a week." So that's how I knew that she had looked into it and that she wanted me to get an abortion.

Thompson (1995) found a similar pattern in her study of teenage pregnancy and parenting, with many of the mothers of the pregnant teenagers in her study encouraging their daughters to have abortions but offering support if the teen decided to keep the baby.

The anti-abortion, anti-adoption sentiment was a pervasive element of the Teen Center culture. When Marci became pregnant with her son, she had no qualms about raising him herself, and she did not even consider adoption or abortion. However, she told me that now that she had firsthand experience of raising a child, her views about adoption had changed. She confided in me that she would never tell anyone else at the center how she felt because she recognized how unpopular it was among most of her peers:

> I'm really careful so that I don't get pregnant again, but god forbid if I were to get pregnant now, I wouldn't tell anybody now. I wouldn't even tell anybody here at the Teen Center. I would wait 'til I graduate [in two months] and then I'd look into putting it up for adoption.

LaNiece told me about a mother at the Teen Center whom she considered irresponsible, exemplifying the widely held view about bearing and rearing one's child as being the responsible thing to do: "One girl who wanted to keep partying and stuff put her child up for adoption. I don't think you should have that option. I figure if you get pregnant, you should be made to grow up. 'Cause it's not fair. Everyone should have to take responsibility for their actions." LaNiece's sentiments were remarkably similar to those expressed by a black middle-class teen in Farber's study of adolescent mothers who said, "I don't care if it's your fifteenth child—you knew what you were doing, and you have to take the consequences" (1991, 709). According to Farber, black teens were more likely than white teens in her study to express the opinion that "having the child, regardless of the circumstances, was the most responsible course" a pregnant adolescent could take (1991, 709).

Amanda, a white twenty-year-old who became pregnant at sixteen, also acknowledged the pervasive peer pressure she felt to do the responsible thing. When I asked how she arrived at the decision to keep her baby, she said, "Oh I *knew* I wasn't having an abortion. I'm totally pro-choice, but I was totally against abortion for myself." Later she told me that she actually got pregnant a second time and had an abortion after she joined the Teen Center, something she did not share with anyone there and did not want them to find out about. In my four years at the center I grew close to a few other adolescent mothers who became pregnant for a second time and had abortions—some kept the entire pregnancy a secret, while others told everyone that they had miscarried. Abortion was something that was talked about in hushed tones in the Teen Center culture.

Seventeen-year-old Jessica, who became pregnant after the condom exploded, had strong feelings about abortion because of her religious upbringing—she was the only teen to whom I spoke who mentioned religion as influencing her decision. I asked her whether she and Patrick had discussed what they would do if she got pregnant. She replied:

> Kind of peripherally, but not really. Since we were using condoms we didn't really expect that to happen, to say the least. And my morals were no abortion, abortion is not an option. You know for me, it was like, I'm a Christian, so I can't have an abortion, but if I see the baby I won't be able to give him up for adoption, so I have to raise him. It's the only thing left.

For Jessica and many other mothers at the Teen Center, parenthood was not considered a choice. Instead, it was viewed as the only way to deal with a pregnancy. Summarizing other studies on teenage pregnancy resolution, Furstenberg came to the conclusion that "many [teens] regard parenthood as a default option. That is, they let parenthood happen because they view their other choices as inferior or difficult" (1991, 134).

The decision to bear and rear their children was one that the teens arrived at by themselves or with varying degrees of input from their parents. Only two of the teens with whom I spoke mentioned anything about the baby's father as being important in their choice to keep the baby, a finding that resembles Farber's (1991) study of black and white teenage mothers, where only one adolescent out of twenty-eight mentioned the baby's father as playing a part in her decision. Eighteen-year-old Marci told me her boyfriend Dion was so adamant about her having an abortion that he threatened her with bodily harm if she did not go along with it. She lied to him and told him she was going to have an abortion and then broke up with him. After the baby was born, she sent him a letter telling him she had changed her mind. Eighteen-year-old Jessica was the only other teen who mentioned her baby's father during a discussion about pregnancy resolution, and she told me she did not know her boyfriend's true feelings about her pregnancy until after their son was born:

> And Patrick told me only like a year ago, right after we had Steven, that's when he tells me, "You know, I didn't want to tell you this because I knew you were so set against it, but I probably would have wanted you to have an abortion." But he totally thought it was my choice and he didn't want to say anything about it.

Although, as part of my in-depth interview, I asked each teen how her baby's father reacted to the news of the pregnancy and what he wanted her to do, only Marci and Jessica mentioned anything about their baby's father preferring one form of pregnancy resolution over another. The other teens described their babies' fathers as being happy, upset, or surprised, but they never mentioned what they wanted them to do about it. These responses make it difficult to discern whether the young men shared Patrick's view that it was the young woman's decision because it was her body, whether the men left it up to the women because they figured they would play a small role in their lives (so it would not affect them one way or the other), or whether the young women did not even consult their babies' fathers because they felt the decision was theirs to make, since it would affect them the most.

MULLING IT OVER

A handful of teens were not as vehement in their convictions—adoption and abortion were possibilities, but for one reason or another these alternatives just did not pan out when it came down to the wire. For example, nineteen-year-old Julie seriously considered relinquishing her second son. She had even gone so far as to make arrangements with an adoption agency. A month before Brian was born, however, she started dating someone who told her she should keep the baby and they could raise him together:

> With Brian, at first I was definitely considering adoption. And then I started going out with a guy and he told me that he'd be there and everything, and he broke up with me a week and three days before Brian was born. But I had already decided to keep him. And my sister was saying, "We can still go to the adoption agency but I'll definitely help you out if you want to keep it." So

I ended up keeping him. It was like, I'd already made my decision and I didn't want to change my mind again.

In deciding to raise her child herself, Julie resembles the approximately 80 to 90 percent of teens who change their minds after initially deciding to relinquish their children for adoption (Cervera 1993).

Sixteen-year-old Linda, the popular cheerleader, seriously contemplated both abortion and adoption. She told me she was ultimately planning on relinquishing her baby for adoption, and she said that was why she did not tell her parents about her pregnancy until she was in her eighth month:

> I thought at first that I was going to give Karly up for adoption because I wanted nothing to do with a baby. So that's why I didn't tell my parents at first. I thought I might not even ever tell them, that I would just go have the baby, give it up, and leave the hospital. And just tell them I was spending the night at someone's house or something. So when my mom asked me, I was like, "Yeah, I definitely want to give the baby up for adoption. I don't want to keep it." Because every time I thought about it, it just reminded me of Ben and the terrible way we broke up. So that was just really tough. I changed my mind when I got to thinking about how I would feel if I were the child and had to be adopted out to another family. And what if this family decided to never tell me and I found out one day, or if they did tell me and I had to wonder who my mom was and why she had given me up, and how much that would hurt. I know people say that, you know, it's not that bad, but when I think about it, I think it would be hard.

In many ways, Linda resembled the prototypical birth mother who relinquishes her child for adoption: she was white (Weinman, Robinson, Simmons, Schreiber, and Stafford 1989) and had educational goals (graduating from high school early and attending a prestigious college) and career plans (becoming an architect) that would be interrupted by early parenthood (Cocozzelli 1989). Linda also resembled the type of woman who considers abortion. She was white, she had well-educated parents (Marsiglio and Menaghan 1990) and "aspirations toward self-improvement and upward mobility," she was of a higher socioeconomic status than most of her Teen Center peers, she was no longer dating the baby's father, and she was unhappy about the pregnancy (Fischman 1975, 222). It is not surprising, then, that she did consider abortion:

I actually thought about having an abortion at first, but I couldn't find money and I was also very scared. And I obviously wasn't going to ask Ben after what he'd put me through. And I called this place in Springfield and this woman, she was just talking to me about, "You know God loves you," and all this stuff, and that just made me mad. I was like, "You know, if God loves me, why am I pregnant?" It was called like "The Pregnancy Center" or something. And I didn't know what to expect, but I thought maybe they would help find an abortion clinic or something, but that's not what they were about. They were about making you keep the baby. And then I called Planned Parenthood, and I was talking to this woman there. And I'm like, "Well I don't have any money, and I don't even have a way to get out there." And she was like, "then we can't help you," and hung up on me.

For a few of the teens, the deciding moment came when they saw ultrasounds of their unborn children. Tracy, who had just turned fourteen when she got pregnant, explained:

Well, my mom said she'd help me with anything I chose and I wasn't really sure for a while what that would be. But after an ultrasound I chose to keep Kevin cause I saw him squirming around in there. That was at five months. And then I decided even more once I started growing and I could feel him kicking. I knew I couldn't give him up.

Andrea, who became pregnant by her boyfriend of three weeks, told a similar story of becoming attached after she saw the ultrasound:

I knew that I wasn't going to abort him. Well, I think I thought about it once when me and Charlie were fighting really bad and I thought that I didn't want Gary to grow up without his mom or dad because I knew what it was like and I thought he would be in a better place if I did that, if I had an abortion. If Charlie wasn't going to be there, I thought maybe the baby would be better off that way. So I thought about that like once, but then I thought, well that's just going to kill him. I was having problems from the very beginning so I had an ultrasound at like four weeks and I could see this little dot and this little heart and I was like, "Oh!" You can't see what it is, but you can tell there's something alive in there. And I never thought about putting him up for adoption because if I'm going to go through all of this I'm not going to give him away because I'm too attached to him to even think about that.

Cervera (1993) posited that *in utero* bonding between the adolescent mother and her child is often overlooked in studies of how teenagers arrive at the decision to bear and rear their children. He argued that as the pregnancy progresses into the second and third trimesters, the teen begins to get the attention of family and friends (and often the baby's father), which may increase her "sense of maternal competency" and feelings of affection toward the baby, making it all the more unlikely that she will relinquish it for adoption (357).

HAVING NO CHOICE IN THE MATTER

Brazzell and Acock (1988) posited that mothers are the most influential figures in shaping adolescents' decisions regarding pregnancy resolution, more so than peers or other significant persons in their lives. At the Teen Center, parental influence was most notable among the younger mothers, teens who were thirteen or fourteen years old when they became pregnant. Although most of the teenage women reported that their mothers gave them support or suggestions for what they should do, the younger mothers reported being the most influenced. Both LaNiece and Kerry told me that their parents made the decision that they should carry their babies to term and raise them. Thirteen-year-old LaNiece told me that she had no idea what to do when she learned she was pregnant:

Well at first, I was just like "God!" 'cause I didn't know anything about the issues and everything. 'Cause I was only thirteen so I wasn't all deep into that "Kill all the doctors who perform abortions" kind of thing. But my mom was like, "No. You are not having an abortion. We are going to keep this child." So it wasn't my decision to make.

LaNiece's account resembles the stories Farber (1991) heard from lower-class teens in her study of adolescent mothers. She noted that lower-class parents, especially mothers, "quickly accepted as inevitable that the young woman would keep and raise her child" and "were actively involved in making this decision" (712). I asked LaNiece, who was sixteen at the time of the interview, whether she agreed with the decision her mother made for her:

Now that I'm older or whatever, I agree with her. I would never, ever give a baby up for adoption. And I would never, ever have an abortion because I'm totally against that unless it was rape. Because I think if you can have a child, you shouldn't just go out, be careless, and like kill all these babies and be like, "Oh whatever, I'll just get another abortion." You shouldn't do that.

I asked what that would mean for her if she were to have another unplanned pregnancy, and she replied, "I'd keep it. I sure would. I'd just have a lot of kids!"

Another Teen Center participant whose parents decided she should keep and raise her baby was Kerry, who had just turned sixteen and was eight months' pregnant when we talked. A white teen from a lower-class background, Kerry told me she was not excited about becoming a parent in the next few weeks, but that her father was making her keep the baby. She explained:

I'm scared. I'm scared I'm not going to be able to do it. Scared that I won't be a good parent. I mean, I've made a commitment to be there and I want to be there, but it's going to be hard and I don't know if I can do it. Some of the people here [at the Teen Center] were telling me about adoption choices and stuff, and I told my dad about it but he said it wasn't an option. The rule in my family is if we get pregnant, that's it, we keep the kid. So that's that.

Farber (1991) noted that teens from lower-classbackgrounds were not only more likely to turn to their parents for advice and have parents who told them how they should resolve the pregnancy, but that they also had parents who leaned toward having their daughters raise the child.

The accounts from this chapter and the last show that in depicting the circumstances of their pregnancies and their decisions to bear and rear their own children the way they did, the teen mothers deflected the stigma cast upon young mothers away from themselves and onto another source. For some, the real deviant was a deceptive boyfriend who duped them into pregnancy; for others, it was a controlling parent who prohibited any outcome other than carrying the child to term and raising it themselves. Another group pointed out the irresponsible behavior of pregnant teens who receive abortions or relinquish their children for adoption, while others denied any deviance in their parenthood—their pregnancy was planned, wanted, and a positive experience. What each of these accounts has in common is the sentiment that the teen mother herself is not deviant.

FIVE

COMPETITIVE PARENTING

The culture created and shared by teen parents involved in a school-based program is a crucial mediator between the structure of the program and the individual participants. It shapes their experiences as they go through the program. The culture at the Teen Center was largely characterized by its competitive nature as the teens tried to prove that they were better parents than other parents, not only other teenagers but also those who delay having children until their twenties, thirties, and forties. The competition encompassed all facets of their parenting: from knowing the most about parenting and child development to providing the greatest number of educational toys for their children. By "winning" these competitions, the teens hoped to combat the negative image associated with early childbearing. In this chapter, I detail the elements that make up the competitive culture of teen parenting.

The feeling of competition in the teen parenting culture was pervasive. Although few mothers openly acknowledged this competition, most were eager to compare themselves with other teen parents and with parents who had children later in life. In both instances, the teen mothers tried to cast themselves in a positive light by pointing out the negative qualities of other parents. The ideology they espoused, then, primarily concerned proving their competence as parents by magnifying their own successes and simultaneously pointing out the failures of other parents. Their concerns as parents revolved around proving that they were financially capable of providing for their children, having children who were developmentally advanced, accepting and rejecting parenting advice as they chose, and viewing themselves as better parents than their own parents and parents who delayed having children until their thirties and forties. By placing themselves as winners in a self-proclaimed competition with other parents, the teen mothers worked to legitimate their decisions to parent at an early age.

HYPERMATERIALISM

The ability to financially support their children was a focal concern, if not an obsession, among the mothers at the Teen Center. An important facet of this hypermaterialism was the ability to live without financial assistance from parents or the government. This financial independence meant living away from their parents (which about half of the teen parents did) and being able to afford rent, food, and diapers. This desire to be independent of financial assistance stands in stark contrast to the reality of most teenage mothers. More than 60 percent of teenage mothers receive AFDC, Special Supplemental Program for Women, Infants, and Children (WIC), Medicaid, and other forms of federal assistance (Miller and Moore 1990), and half of all AFDC payments go to adolescent mothers (Ortiz and Bassoff 1987). As Horowitz (1995) pointed out, however, teen mothers, often reluctant to admit their poverty, tell others that they are more financially secure than they really are. In keeping their poverty a secret and setting forth an image that they are financially stable, if not wealthy, the teen mothers seek to place themselves in a position of superiority over other teen mothers and to cast off the criticism that they are too young to adequately provide for their children.

Several mothers drew sharp contrasts between themselves and the stereotypical welfare-dependent teenage mother. For example, nineteen-year-old Brooke took pride in her financial situation, which she felt distinguished her from other teen mothers. Brooke, a white mother from a middle-class family, lived with her nineteen-year-old fiancé Mark and their eleven-month-old son Chris. Mark's income as an electrician allowed them to buy a mobile home and live quite comfortably. Brooke explained that she and Mark were different from other teen parents because they were not financially dependent on others: "I'm sure for a lot of girls it's that way, but I'm not on welfare. We're making it on our own. My fiancé works, we own our own place, and we're not mooching from my parents."

Other teens were upset with the pervasive media image of the welfare-dependent teenage mother. Tracy, the fifteen-year-old white mother from a working-class family, explained why this image bothered her:

They're just going by the statistics. [They think] that we're all bad people, that we'll all amount to nothing, and that we'll all be living in the streets. It upsets me. Sometimes I just want to give them a call and say, "Hey, look, this is what I'm doing and I don't think I'm having much trouble." I get mad when people say, "Just because you're a teen parent, you can't take care of your child."

Brooke told me that she was in the process of staging a letter-writing campaign to network talk show hosts to plead with them to portray teen parents in a more positive light by showcasing self-sufficient mothers like herself and some of her peers from the Teen Center.

Many teen parents were optimistic when they described their financial situations, even if they were experiencing hardships. For example, I learned firsthand that Brooke and Mark were having financial difficulties when Brooke asked me to drive her to an appointment to apply for Emergency Family Assistance. Apparently Mark's salary was not making ends meet, and they found themselves short $120 for their monthly utility bill. Nonetheless, Brooke remained proud of the fact that she and Mark were different from other teen parents who relied on welfare. Tracy, too, was more dependent on her mother than she liked to admit; only days after telling me why the media image of teen mothers upset her, Tracy and her six-month-old son Kevin moved back with Tracy's mom because she could no longer afford to live on her own. For Tracy, the reality of her financial situation was that she could not survive without financial assistance. In her mind, however, she stood in sharp contrast to other teen mothers who "all live in the streets." For many mothers, contrasting their financial situation with that of the stereotypical welfare-dependent teenage mother was a way of affirming that they should not be perceived as belonging to that stigmatized group. They were dramatically different from this image.

Merely getting by financially was not satisfactory for the teen mothers; it was important to have enough money left over after paying bills to buy expensive clothes, toys, and gifts for their children. Horowitz (1995) noted in her study of adolescent mothers that having a "spoilt" child was a source of pride for teen mothers, a pattern that was evident at the Teen Center as well. At Christmas, the teen mothers compared how much money they had spent on their children. In one conversation, three mothers bragged that they had spent between $300 and $500 on gifts for their children; a mother who spent considerably less than they did was put on the defensive and felt guilty for not being able to match their lavish spending. To pay for these extras, the teen mothers maxed out their credit cards and bought things on layaway. Other mothers spent their paychecks and AFDC checks on toys and clothes for their children. Jill, a Latina from a working-class family, talked endlessly about the $200 in new toys she was going to buy (for no particular occasion) for her twelve-month-old son Henry, as soon as she received her next paycheck from her part-time job as a medical assistant in a nursing home. The sixteen-year-old sophomore frequently reminded the other mothers of her plans by asking their opinions about where she should go shopping with her $200. At the same time, she confided in me that her husband's salary from his landscaping job provided barely enough income to cover the essentials, and that they were constantly short of cash. Like Brooke and Tracy, Jill was not as affluent as she wanted others to believe.

In addition to shopping sprees, several mothers talked of buying a toy or an outfit whenever they went shopping. Linda, who became pregnant at sixteen, recalled spending a lot of money before her daughter was born. She explained that "once I found out about all the kinds of stuff you can buy them at the store, I just started going out and spending money left and right." Seventeen-year-old Stephanie said that she bought toys for her eleven-month-old son "every time I go to, like, Walmart or somewhere," something she said she did several times a week. She also described how much she bought him before he was born: "When I found out he was a boy, oh god. I went and bought anything that—I bought the store. I had a clothes fetish, and I bought him so many clothes. Before he was born he had enough to last him for a year." In her study of teenage mothers, Horowitz (1995) also noted the importance of having a well-dressed child; specifically, she found that adolescent mothers equated having well-dressed children with good parenting, whereas children with mismatched or dirty clothes were presumed by the teens to have bad mothers.

Although it was important to accumulate toys, clothes, and gifts for their children, the teen mothers were discriminating about where these gifts should come from. Gifts bought with money from their own or their partners' salaries (or other income) were ideal, as were the new gifts donated to the Teen Center by local stores. Unacceptable for many of the mothers, however, were hand-me-down clothes or used toys or any other gifts that might be construed as charity. As Horowitz (1995) found, for a mother to dress her child in used clothes or accept charity would be like saying she could not afford to raise her child without help, which would make her feel like a bad mother. As a consequence of this attitude, there were always several boxes of untouched donations (used clothes and toys) sitting near the entrance of the Teen Center that only a few teen mothers bothered to look through. Gifts from parents were also highly suspect, for if a teen mother's parents bought her baby more than she did, she felt like a failure as a parent. Eighteen-year-old Andrea, a white mother from a middle-class family, explained how her mother's extravagant gifts made her feel like a bad mother to eleven-month-old Karly:

> My mom buys her everything. I bought her a high chair, then my mom bought her the top of the line high chair. I bought her shoes, she bought her, you know, LA Gear. I bought her a toothbrush, and my mom buys her a yellow and purple, glow-in-the-dark toothbrush. So how can I compete? I buy her the simple stuff, and my mom buys her the awesome stuff.

Unwelcome gifts and anything perceived as charity were more likely to be met with hostility than gratitude. To many teen mothers, extravagant gifts from other people were a constant reminder that they could not afford these things themselves, which made them feel like they fit the bad mother image they were trying so hard to distance themselves from.

To afford new clothes and toys, the teen mothers employed several strategies. The most common technique for getting the most out of a limited budget was to divert money from other areas. Specifically, the teen mothers denied themselves clothes, makeup, and entertainment so they could buy things for their children, a pattern identified in other studies of teenage mothers (Horowitz 1995) and single mothers of any age (Boyle 1989). Nineteen-year-old Julie, the mother of three sons, exemplified this self-denial. Julie told me she could not remember the last time she bought something for herself, but guessed that it might have been the pair of snow boots she purchased the previous winter. In contrast, she bought new toys or clothes for her sons every time she went to the store. Other mothers scrimped on diapers—making each one last as long as possible—or avidly clipped coupons and watched for sales on food. Swanson (1988) noted that the teen parents in her study did not cut corners by buying generic food or diapers for their children, because buying expensive items was equated with being a good mother. Several mothers at the Teen Center held part-time jobs at the local mall or fast-food restaurants, but most relied on their AFDC checks or money given to them by their parents to purchase things for their children. For all, spending this much money on their children was a significant hardship, regardless of whether or not they admitted it.

DEVELOPMENTAL DOMINANCE

The children themselves were viewed as important indicators of whether or not teen mothers were parenting effectively, because mothers perceived their children's development as a way of assessing their own competency. Denzin (1973) pointed out that children are seen as a reflection of their parents and whether or not their parents have done a good job of raising them. To most teen mothers, part of proving that they were good parents involved having children who were developmentally advanced. Thus many mothers exaggerated what their children could do. When comparing their children to other children in the nurseries and the children of other teenage parents, the teen mothers made sure that their children came across as sounding developmentally advanced, in both their physical and their cognitive abilities.

Several studies have suggested that adolescent mothers often overestimate the physical capabilities of their infant children (Field, Widmayer, Stringer, and Ignatoff 1980; Vulkelich and Kliman 1985). Vulkelich and Kliman (1985), for example, found that teenage mothers were more likely than older mothers to expect their children to perform certain behaviors earlier than child development experts suggested. The adolescent mothers at the Teen Center had similar expectations. Tracy's son Kevin was just learning to sit up when she told me, "He's trying to get the crawling thing down." Kevin was unable to sit unsupported without falling backward and was clearly several months away from crawling, but it was important for Tracy to think he was near crawling, because her best friend's infant daughter (who was three days younger than Kevin) had just begun to crawl. Sixteen-year-old Jill did not have to exaggerate about twelve-month-old Henry's accomplishments, but they still served as a source of pride for her. She bragged, "He's been walking since he was nine months. He crawled at six. He held his head up at two weeks. That's like, too early!" This developmental superiority enabled the mothers to feel as though they were doing a good job and, as Vulkelich and Kliman (1985) noted in their study of teen mothers, mothers with developmentally advanced children were regarded by their peers as "exceptionally talented" parents.

When their babies' physical development did not meet with their often unrealistic expectations, the mothers blamed themselves. In this way, they viewed their babies' physical development as directly related to their own parenting skills, much like the adolescents in Vulkelich and Kliman's (1985) study of teenage mothers. Nineteen-year-old Kristina, a high school senior, verbalized how her daughter Lea's falling behind developmentally made her feel like a failure as a parent:

I've just been very bad to myself because she's not crawling. 'Cause I have this book and these exercises that I do with her, and she has just been, I mean, a couple of weeks, three weeks, maybe a month ahead of the whole book, and now she's two months behind on crawling. And I'm just like, I'm falling behind, and I'm not catching up.

The physical development of their children was viewed as an indicator of their relative competence as parents, and a competition to have the most advanced child (and thus be the best parent) was reflected in their constant comparisons with each other about what their children could and could not do. Swanson (1988) found a similar pattern in her study of adolescent mothers and noted that mothers tried to outdo each other by comparing which foods had been introduced into their babies' diets. Babies who ate more solid foods were viewed as being more "accomplished," and their mothers better parents.

In addition to exaggerating their physical development, mothers also were likely to use unrealistic descriptions of the cognitive development of their children. Often, infants were endowed with the personality characteristics of young children. Brooke described eleven-month-old Chris as follows:

He's so unique. He's really different than a lot of the other babies. He's got a great personality, and he's had that since he was born. I never really looked at him as a newborn because he was always so aware, so aware. Like he knew what was going on.

Other teen mothers talked about the likes and dislikes of their infants as if the infants themselves had vocalized their preferences. For example, Jennifer was continually asked by the nursery staff to stop putting necklaces on eight-month-old Andi, but Jennifer would not do it because she said Andi really liked to wear necklaces and got upset if Jennifer did not put one on her every morning. Other teen parents spoke to their infants as if they could understand them, giving them directions to "come over here," "don't hit her," or "don't put that in your mouth," overestimating the extent to which their infants could understand them. Other studies of adolescent parents have also revealed this pattern. For example, Horowitz (1995) noted that the mothers in her study disciplined their infants and toddlers, believing that the children understood what they had done wrong. Swanson (1988) pointed out that adolescent mothers described their infants' food likes and dislikes as though the babies themselves had expressed them.

Just as they were bothered with the media image of teenage mothers as financially dependent, the teen mothers also were angered by the notion that their children might be behind the children of thirty- or forty-year-old mothers in terms of their cognitive development. Jill was particularly upset about something she had seen on television regarding the children of teenage mothers:

> 'Cause, I don't remember which show it was, but they said something about if you're a teenage mother, then your child will not be intelligent when they grow up. I don't believe that. They say it's because the child doesn't get enough attention. My child gets tons of attention. That doesn't make any sense: Just because you're a teenage mother, your child is not going to be smart. They just make up all these kind of guess things. I don't understand how they just come up with these lies. When I watch these shows, it just makes me so mad 'cause, I mean, I'm totally different to the girls they show on the shows. 'Cause, I mean, they're too young, twelve or thirteen, and they're having a kid. And they're in gangs, and they're gonna raise their kids in gangs. It's like, you don't do that.

Although she herself became pregnant at fourteen, Jill felt as though she was more mature than the twelve- and thirteen-year-old mothers she believed were the source of the negative image of teen mothers. By pointing out their immaturity, she distanced herself from them, and in so doing, she also distanced herself from having to worry that her decision to parent at a young age might result in negative consequences for her son. Although Jill focused on her mature age as the factor that distinguished her from the teen mothers on television, it is possible that she was also trying to distance herself from them in terms of class and race. Jill, a Latina from a working-class background, was working to combat three stigmatized images at once: her age, race, and class. Despite her similarities to other teen mothers with respect to social characteristics, Jill was confident that her parenting, evidenced by Henry's developmental accomplishments, set her apart from everyone else.

ADVERSARIAL ADVICE

The teen mothers were besieged with advice from their own parents, as well as from their doctors, teachers, and the books and magazines they themselves consulted. The advice they were given dealt with topics ranging from child-rearing strategies to postpartum health tips and whether or not they should continue a relationship with the father of their child. Depending on the source, the advice was either accepted as the final word on a subject or rejected outright as wrong. In selectively accepting advice, the teen mothers demonstrated that, despite their age, no one could know better than they how to best raise their children. Perhaps the most important determinant of whether or not advice was accepted was whether it was presented as a suggestion or a command. The prevailing attitude was that it was acceptable to be given suggestions, but in the end mothers should decide how to raise their children. The teens frequently echoed Kristina's sentiments that "everyone gets to raise their kid the way they want." Horowitz (1995) noted a similar pattern in her study among the adolescent mothers, who adamantly voiced their responsibility for raising their own children.

Because they felt as though they knew how to best care for their children, the teen mothers saw themselves as better parents than the advisors, whose suggestions they often rejected. In this sense, the teens could be viewed as engaging in a competition with advice givers. Although most teen mothers felt that other mothers should be given the independence to raise their own children, they competed to provide the best advice, arguing over tips and practices they had picked up from their doctors, mothers, or something they had read. Julie, the mother of two sons and pregnant with her third child, felt proud that she could share her wisdom with other mothers. In fact, when asked what she liked most about school, she told me:

> I like the fact that there's a lot of other girls who I can help out, seeing as how I have the oldest one there, and I'm gonna have my third one. I think it's nice that I can help the other ones out, so they can know they're not the only one who's gone through this, even though it feels like it's the first time.

Her willingness to share her experiences was based on a desire to make motherhood easier for the younger girls, but it also gave her a certain amount of status, which helped her combat the stigma of having three children.

Many teen mothers went along with everything their own mothers suggested or told them to do, even if it contradicted the advice of doctors or other experts. Their mothers were deemed trustworthy not because of special training or technical expertise but because they had experience raising children, and the teen mothers themselves were living proof of what a good job they had done (Swanson 1988). Some teen mothers took the advice of their own mothers, and others did everything they could to prove their own mothers wrong. Several studies have suggested that adolescents often reject the parenting advice of their own parents because they are struggling for their own independence (Barratt, Roach and Colbert 1991; Swanson 1988). Thus mothers who were living on their own followed what their own mothers said, but teen mothers who still lived with their parents were concerned with proving they could get along without their parents' advice.

Sixteen-year-old Angelica, the Latina who became pregnant at age fourteen, revered her mother and the advice she gave. Although Angelica lived in her own apartment with her twenty-two-year-old husband, she spent almost every afternoon with her mother, acting "more as friends than anything else." When asked where she learned to parent, Angelica responded:

> I learn from my mother. Because I think she's the best. She tells me—she gives me suggestions, she doesn't tell me—and I take them, because I know my mom knows what she's talking about. But if other people come up to me and say, "Well, you're not supposed to be doing this," it's like, "This is my child. If you want to give me suggestions, you can, but just don't tell me how to raise my child."

Angelica relied heavily on the advice offered by her mother and took no offense when the advice was unsolicited.

Kristina, on the other hand, was in a constant struggle with her mother over how to raise Lea. At nineteen, Kristina found herself back in her parents' house when her husband of two years went to jail and she could no longer afford to live on her own. Kristina's mother constantly urged Kristina to wean Lea off her breast milk and to start putting her in her crib at night (rather than sleeping with Kristina), but with each suggestion Kristina became more determined to do the opposite. For Kristina, accepting her mother's advice was equivalent to admitting that she was not ready to parent, and she was already filled with doubts because she was not financially independent from her own parents. In Kristina's eyes, the best advice came from credentialed experts.

In addition to their own mothers, teen mothers also received advice from a host of experts, including health professionals and social service employees. Many mothers accepted the advice of these experts without question and often sought the program nurse, social worker, or the coordinator of the Teen Center for answers to their questions about diaper rash, feeding a sick baby, or how they should act the next time they saw their baby's father. Other mothers distrusted doctors and other experts and were angered by advice that was perceived as meddlesome. For example, one young woman dropped out of school after the nurse told her that giving her daughter a bottle while she slept might cause the baby to develop ear infections. Many teen mothers supported her decision to drop out, but others actually laughed at the thought of someone being so unwilling to take the advice of a medical professional. Swanson (1988), noting a similar pattern of skepticism about medical expertise, found that many adolescent mothers believed that doctors do not know anything about the proper diet for infants.

Although mothers like Angelica believed everything their mothers told them, they were reluctant to take the advice of doctors and often thought their suggestions were completely wrong. Mothers like Kristina, on the other hand, were more likely to have total faith in doctors, books, and other experts. Kristina's doctor knew her on a first-name basis because she called him so often with questions about Lea.

GENERATIONAL SUPERIORITY

An important facet of competitive parenting was the constant comparison to other mothers. Not only did teen mothers compare themselves to other teenage parents but also to mothers who delayed having children until their twenties, thirties, or forties, including their own parents. In comparing themselves to these older mothers, the teen mothers found reason to criticize and discredit them, while legitimizing themselves.

One of the ways the teen mothers legitimized having babies at a young age was by pointing out negative qualities of parents who have children later in life. As eighteen-year-old Andrea said:

> I've got an aunt who's forty-four, and she's got a three-year-old, so I see a lot of these teenage moms better than her. Because I think teenage moms—we all share energy. We've got a lot more energy than a thirty- or forty-year-old woman. She throws her kid in front of the TV and expects that to entertain him because her body's old. She really does not have enough energy to be chasing him. Or going to the grocery store with him kills her. It's just, that's all the energy she'll have for the entire day. The zoo is extremely hard on her. I think we're all very lucky that we have our bodies that are young.

Other studies of teenage parents have also found that young mothers tout the virtues of being young and point out the hardships of being an older parent. Schofield (1994), for example, quoted teenage mothers who said that young mothers do not mind living with the economic hardship of raising children; to them, living independently is exciting, so they do not mind if their living conditions are not very fancy. Horowitz (1995) noted that young mothers cited "growing old together" as a positive character-istic of early childbearing, a sentiment echoed by many of the mothers at the Teen Center as well.

Mothers at the Teen Center criticized older parents for being too rigid and authoritative in their child rearing. For example, fifteen-year-old Tracy suggested that one of the biggest differences between teen parents and older parents was that older parents "feel more that [their children] need to do what they say. Like, they do what my parents did with having lots of rules and being really strict."

Not only did teen mothers compare themselves to older mothers in general but, as Tracy illustrated, they also compared themselves spe-cifically to their own parents. The theme of parenting differently than their own parents is common in the teen parenting literature (see, e.g., Carlip 1995), but it is also an attitude held by older mothers as well (Hansen and Jacob 1992). In most cases, the teen mothers hoped to have dramatically different relationships with their children than they experienced with their own parents. Many talked of being more lenient and permissive and commented that they would never force their children to do things they did not want to do. For example, Jennifer vowed that she would never make Andi take ballet or play in the marching band as she was forced to do. Instead, she hoped Andi would follow her heart and find something on her own that interested her. Carlip's (1995) study of adolescent mothers revealed a similar pattern; the young women in her study lamented their own parents' restrictive behavior.

Another way that teen mothers expected their relationships with their children to be different from their own relationships with their parents was through the unconditional love they planned to have for their children. That is, they wanted to love their children no matter what they did, and they hoped their children would love them no matter who they became. Kristina told me she often recorded these thoughts in Lea's baby book:

> I find myself writing, "Will you just be close to me? Will you just communicate with me? And that's all I ever expect. If you're a punk rocker, just please still love me. If you're a hippie, an astronaut, a scientist, whatever, will you please still have enough

time to love me?" I always want her to love me because I never had that.

In Carlip's (1995) study, several adolescent mothers commented that they too were seeking a relationship of unconditional love, and, like Kristina, they noted that this type of relationship was one they never had with their own parents, who were often abusive (as were Kristina's parents).

Other teen mothers hoped to differ from their own mothers by paying more attention to their children. Julie, the mother of three sons, told me that her mother neglected her and her older sister and put the needs of different boyfriends before the needs of Julie and her sister. When describing her parenting, Julie referred to her own mother:

> I think I put a lot more effort into it just because I saw the way my mom raised me and my sister, and I don't think she did a good job with us. So I try and give them something that I never had, and I try and do better than what I think we had. Actually, I try to be exactly the opposite as my mom was. I actually think, "What would my mother do?" And then I do the exact opposite.

Fifteen-year-old Tracy told a similar story. For two years, Tracy rarely saw her mother, who was busy partying and dating. In fact, Tracy told me that their only communication was the occasional five-dollar bill and a note left on the kitchen counter telling twelve-year-old Tracy to buy food with the money. The teen mothers in Carlip's (1995) study reflected a similar pattern. Several young women told her that they planned to parent differently from their own parents, whom they criticized for being neglectful, for never being there, and for not paying any attention to them. Comparing their own parenting styles to their own parents' and to other older parents' styles resulted in the young mothers being cast in a positive light, for they compared themselves to older parents who were depicted as lacking in energy, being too strict, and being uncaring, neglectful parents.

The culture of teen parenting displayed in this setting emphasized competition to be the best parent above all else, whether in the form of having the most developmentally advanced or best-dressed baby. By competing with one another and with other parents not in the program, the teen mothers worked to prove their competence as parents in an effort to contradict the widely held view that teenagers should not be having children and to validate their decisions to bear and rear their own children. The teen mothers' age as adolescents fueled this competition, which was shaped in different ways by their gender, class, and race.

SIX

TEEN MOTHERS'
CONCEPTIONS OF FATHERHOOD

The literature on fathers of children born to teen mothers is scant; the limited literature that does exist looks primarily at adolescent fathers. Given that 60 percent of children born to teen mothers are fathered by men over age twenty (Oberman 1994), a focus solely on teenage fathers ignores a significant number of fathers. In addition, studies of adolescent fathers usually focus on young men's experiences before becoming parents. Thus we know about adolescent fathers' sexual histories (Robinson 1988), risk factors for becoming teen fathers (Thornberry, Smith, and Howard 1997), how young fathers responded to their girlfriends' or wives' pregnancies (Barret and Robinson 1982; Sullivan 1989), and what they plan to do as fathers (Barret and Robinson 1982; Sullivan 1989). We know little about what they do as fathers after the baby is born, or how the young mothers feel about their parenting. In this chapter I examine these questions as they pertain to both adolescent fathers and older men who have fathered children born to teenage mothers.

The data I present come from adolescent mothers' descriptions of fatherhood—of what their babies' fathers do as parents, what the young women wish they would do, and where their ideas about fatherhood originate. Robinson (1988) noted the shortcomings of using adolescent mothers' accounts to assess what fathers are doing, positing that these responses are often negatively biased and invalid. My purpose here, however, is to learn about teen mothers' expectations for and experiences with their babies' fathers, a question that can best be addressed from the mother's perspective.

An extensive body of literature details the inferior family situations of girls who become parents as teenagers, and most of it points to absent, uninvolved, or abusive fathers (Landy et al. 1983; Oz and Fine 1991; Schamess 1993; Zongker 1977). Given that teen mothers often come from homes where fathering is substandard, it is important to see how their experiences shape their perceptions of what fathering means and whether they look for something different for their children than they experienced themselves. Thus the questions I examine here are how teen mothers define fatherhood, how they view the contributions of their babies' fathers, and whether they break the cycle of substandard fathering with which they were raised.

DIMENSIONS OF FATHERHOOD

The adolescent mothers at the Teen Center had clear ideas of the kind of men they wanted as fathers for their children. Like Furstenberg (1988), they called this man a "good dad," although they were not necessarily referring to the new, androgynous father he described. Discussions of good fathers centered around the extent to which the men wanted to be fathers and how they carried out that role once the baby was born. Their notions of what constituted good fathering were rooted in their experiences with their own fathers, in the things their babies' fathers did (or, more often, did not do), and in their expectations for sex-role appropriate behavior. In many instances, the men in their lives contrasted sharply with their image of a "good dad."

EMBRACING FATHERHOOD

Good fathers showed that they embraced the role of father from the outset by showing enthusiasm about their girlfriend's or wife's pregnancy and the birth of the baby. Like the young men in Sullivan (1989) and Vaz, Smolen, and Miller's (1983) studies, many of the fathers of Teen Center babies were described as participating in the excitement and events surrounding the pregnancy, living up to the good dad ideal. Of all the dimensions of fatherhood the teen mothers defined, enthusiasm about the baby's arrival and the new role of father was the one area in which more boyfriends were described as meeting the ideal than not. In this way, the fathers resembled the adolescent fathers in other studies (Sullivan 1989; Vaz, Smolen, and Miller 1983).

Eighteen-year-old Kristina described her husband, eighteen-year-old Kyle, as "the perfect dad" because he was thrilled about the prospect of becoming a father:

> He was shocked, he was scared when I got pregnant because she was my fifth pregnancy. We had lost a set of twins and had a miscarriage, and I had a miscarriage before I met him, so he was scared that we might lose her too. And then when he saw her on the, you know, the screen for the amnio, he was just excited, he was overwhelmed with joy. He put the pictures in his wallet and showed them to everyone. And he went to every doctor appointment, to everything. He hated Lamaze, but he went anyway. And he went to parenting classes and childbirth education classes with me.

Seventeen-year-old Andrea told a similar story about her boyfriend embracing fatherhood from the beginning. She was nervous about telling nineteen-year-old Charlie about her pregnancy because they had been dating for only three weeks, but she told me she was pleasantly surprised when "he was so excited!" She told me she would not have expected a positive reaction from any boyfriend, let alone a new boyfriend, and she felt his enthusiastic acceptance of fatherhood guaranteed that he would be a good dad. She had further confirmation of his excitement for his new role when he showed more emotion than she did at the birth of their son:

> He cried when he was born. I *never* cried. I didn't see it, but all my friends were telling me—'cause I had lots of friends that were in there—and they said, "Oh you should have seen him, it was so cute, he was holding him and crying." And he was like, "Oh my little buddy!" This big guy holding this little baby. So he was happy, really happy.

Schofield (1994) noted a similar finding in her study of teen mothers, with several of the boyfriends being excited about the baby while the mother herself had mixed feelings. She noted, however, that the only men who showed more enthusiasm than their girlfriends were men who felt their relationship had a future. Thus while Andrea thought of Charlie as just a new boyfriend, perhaps Charlie perceived their relationship as more permanent (which it was—they married two years later).

Blair, the seventeen-year-old Latina, described her fiancé John as someone who was excited about fatherhood because he mentioned to her that he had specific plans for how he wanted to raise their soon-to-be-born daughter. When I asked her to elaborate, she said, "Well, John wants to spoil the baby. He's already said that." To Blair, plans to spoil the baby with clothes and toys were a signal that John would be a good dad, for he was already assuming the gender-appropriate role of provider (Teti and Lamb 1986).

For many teens, evidence of a man's embracing fatherhood was a willingness to do it again. Vanessa told me her image of the ideal father was someone who would "Want to have children, or want *me* to have children, or I guess have *more* children." Andrea thought Charlie was a good dad because although "He says he doesn't want to have any more—he says that once in a while—but then he'll say, 'Well, as long as we stop at three.' He told me that one time! I'm like, OK!," she took this as evidence that he was eager to become a father, and hence, that he must be a good dad.

In addition to being excited about raising their own children, many teens explained that their babies' fathers were good with other people's children as well—that the love they had for their own children was an extension of their love for children in general. In fact, Kristina explicitly said that Kyle's interactions with other children convinced her that he would be a good dad:

> The reason I wanted to have kids with him is because we lived with a lot of other families in one household and the kids loved him. Or other kids would knock on the door and say, "Is Kyle there?" The little kids from all the way down the street, or even two streets down, "Is Kyle there?" He loves kids.

Tracy echoed this sentiment when she told me that a good father is "Someone who loves kids. It doesn't matter whose they are, they just like kids." Andrea, too, said one of the reasons Charlie was such a good father was because "He's just good with kids, period." Vanessa told me the ideal boyfriend would be someone who loved children, because that meant he would love her daughter. She explained, "If he didn't want anything to do with Hope, then he wouldn't have anything to do with me." Vanessa was single when we spoke, but she made it clear that she would evaluate future boyfriends based on whether or not they embraced fatherhood.

In contrast to the mothers who described their husbands and boyfriends as ideal dads because of the enthusiasm they showed for becoming fathers, other teens complained that their babies' fathers were so disinterested in being fathers that they would not even acknowledge paternity. Sixteen-year-old Kerry told me her baby's father was denying paternity and demanding a test, as was eighteen-year-old Marci's ex-boyfriend, who moved out of state without leaving word of where he could be contacted to avoid taking a paternity test. He returned when the baby was eight months old and, according to Marci, wanted custody of the child he had previously denied fathering. Seventeen-year-old Sunshine was not sure which of two men had fathered her son, but both disappeared without forwarding addresses when she asked them to take paternity tests. Gershenson (1983) noted a similar pattern in his study of adolescent mothers and their babies' fathers, commenting that some of the fathers "were expert at giving strong signals to the mothers that they had no interest in fatherhood" by doing things such as moving out of state upon hearing of the pregnancy (593). The young women at the Teen Center also resembled the adolescent mothers in Schamess's (1993) study, who made frequent reference to the idea that their babies' fathers "had just walked away without even thinking about it" once they found out the young woman was pregnant (433).

Putting Family First

No matter what the circumstances, good fathers made spending time with their children a priority; their commitment to their children was stronger than their individual needs or interests. Several of the teens explained that a father who put his children first would be ideal, but the reality for them was someone who was more interested in himself than in spending time with his child. In Gershenson's (1983) study of fathers of children born to teen mothers, ex-husbands and ex-boyfriends were less likely to spend time with their children than current partners; ex-partners had infrequent, irregular contact with their children, if any at all. The mothers at the Teen Center told similar stories of their ex-partners, and their current partners as well.

Several teen mothers described their babies' fathers as men who were not interested in being fathers because they never wanted to spend time with their children. For example, twenty-year-old Amanda characterized her son's father, Robby, as the opposite of the kind of father she wanted for Matthew because he showed no interest in the role of fatherhood or his son, even when the baby was a newborn. When I asked her what fathering meant to Robby when Matthew was a baby she said, "Nothing. It meant nothing." She went on:

> He would sometimes hold him, and it was cute, but it was never like he really *wanted* to. I don't know, it was kind of like, "This is

my kid" [frowns and shrugs shoulders disinterestedly]. And he was always at his parents' house, always with his friends. He was never with us.

At the time of our interview, Amanda and Robby were no longer living together. Despite the fact that he lived only fifteen minutes away from them, Robby saw three-year-old Matthew only one day each month, which indicated to Amanda that Robby had not made fatherhood a priority: "So it works out that he only sees him around once a month, on the weekend. And even then he usually takes him to his parents' house so *they* can watch him. And then Robby sits and watches TV the whole time." She gave more examples of why Robby was not a good father:

> A good father is not just a plaything. It's someone who's always there. Someone who always wants you. Someone who makes the kid their number one priority, not themselves. And these qualities aren't from my childhood, they're from the fact that Robby is such a bad dad that I know what I want for Matthew. Just someone who will go outside with him when he wants to go outside, 'cause Robby never wants to go outside with him. Our neighbors used to think that my dad was my boyfriend because he was the one who was always outside with me and Matthew. They never saw Robby, they *never* saw Robby, even though he lived here too.

Like Amanda, fifteen-year-old Tracy also spoke of the ideal father as someone who made plans to go out and do things with his children, and who followed through on them: "He's someone who likes to do things as a family. The zoo, golfing, you know, miniature golfing. You know, just going out. He occasionally likes to do things alone with his partner. Isn't out with his friends every night. Doesn't break promises." When I asked her how her baby's father, Eddie, measured up to this image, she told me: "These are all the things Eddie *isn't* doing." Tracy often came to school in tears because Eddie had canceled plans with her and Kevin to go out partying with his friends. Several other teen mothers complained that the thing standing between their baby's father and their child was the father's partying—he would not give up drinking and doing drugs with his friends to spend time with his child. As a consequence of their partying and subsequent convictions for drunk driving, vandalism, fighting, illicit drug possession, sales, and/or use, many of the babies' fathers could not see their children even if they wanted to, for they were incarcerated. Fathers of children born to teen mothers are more likely than other men to be incarcerated (Elster et al. 1987), and the Teen Center fathers were no different. Although the teen mothers were not ashamed of their babies' fathers' brushes with the law—they talked about them openly and unabashedly—they did express that the fathers' irresponsible actions showed that they had not put their babies' interests first, preventing them from being ideal fathers.

Vanessa's boyfriend Marcus was not incarcerated, but she complained that he had not made Hope a priority because he made no effort to see her. When I asked fifteen-year-old Vanessa what she would tell Hope about her absent father when she was older, Vanessa said this:

> That he just wasn't there. I'm gonna save his picture and if she wants to see it she can see it. If she wants to go find him she can. But I don't think he'll ever try to contact her. I'll tell her that being a father wasn't important to him. All he cared about was himself, and that was it.

When she was still pregnant, Vanessa thought her boyfriend Marcus would be a good father because he seemed to agree with her plans for raising their child, including her plans to breast-feed for the first year. She told me, "Like, before she was born, I told him that I was gonna nurse Hope, and he was like, "OK, that's fine." However, like other mothers who find their babies' fathers are excited about the pregnancy and impending fatherhood, only to become less and less involved as the baby grows (Hardy, Duggan, Masnyk, and Pearson 1989; Sullivan 1989), Marcus too became increasingly removed from Vanessa and Hope's life. They were separated by 300 miles in the seventh month of Vanessa's pregnancy until the baby was eight months old, at which point Marcus finally came to see Vanessa and the baby. Vanessa expected him to follow through with his plans to be an involved father but was confronted instead with a man who was more concerned with her body as his sexual arena than the well-being of their infant daughter, which surprised Vanessa: "He was like, 'Oh, you're nursing her?' And he got really mad because he said that she was going to mess up my breasts for *him*. And he also got mad because he didn't know how to quiet her down when he held her, because she'd just cry more." Not only did Marcus show no natural aptitude for fathering, he also showed no interest in trying to become a better father. Fatherhood was not a priority for him. Vanessa's eventual decision to break up with Marcus and downplay his existence to her daughter resembles a pattern identified by Schofield (1994). In her study of teen mothers, she found that the young women who were no longer dating their baby's father "tended to dismiss him as rather an irrelevance"

(102). While Vanessa wished Marcus would have been a better father, she washed her hands of him once he demonstrated to her that he was not interested in fatherhood.

The idea of good fathers putting their families first was something that many teens discussed in the context of their own fathers, whom they described as never being around. As Tracy said, "I know I have a dad, but I don't want a dad. I don't feel . . . I feel like he's an uncle or something, not a dad. And he's not a huge part of my life, or my son's life for that matter. But it doesn't matter now." She went on to explain that her father had blown the opportunity to be a good dad when she was younger, when instead of spending time with her he devoted his time to his newly active social life as a divorced man (and, eventually, to his new wife). And although Amanda said her desire to have Matthew's father be someone who put family first was not a result of her own childhood experiences, the topic of her own dad's seeming disinterest in her came up frequently while we were discussing her baby's father, Robby, and his tendency to cancel plans:

> I think they're exactly the same, Robby and my dad. My dad hates Robby but he should see that he has those same qualities in himself. Robby would say we'd do things so I'd get all happy and excited and then he'd say, "Well, I don't want to go now." My dad does the exact same thing. He always gets pissed at Robby but he does the exact same thing. My dad was never there when we were growing up. He always worked at night so we never saw him. He was never there for anything that was important to me.

Just as Robby was a bad dad for putting his own interests before spending time with his child, Amanda felt her father had put his own interests (which in this case was providing for the family financially) before spending time with Amanda and her brother when they were young. In Schamess's (1993) study, adolescent mothers also made frequent reference to their own fathers not being around while they were young. When asked to complete the sentence "My father . . ." more than half of her respondents made what she called "neutral comments," many of which referred to fathers being overinvolved with work, or made specific reference to his absence, both physical and emotional.

A few Teen Center fathers were exceptions to this pattern of limited interest, limited-involvement fathers. Most notably, the fathers who were enrolled in the program were usually pointed to as examples of fathers who *did* put their children first. Throughout my three years at the Teen

Center, I saw a high turnover rate of teen parents, but every year there were exactly two fathers enrolled, and every year, those fathers were idolized by the mothers in the program. In the last year of my study, the two fathers were both seventeen years old. Anthony, an African American from a working-class family, won the respect of all the mothers at the Teen Center when he fought for and eventually won full custody of his infant daughter after he witnessed her mother abusing her. He was the only father in the history of the Teen Center to enroll in the program alone. The girls revered him for recognizing that the baby's mother was an unfit parent, for fighting for custody, and for assuming the responsibilities of full-time parenthood. Clearly he had put the interests of his daughter before his own. Unlike Anthony, Tim was still dating his baby girl's seventeen-year-old mother, Jen, who was also enrolled in the program. Tim, a white father from a middle-class family, was admired because he spent so much time in the nursery with the baby, skipping lunch with his friends to play with her or put her to sleep, telling her he loved her and calling her affectionate names (like "my little tater tot"), and taking her home with him every other night. Tim was in the nursery as often as most of the mothers, so they had frequent opportunities to view his parenting and observe how he made Emma the number-one priority in his life. In this way, Tim—and the other involved dads like him at the center—were important contributors to the Teen Center culture, as their presence set a standard for good fatherhood.

PARTICIPATING IN EVERYDAY LIFE

Good dads participated in their children's everyday lives, such as mundane child-rearing duties, for example, feedings and diaper changes, and they made the time with their children meaningful by teaching them important lessons. While none of the mothers specifically mentioned this everyday participation as a quality of an ideal father, the idea came up often enough in the context of other questions that it became clear that they did view it as an important dimension of fatherhood.

Participation in mundane child-rearing duties was tangentially mentioned by several young women when they discussed the "type of dad" their babies' fathers were. When I asked Amanda what kind of father Robby was when Matthew was a baby, she referred to his lack of involvement in these everyday activities: "Well, actually, he wasn't a very good dad at all. He didn't ever change him, he never fed him, and he didn't ever get up in the middle of the night. He'd just shove me if I didn't hear Matthew crying." By logical extension, a good dad is someone who does take responsibility for those things: a father who changes his baby's diaper and gets up for middle-of–the-night feedings. Thus although she did not explicitly describe the ideal man as one who does participate, her disappointment in Robby's behavior makes it clear that she expected him to get involved at some level. In this way, Amanda resembled the transitional women in Hochschild's (1989) study. While they assume the majority of child-rearing responsibility, transitional women expect their partners to participate to a small degree. Fifteen-year-old Tracy could also be characterized as transitional, for she described Eddie as a good dad because he did participate, albeit minimally, in eight-month-old Kevin's feeding:

> He's a pretty good dad. He doesn't feel too comfortable being alone with Kevin that much 'cause he's afraid that he might die or something while he's with him, so he doesn't do that too often. But he likes giving him his jar food, he likes to cuddle him when he's eating.

Although Tracy was proud that Eddie liked to feed Kevin his baby food, she went on to describe how she had to select the food, get Kevin ready to eat (put him in his chair, put a bib on him, get him a spoon, give Eddie the food), and clean up after the meal. However, relative to what she knew other fathers did—including her own father and the fathers of her friends' babies at the Teen Center—she felt like she was getting a good deal. The women in Hochschild's (1989) study also felt "lucky" to have husbands who did any child care or housework at all, since they knew women whose husbands did even less. Nevertheless, when I interviewed Tracy again when Kevin was a year old, she told me that she was getting tired of doing more than her share of child rearing:

> We only see Eddie on the weekends. Eddie and I had a big talk about this last night, actually. I've been getting mad at him because he wouldn't come over and see us during the week because he would like to hang out with his friends and stuff. He said he'd spend more time with us when I get out of school and have more free time.

As a high school sophomore, the reality of how long it would be until she was out of school hit home as Kevin got older and demanded more time and energy. Eddie's once-a-week visits, for which Tracy was always present because Eddie did not want to be alone with Kevin, were just not enough. And though Eddie offered to "babysit" Kevin if Tracy wanted to go out, that was not satisfactory for Tracy; a father was not a babysitter, she told me, he was someone who wanted to spend time with his child. Perhaps because they were still dating, Tracy was able to explain this notion to Eddie, who subsequently took on a much more active role in Kevin's upbringing—spending three nights a week with him and taking full responsibility for feeding, clothing, and watching him while he was in his care.

In addition to feeding and diapering their children, good dads taught their children valuable lessons. When she was eighteen, Jessica described her eighteen-year-old boyfriend Patrick as an ideal father because of the kinds of interactions he had with one-year-old Steven: "Patrick's more playful than I am. I'm more of the comfort giver. Patrick's a lot more fun, more of a fun person. They do a lot more physical things together, more interactive and learning things." When I asked her for an example of such a lesson she told me:

> Well, they take baths together, and last week Patrick taught Steven how to put something "in"—'cause Steven takes everything out of his toy bucket in the bathtub but doesn't put anything back, so Patrick taught him the concept of in, then out. He does a lot of neat things like that.

Like other couples, Jessica and Patrick had defined the responsibilities of fatherhood as playing with their son and teaching him how to do things, leaving the "comfort giving" to Jessica.

FULFILLING THE PROVIDER ROLE

Perhaps the most significant indicator of responsible fathering was contributing financially to the child's upbringing. In general, noncustodial fathers are more likely to provide financial support to their children than any other form of support, such as providing them with clothes or driving them to dental appointments (Paasch and Teachman 1991), but few noncustodial fathers of babies at the Teen Center paid any child support. Those who did contribute did so only when forced, and even then their contributions were minimal. In this regard, the babies' fathers were similar to other noncustodial, never-married fathers, who are less likely to provide money for their children than noncustodial fathers who were married to their children's mothers (Paasch and Teachman 1991).

Like the young fathers in Barret and Robinson's (1982) study, many of the fathers of Teen Center babies stated their intentions to provide for the child financially before the child was born. However, the reality at the Teen Center was that most ex-boyfriends did not contribute anything. Twenty-year-old Amanda explained that getting any money from Robby was a struggle, despite the fact that he was a twenty-seven-year-old single man with a full-time job. Robby planned to provide support for Matthew, but when Matthew was three years old, Amanda finally got fed up with his promises:

> He's given me crap Matthew's whole life for child support, so I finally had to get AFDC. We're going to court about it next month, because he should be paying child support; I shouldn't have to get AFDC. But going through the courts is the only way I could get him to pay anything. Before, when he first moved out [when Matthew was four months old] he would give me money every once in a while, but he would always give me crap about it and blame me for spending too much, and then he stopped. When I threatened to go on AFDC [and take it to the courts] last summer he was like, "I'm going to give you $100 every month," and he did it like twice. In October he didn't give me anything, in November he gave it to me in the middle of the month, and he gave me all these excuses for why it was late, and then he didn't give me anything in December. So I got on AFDC in January.

Robby was a prize compared to other fathers, who disappeared altogether once the issue of money came up. For example, Julie, the mother of three sons, told me her oldest son's father also had a daughter for whom he was paying child support. Julie told me he disappeared once she told him she was pregnant, because "He's more worried about paying more child support than having a kid." Like Amanda, she could not understand why a grown man with a job ("He's in the Army Reserves so he makes a lot of money") had trouble with the notion of financially supporting his child. Sorensen's (1997) research supports the young women's claims that their children's fathers are not providing as much support as they could. Sorensen revealed that approximately 50 percent of nonresident fathers do not pay any child support; those who did provide child support make payments totaling only about 7 percent of their income. Based on the incomes and expenses of the men in her study, she calculated that most men could comfortably contribute closer to 20 percent of their incomes to their children.

Sunshine was not sure which of two men was her baby's father, but she said the chances of figuring it out were slim after she told them both that they would have to report to Social Services to resolve paternity and child support issues. She explained what happened when she discussed these issues with the man who had been her on again-off again boyfriend for two years:

> Well, I think we're "off" for good now because as soon as I mentioned Social Services he hasn't been around. But before then he was wanting to know if it was his kid, and he was even going to come here to visit in July and he was going to take us back to Alabama with him to visit his family. I mean, he was saying all this stuff, and as soon as Social Services and child support was mentioned, he's never been around.

The man she called "father possibility number 2" also disappeared when she mentioned that he would need to contact Social Services. She told me that because both of these men were so irresponsible she did not think either would make a good father, and she subsequently abandoned her quest to track them down.

Men who were described in glowing terms, like Kyle ("the perfect dad"), fulfilled the provider role without making a fuss. When Kyle and Kristina's daughter was born, Kyle worked overtime at a fast-food restaurant to support the family financially. Kristina beamed when she talked about how he put in so many hours yet still made time to show affection for the baby, telling me, "He was working as a manager at Wendy's, and he was working way too many hours, but he still would wake up in the middle of the night and sing to her." For Kristina, the provider role was not the only element of good fathering: getting up in the middle of the night was important too.

DISCIPLINING APPROPRIATELY

Many teens pointed to one specific parenting practice as being significant in determining the relative "goodness" of fathers: the discipline strategies they used. Perhaps because their children were too young to have been disciplined, the teens' notions for appropriate and inappropriate discipline methods were rooted in their own childhood experiences. Most of the young mothers at the Teen Center had in common an abusive, overly strict father, which may have influenced their decision to think about discipline and spanking, despite the fact that their children were so young.

Many of the teens described their own fathers as having absolute authority in their homes. Tracy told me her dad was "Really strict. My dad didn't let my mom have any say in anything." Eighteen-year-old Kristina's dad held a similar position in the family, "hitting the roof" when his children did something that disappointed him. Kristina's father was not only a stern disciplinarian, he was also a physical disciplinarian. On one occasion, when she arrived home from a date with an older boyfriend of whom he did not approve, he met her at the front door, pushed her down to the tile floor, and sat on her with the full weight of his 300-plus-pound body, breaking several of her ribs. When she told me this story, she emphasized that this was just one instance of the type of physical abuse she incurred at his hands.

Several other girls told me about their fathers using physical punishment. In fact, when I asked them whether they would do anything differently than their own parents had done, the issue of violence frequently came up. Sixteen-year-old Kerry told me, "I'm not going to beat them upside the head! My dad used to do that. He used to hit us with a belt." Twenty-year-old Amanda said, "Hitting. Spanking. I won't do it." When she reflected on her relationship with her father, Amanda realized that most of her memories were of his punishments and her fear of him:

> I always feared him because the only time he did talk to us was when he was yelling at us for being bad. And he'd spank us with a belt when we were little, as far back as I can remember. And I remember my brother was really naughty, and I always took the blame for him because I hated hearing him cry, I couldn't handle it. I remember standing in the corner all day, all day. He wouldn't let us sit, he'd make us stand all day.

When I asked her to elaborate on who did the spanking and why, she told me her mother never hit her; it was her father who spanked her and her brother, striking them with his belt or hitting them with a wooden spoon. She explained that her father hit them for virtually everything:

> I got the belt for peeing the bed. And that is something that is psychological, it is not something that you purposefully do. And I got spanked all the time for doing that. I got spanked again for crying after the spanking! I got the belt for everything. And my dad feels really guilty about it now, but that's one of the strongest memories that I have: him with the belt and then being forced to stand in the corner all day.

After describing her own father and his yelling and violence, she told me she was wary of Matthew's father's parenting practices: "I see Robby being totally like that, that's why I'm glad he only sees Matthew once a month, because then he appreciates the time he has and doesn't lose his temper." Not only was she afraid of Matthew being physically harmed, she was also afraid of perpetuating the cycle of violence by having him learn to hit:

> I look at my brother who is always like, "I'm going to kick his ass. He started this . . ." and blah, blah, blah. I mean, kids learn to hit. He learned from my dad. So once when Robby was over to pick up Matthew, he wanted to slap Matthew on the hand. I told him that I was against it, but that I wasn't going to tell him not to do it because it's his child too and he has every right. But once he got to the point where he wasn't just slapping his hand, when he was slapping him on the back, I'm like, "No." And then he started thinking about it and he realized it was wrong. So he doesn't do it anymore.

In her concern over Robby's discipline style, Amanda resembled the teen mothers in Gershenson's (1983) study, who felt their babies' fathers were too strict and harsh in their discipline. In fact, Gershenson noted that this was the one parenting issue over which there was the most disagreement between adolescent mothers and new boyfriends (who were not the babies' fathers).

The mothers at the Teen Center imagined a "good dad" to be someone who was involved with his children, a good provider, and an appropriate disciplinarian. In most instances, the men in their lives contrasted sharply with their image of an ideal father for their child. By contrasting their idealized expectations with the actual practices of their babies' fathers, the teen mothers further demonstrated their competence as parents, for a good mother is someone who recognizes what is important in a father. This not only further legitimated their (typically) nonmarital childbearing, it also deflected the stigma cast upon them to a new target: their babies' fathers.

SEVEN

DEFINING, EXCUSING, AND JUSTIFYING DEVIANCE

Teen Mothers' Accounts for Statutory Rape

In all fifty states, laws distinguish between legal and illegal sexual relations based on the age difference between the participating man and woman. These statutory rape laws vary from state to state; while most view sexual relations between an adult male (over age eighteen) and an "underage" female as statutory rape, the age of consent for women ranges from eleven to eighteen. Despite the fact that statutory rape laws exist in almost every state, they are rarely enforced, and perpetrators are infrequently prosecuted (Oberman 1994). In recent years, however, these laws have come under increased scrutiny, which means that changes may be on the horizon (Lauer 1981; Oberman 1994).

While existing laws and public opinion stigmatize the older boyfriend-younger girlfriend relationship, the young women involved with these men often do not view their relationships, or themselves, in a negative light. This chapter asks the following question: How do teenage girls involved with older boyfriends view their relationships? I address this question by providing a conceptual framework for understanding the different ways that teenage mothers account for their involvement with adult boyfriends.

In many ways, the issue of whether or not young women view their behavior as deviant can be conceptualized as an accounts application. Like other forms of aligning actions (Stokes and Hewitt 1976), such as Sykes and Matza's (1957) "techniques of neutralization" or Mills's (1940) "motive talk," Scott and Lyman's (1968, 46) "accounts" are also meant to "verbally bridge the gap between action and expectation" by offering an explanation for why the deviant engaged in behavior that was not congruent with normative expectations. Scott and Lyman distinguish between two types of accounts: justifications and excuses. They describe justifications as "accounts in which one accepts responsibility for the act in question, but denies the pejorative quality associated with it" (1968, 47). Excuses, in contrast, are "accounts in which one admits that the act in question is bad, wrong, or inappropriate but denies full responsibility" (1968, 47). Accounts, in the form of justifications or excuses, are the deviant's effort to minimize damage to his or her identity after the deviant act has been performed or discovered.

Researchers have used Scott and Lyman's accounts to analyze deviants' explanations for their behavior in a variety of contexts. Kalab (1987) studied accounts used by college students who did not attend class by analyzing the notes they were requested to turn in following an absence. She found that most students' explanations for their absences were excuses; they acknowledged that absence was deviant but reported that something beyond their control (such as illness) prevented them from coming to class. Ray and Simons (1987) used accounts to analyze the explanations that convicted murderers gave for their crimes, and they also found a preponderance of excuses. Like Kalab, they found that most of their informants accepted the normative expectations for behavior (i.e., they agreed that what they did was deviant) and therefore felt compelled to excuse their behavior by attributing the murders to accident, intoxication, or stress. In contrast, Scully and Marolla's (1984) research on convicted rapists revealed a preponderance of justifications. They found that some rapists viewed their behavior as criminal and made excuses for their behavior, but most justified what they did on the grounds that the behavior was appropriate, acceptable, and/or deserved. Scully and Marolla noted that these accounts allowed 83 percent of their research subjects (who were incarcerated for the crime of rape) to view themselves as non-rapists.

In this chapter, I use Scott and Lyman's two forms of accounts as an organizing framework to conceptualize the different explanations given by teenage mothers regarding their involvement with older boyfriends. Their framework is helpful for two important reasons. First, it takes into consideration that the accounts are reactive (i.e., employed after the deviance has occurred). Second, this framework distinguishes between people who view the act as deviant and those who do not, as well as between people who assume and deny responsibility for their behavior, a source of significant variation among the teenage mothers with whom I spoke about statutory rape.

While this framework is helpful, it is also limiting in one major respect: this type of analysis assumes that the act in question is deviant. Many of the young women I interviewed felt that dating an older boyfriend was not deviant. For this reason, I have divided my analysis into three major sections. In the first section, I examine the justifications used by the young women who do not view having older boyfriends as deviant. In the second section, I analyze the responses of the young women who do view this behavior as deviant. Here I look at why they define younger girlfriend-older boyfriend relationships as deviant. In the third section, I examine the different excuses given by the young to account for their involvement in behavior they define as deviant. Finally, I offer explanations about why the young women may have different ideas about whether the act is deviant, and I discuss the implications of my findings for the accounts literature and for statutory rape laws.

JUSTIFYING DEVIANCE

Teen mothers who used justifications to account for their relationships with older men claimed responsibility for being involved with them, but they denied that the relationship was deviant in any way. They used justifications to explain why dating this older person was "no big deal." The teen mothers who used justifications were either still dating their older boyfriends or had parted ways but were still on amicable terms. Because they felt that older boyfriend-younger girlfriend relationships were not deviant, and because they had come out of them unscathed, they viewed statutory rape laws as unnecessary. There was no victim, so there was no crime. Older boyfriends were simply that, boyfriends who happened to be older, and their justifications supported this belief that they were not engaging in deviant behavior.

Age Is Meaningless

Several of the teen mothers felt that the fact that their boyfriends were significantly older was of little or no importance. Because they viewed their boyfriends' ages as meaningless, they drew no distinction between dating someone who was sixteen and someone who was twenty-six; a boyfriend was a boyfriend. Tracy, the fifteen-year-old mother of one-year-old Kevin, started dating her boyfriend Eddie when she was thirteen and he was eighteen. She told me that Eddie's age was "no big deal," adding that, "It's just like you have this boyfriend and he happens to be older." Crystal, a fifteen-year-old mother, concurred. She explained to me that dating a twenty-year-old when she was fourteen "didn't bother [her] at all" because "after all, age is just a number." Sunshine was nineteen when we talked about her dating experiences, but she had dated older men when she was younger. Her first sexual experience was with a thirty-year-old man when she had just turned sixteen. She told me that age differences between boyfriends and girlfriends were irrelevant, and that "as long as she felt good enough to be with him or liked him or whatever, then age doesn't really matter."

While Tracy, Crystal, and Sunshine told me that age was meaningless, they all qualified their answers. Tracy felt that a five-to-seven-year age difference between a girl and her boyfriend was harmless but added, "I mean, I can understand someone freaking out if the girl was fifteen and she was dating, like, a forty-five-year-old. That's just gross. It's like screwing your dad." Crystal also qualified her response, explaining that "a couple of years difference is okay, but if it's like five or six, then that's just not right." Sunshine told me, "I have a thing about certain ages. I don't have like a limit, but I wouldn't be with a guy that was my dad's age, because I would feel like I was with my dad, you know, and that's just gross." In qualifying their justifications, Tracy, Crystal, and Sunshine hoped to make their account sound more plausible; the differences between their ages and those of their boyfriends should be viewed as insignificant relative to what they *could* be.

Other teen mothers felt no need to qualify their answers, believing that age was meaningless no matter what the age difference. Eighteen-year-old Kelly, who had dated a high school senior when she was still in middle school, stated, "I really don't care how old a guy is." She went on to say, "I think that you can find somebody, and whether they're forty or not, it doesn't really matter." The justification that age was not important held true under all circumstances.

For both the "qualifiers" (like Tracy, Crystal, and Sunshine) and the "everyone is fair game" group (exemplified by Kelly), the only thing that made their relationships deviant—the age difference between themselves and their boyfriends—was discounted as an irrelevant characteristic. In that way, they claimed responsibility for their involvement yet denied partaking in anything deviant. Since the act was not defined as deviant, they felt statutory rape laws were unnecessary.

Everyone Does It, Nobody Minds

The knowledge that many of their peers at the Teen Center had older boyfriends was the source of a justification used by many of the teen mothers. Fifteen-year-old Tracy illustrated this type of justification well when she explained that none of her peers gave her a hard time for dating twenty-year-old Eddie, "cause a lot of them are dating guys who are older too!" The phrase many teen mothers used to describe the prevailing attitude was that dating an older guy was "no big deal" to them or anyone else they knew at the Teen Center, because "everyone does it." The young women at the Teen Center were not the only young mothers dating older men. Between 60 and 70 percent of teenage mothers in the United States become pregnant by men in their twenties (Oberman 1994; Phoenix 1991). Because so many teen mothers at the center had older boyfriends, and because it was widely approved in their teen parenting culture, it was not viewed as deviant.

Several teen mothers who had not been involved with older men themselves saw nothing wrong with their peers' decisions to date older men, supporting the justification that these relationships were not deviant, because "nobody minds." Seventeen-year-old Blair was eight months' pregnant when I spoke with her. Although her boyfriend was also seventeen, she stood up for other young women who dated older men: "If she said 'yes' then I don't think anyone should go after him because she gave in to him. In other words, I mean, if she was pressured into it, then maybe I would see something wrong with it, but if she wanted to [have sex with him], then they shouldn't get in trouble for it." Eighteen-year-old Jessica's boyfriend was five months younger than she, and she had never actually dated an older guy, but she told me that she had been interested in older guys in the past and was surprised when she found herself attracted to Patrick: "I *never* thought I would date a younger guy!" While they were not partaking in the behavior themselves, both Blair and Jessica voiced their approval of older boyfriend-younger girlfriend relationships, suggesting that such behavior was acceptable in their teenage parenting subculture, regardless of whether or not one was involved in this type of relationship. Thus when teen mothers used the justification "nobody minds," they were correct in that it was acceptable in their peer group.

Another form of the "everyone does it, nobody minds" justification was rooted in the approval of adults, such as parents or teachers. Linda, a junior, dated an eighteen-year-old when she was fourteen. She explained to me why there was nothing deviant about their relationship: "His name was Justin. I dated him when I was in eighth grade and he was a senior in high school. But our parents were good friends, so it was cool." In addition to her mother's approval, Linda also commented on the community sanctioning of older boyfriend-younger girlfriend relationships, thereby further justifying her decision to date Justin: "Everybody knew each other in my town. I went to parties sometimes with people that were my mom's age! So everybody just kind of hung out, no matter what their age. It was no big deal to anyone."

The approval of others may be rooted in mate selection norms. Until recently, it was common for women to marry "up" by choosing mates several years their senior (Atkinson and Glass 1985). While these patterns of marital age heterogamy are decreasing—that is, as men and women are increasingly likely to marry someone close to their own age (Atkinson and Glass 1985)—men are still more likely to report that they would like to marry someone younger, while women report a greater willingness to marry someone older (South 1991). Thus the teen mothers and the people who approve of their relationships with older boyfriends may simply hold traditional values about men and women, making it not only nondeviant for the teens to date older boyfriends but desirable. In saying that all of their peers date older men, and that nobody minds that they do, the teen mothers justified their deviance by denying the pejorative content of their behavior. Because nobody is telling them that these relationships are deviant, they see no need for them to be criminalized through statutory rape laws. As Linda stated, "As long as everybody is all right with it, I don't think it should be a problem. I don't think the guy should have to serve time for it or anything."

True Love Is Never Wrong

As Christian-Smith (1995, 211) pointed out, most young women view romance as "the only legitimate context for sexual expression." The young women at the Teen Center subscribed to this view, qualifying their sexual relations as acceptable if the relationship was based on love. Relationships were not construed as deviant if they were serious, for a couple in love could not be doing anything wrong by simply being together. Fifteen-year-old Tracy illustrated this viewpoint when she explained that it was okay for older men to date younger women, "If there's a real emotional feeling, and not just like, 'Wow, I like your body.'" This notion of romance as the proper context for sexual relations stands in contrast to the historical roots of romantic attachment. In colonial America, the norm was for suitable mates to be found through matchmaking, parental selection and approval of prospective mates, or compatibility between a young man and woman; the notion of romantic love and intimacy serving as the foundation for mate selection was deviant (D'Emilio and Freedman 1988). Now, love and intimacy have not only come to the fore as the normative basis for mate selection, they have totally displaced matchmaking suitability; the only deviant relationship is the relationship based solely on lust. Just as their colonial counterparts distanced themselves from the type of relationship that contemporary teens desire, these contemporary teens distance themselves from the notion of mate selection based on lust, thereby legitimating their relationships in contrast to what they identify as a deviant mode of attachment. For contemporary teens, romantic relationships are viewed as the only appropriate context for sexual relations.

Several teen mothers explained that they had reservations about dating someone so much older and were relieved when their boyfriends expressed serious affection. For example, Tracy remembered that when they first started dating she was afraid to tell eighteen-year-old Eddie that she was only thirteen. When she finally told him her real age, he alleviated her fears by telling her, "Well, it doesn't matter now because I'm already in love with you." His expression of love confirmed that their relationship was legitimate. The same was true of Crystal and her eighteen-year-old boyfriend Richard. When Richard learned that Crystal was only fourteen, his response was, "Okay, well, it doesn't matter now." His unspoken message, Crystal thought, was that it did not matter what her age was because their relationship had developed into something serious, for she interpreted the "now" to mean "now that I'm in love with you."

Both Tracy and Crystal claimed that a mutual feeling of love was a satisfactory justification for dating older boyfriends, and this contention allowed them to avoid defining their relationships as deviant. However, Tracy's and Crystal's words belied a different reality: the crucial aspect of the justification was that their boyfriends loved *them*. Their boyfriends' expression of love provided evidence that their relationship was not deviant; the young women were not being sexually exploited if their boyfriends loved them. In this way, the young women used their boyfriends' feelings, not their own, to distinguish between acceptable and unacceptable behavior. As long as an older boyfriend truly loves his younger girlfriend, their sexual relationship should not be viewed as deviant. This account resembles Scott and Lyman's (1968) description of the self-fulfillment justification, wherein deviants justify their wrongdoing by arguing that the deviance makes them happy or complete. For the teen mothers, being in love (and being loved by somebody) was a sufficient justification on the grounds that romance (and the concomitant sexuality) was perceived as being vital to one's happiness.

Consensual Sex Is Not Rape

The young women at the Teen Center told me that sexual relationships entered into by willing partners cannot be deviant. This type of relationship was viewed by the teen mothers as consensual, and it stood in sharp contrast to the other forms of rape, which they thought of as nonconsensual. Thus consent is the key to their definition of deviance, or as Burt and Albin (1981, 213) pose the question, "Did she want to or did she have to?"

Fifteen-year-old Tracy explained that consensual relationships between older boyfriends and younger girlfriends are not deviant "Because the girl is willing to go with the guy. If you were raped, you wouldn't be willing." Fifteen-year-old Crystal felt that even young adolescents can make rational decisions about whether or not they want to have sex. She said sexual relations between older boyfriends and younger girlfriends should not be considered deviant "Cause it's something that both people give consent to. Even if you're thirteen, you know what you're doing." Nineteen-year-old Sunshine agreed that consent made relationships legitimate, and she felt that accusing older boyfriends of statutory rape was wrong in cases where the girlfriend was a willing partner: "The laws are stupid. I mean, unless they were raped, then, you know, it takes two to tango and they agreed, so it shouldn't be any big deal. It's their life."

The teen mothers felt that their consensual involvement with their boyfriends negated any deviance. While they admitted responsibility for getting involved with older men, they denied that the relationship was deviant because it was entered into willingly by both partners. Because they did not perceive the relationships as deviant, they felt that statutory rape laws were unnecessary. Using the justification that they consented to sex reinforces the idea that no crime was committed, because they wanted to have sex just as much as their boyfriends did. In addition, they would argue that they are mature enough to give informed consent. The idea that they are too young to consent suggests that they are similar to other people who cannot give informed consent—children, people who are alcohol- or drug-impaired, or people who have impaired mental capacity—a supposition that threatens their identities as mature adults who can make informed decisions. The justification that their consent makes the relationship legitimate reinforces the idea that they are mature enough to make decisions about their sexuality, that they can make decisions in their own self-interest. Their justification resembles the technique of neutralization "denial of injury," for the teen mothers reasoned that "it was permissible to do this act since no one was injured by it . . . since the act resulted in consequences that were trifling" (Scott and Lyman 1968, 51). Since nobody was hurt by what they did, and since nobody minded, the relationship should not be viewed as deviant. This justification is ironic, in a way, because the teens argued that no one is hurt by their involvement with older men, despite the fact that many critics of younger girlfriend-older boyfriend relationships argue the opposite: that statutory rape laws protect young girls from being sexually exploited by older men, a stance that assumes younger girlfriends (and any children resulting from the union) will end up being hurt in the long run (Oberman 1994).

DEFINING DEVIANCE

In contrast to the teens who used justifications to explain why dating older boyfriends was not deviant, another group of young women who had dated older boyfriends in the past offered specific reasons for defining these relationships as deviant. These explanations focused on specific characteristics of older boyfriends as well as an awareness of laws and societal attitudes prohibiting such relationships.

Only Dirty Old Men Date Young Girls

One of the most common explanations for why dating older boyfriends was deviant was the assertion that the kinds of men who date young girls are sick, for there must be something wrong with them if they are attracted to young girls. These boyfriends were characterized as "dirty old men" and "perverts" who exploit young, naive girls for sex because they cannot find any willing partners in their own age group. Eighteen-year-old Kristina summed up this feeling when she told me that "in a lot of cases I've heard of, the older person wants to take advantage of the younger person for sexual reasons." Amanda, the twenty-year-old mother, viewed these relationships the same way, and she was furious that older men got away with this exploitation:

> I was watching this talk show the other day, and they had these really old women and younger guys, you know, and I'm like,

power to all of them. But there was this one guy that was like forty-five—maybe fifty-seven—with this sixteen-year-old. I'm like, *that* is not okay. And when she's eighteen, that's fine. But you are molesting her. She is a child. Because really, at sixteen, you're still just a tiny little kid; you don't know anything. There was another girl who was thirteen. And I was like, this is sick! This was like thirteen and thirty-nine. That's way beyond sick. And actually, a fourteen-year-old and a twenty-five-year-old is pretty sick too. She is obviously a little girl, and he is an older, older man.

In addition to pointing out that older men in general are "sick" for dating younger girls, Amanda was also angry that her ex-boyfriend, the father of her baby, dated her when she was younger, implying that it was his responsibility as an adult to know better:

I just think the older person—I think Robby's an asshole for going out with me when I was sixteen. I think that's horrible. Seven years difference! I was sixteen; he was 23. He was a total adult, I was still in my adolescent years, you know? Wanting to ditch school and get drunk all the time, and he's an adult working full-time. He knew better, and he should have, I mean, I never came on to him, but when I wrote him poems, even with that he could have said, you know, "Come back when you're eighteen." The older person should do that. I would never go out with a sixteen-year-old, never. I couldn't do it. I think it's disgusting; I think it's sick.

LaNiece, who was sixteen when we spoke about her dating experiences, also blamed her older ex-boyfriend for letting their relationship get started. She told me that she was dismayed when she found out her boyfriend's real age, for at thirteen, she thought she was dating a fifteen-year-old: "I found out [his real age], 'cause my friend, she said, 'Well, I'm just going to tell you this: he's really 20.' And I was like, 'No he's not.' So I asked him, and he admitted it, and I didn't want him to, you know? I wanted him to lie to me." When I asked why she did not want to know his age, she offered the following explanation:

I guess 'cause I was kind of a little creeped out because he was so much older than me. I think guys who date younger girls are sick, sick, sick. For most people, it's like the guy taking advantage of the girl. It is almost every time. Or he can't get anyone his own age because there's something wrong with him.

Like Amanda, LaNiece also felt that older boyfriends were "sick" because they took advantage of young girls who do not realize they are being exploited: "I mean, if you know someone is that young, they don't know anything about *anything*, and you shouldn't even be, like, thinking about it. Thirteen and twenty? That is like a man and a little girl! Seriously, like, that is so much older." Eighteen-year-old Marci, the mother of an eight-month-old boy, told me she was attracted to older men and felt like she had to be cautious to avoid being exploited in the way Amanda and LaNiece described:

> Um, I have to be careful because I have to realize that a lot of times people that age, you know, it's either out there for sex or someone to make them feel like they're still attractive and desired and everything else. Nothing like a forty-five-or-something-year-old man being desired by an eighteen-year-old.

For Amanda, LaNiece, and the other girls who described older boyfriends as "sick" (or in Marci's case, potentially sick), the intentions of the older boyfriend made younger girlfriend-older boyfriend relationships deviant. While their peers justified their relationships with older boyfriends by pointing out that their older boyfriends really loved them, these girls voiced different opinions. In their view, older boyfriends exploit naive girls who are too young to realize they are being taken advantage of, and this exploitation made the relationships deviant.

Older Boyfriends Are Abusive

Another explanation for the deviance in dating older boyfriends was based on the experiences the teens had with older boyfriends. The girls who were the most adamant about the relationships being deviant were those who had been physically abused, controlled, and/or manipulated into getting pregnant.

Sixteen-year-old LaNiece told me that the typical older boyfriend-younger girlfriend scenario involved control and domination by the boyfriend: "They want to be able to tell someone what to do and when to do it. That's why they date younger girls." Her own relationship with her baby's twenty-year-old father ended when "he just kept being bossy." She explained that he was controlling every part of her life and cheating on her at the same time:

> He was just like, controlling everything. "Where are you going?" Or, "Why are you combing your hair like that?" I was like, "Because I want to." And he would tell me, "Oh, I *know* you're not wearing that to school." Or, "I *know* you're not doing that." So really controlling. And he was with all these other girls.

Fifteen-year-old Vanessa, the mother of a baby girl, told me her twenty-year-old boyfriend cheated on her while she was pregnant and living with him, often disappearing for days at a time while he had sexual flings with other girls (and grown women). When the baby was born, he disappeared for eight months. When he eventually returned, he insulted Vanessa by repeatedly commenting on how much weight she had gained, told her that breast-feeding was disgusting and that she had to quit doing that to "any baby of mine," and chastised her for spoiling the baby. Vanessa broke up with him one week later, commenting that, "He changed. Or at least I think he changed. All he wanted to do was tell me what to do. And nothing I did was right." Like LaNiece, Vanessa believed that the basis for his dominating personality was his age.

Several mothers told me stories about their older boyfriends "tricking" them into getting pregnant, which they saw as comparable to the other forms of abuse and domination. For example, when she was thirteen, Diana's eighteen-year-old boyfriend Matt told her that he had been diagnosed by his doctor as infertile, so he did not need to use a condom. Similarly, LaNiece's twenty-year-old boyfriend told her that he couldn't get her pregnant:

> Well, I was only thirteen, keep that in mind, 'cause he told me, "Oh I can't have kids, I can't have kids." And I believed him! I was like, "Oh, okay." You know, I didn't know anything about the reproductive system—I was only thirteen. So he said he couldn't get me pregnant and I believed him. And that was his intention, all along, to get me pregnant. 'Cause I asked him once, when I was complaining that I was all fat and my feet were all swollen, I'm like, "You probably knew you could get me pregnant. You probably just wanted to trick me so I'd get pregnant." And he got this big smile and he was like, "Well, what if I did?" And I was like, "Oh my god!" I wasn't expecting

that at all. I was thinking he'd say something like, "It was an accident," or "I'm just as surprised as you are."

Both girls told me that they were tricked only because their boyfriends were older and they trusted their "judgment," but they realized later that the men used this maturity to manipulate the girls into getting pregnant.

Eighteen-year-old Kristina was physically abused by her older boyfriend. She told me that she felt like her former boyfriend duped her into thinking she was in love with him, and that his physical and sexual abuse were signs of love from him. Looking back, she was angry: "How does anybody at age thirteen know they're in love? He nailed it into me that I was in love with him. He gave me all these things. He took me out to dinner. He told me this is what it means to be in love." Later, she told me what else her eighteen-year-old boyfriend did: he physically abused her during sexual intercourse to "prepare" her and "toughen her up" in case she was ever raped. Because she was not able to see past the dinners and the gifts at age thirteen, Kristina felt strongly that other young women would not either. Statutory rape laws, she thought, could be used to intervene in relationships like hers where the girl was too young to realize she was being abused.

Dating Older Boyfriends Is Illegal

A pragmatic explanation for why dating older boyfriends was deviant was one based on the law: because the law defines these relationships as illegal, they are deviant. Even though most of the girls had only vague understandings of what the actual law was in their state, they all had an awareness that a law existed, and as a result, they viewed their relationships with older boyfriends as deviant.

Twenty-year-old Amanda told me that when she was sixteen she and her twenty-three-year-old boyfriend Robby were so concerned about breaking the law that they looked up the statute in the state where they lived:

> That's one of the things that me and Robby were talking about before we got together, was what are people going to think, and is this okay. I went to the library and looked in the law book and saw that it was fifteen and nineteen, you know, a fifteen-year-old girl-nineteen-year-old boy is the limit. If you have a fifteen-year-old and a twenty-year-old, it's statutory rape. But once

you're sixteen, you can go out with someone who's any age. We made sure of that before we started really going in public and doing whatever.

Because they worked together, their primary concern was that their coworkers would think they were doing something wrong. Before they started officially "going out," they discussed the potential problems that might arise:

The biggest problem was the age difference. It was important because—well, he was twenty-three and I was sixteen, and that's a huge gap in the things you do and the things you like. We were really worried about other people and what they'd think. Other people at work who would think he was a pervert, 'cause he was twenty-three and I was sixteen, and at that age—actually, at any age—that's a big difference. People were already talking about us, which made it kind of weird.

Other young women did not take the initiative to look up the specific laws regarding statutory rape, but they did feel that what they were doing was deviant, if not illegal. They showed their awareness of the deviance by lying about their ages to their boyfriends—either because they knew it was illegal or they knew such relationships were socially stigmatized. Many young women began relationships with their older boyfriends under false pretenses, either blatantly lying about their ages or subtly steering the conversation away from the topic of age. Indeed, LaNiece told me that lying was very common among her peers: "I thought it was all cool because I was like in eighth grade and everything and, like, all my friends were dating older guys and we all lied about our ages. We'd be all, 'How old are you?' 'Oh, I'm 16.' 'Oh yeah, well I'm 17!' So we were all lying, you know?" Even though they lied about their ages, the girls told me that their boyfriends knew their real ages—or at least knew they were younger than they said they were—and that did not stop them from dating them or having sex with them. When she was thirteen, LaNiece lied about her age to her boyfriend, but she pointed out that her boyfriend, who was twenty, knew her real age and should have known better than to seduce a young girl: "I told him I was fifteen and he never seemed to care, so I just told him later that I was really thirteen and he said, 'Yeah, I knew all along you were thirteen.' He said, 'Yeah, I already knew how old you were, I just wanted to see how long you would wait to tell me.'" Although she went to great lengths to hide her true age—thereby showing an awareness of the deviance of dating someone so much older than herself—LaNiece found out her boyfriend knew her age all along. Thus while she altered her behavior (or, more accurately, her age) to avoid a deviant identity, he seemed to feel that there was nothing wrong with dating someone so young. Fifteen-year-old Diana told me a similar story. When she was thirteen, she told eighteen-year-old Matt that she was fifteen. Three weeks later (and after she became pregnant with his child), she revealed her true age, only to have him tell her that he knew all along. Like LaNiece, Diana had a sense that her real age would make the relationship deviant, a feeling that was not shared by their boyfriends.

Excusing Deviance

The young women who defined younger girlfriend-older boyfriend relationships as deviant had been involved with older boyfriends. Thus they had participated in an act they defined as deviant. Because they viewed these relationships as deviant, and because they did not want to lose face by assuming responsibility for the deviance, they denied responsibility for their involvement with older boyfriends. In contrast to the teens who used justifications and assumed responsibility for their involvement with older boyfriends, the young women who viewed dating older boyfriends as deviant excused their behavior as something that was beyond their immediate control. The two groups differed in another important respect as well: while the justifiers were still involved with their older boyfriends, the girls who defined that behavior as deviant (and therefore felt compelled to use excuses to account for their behavior) were no longer with their older boyfriends. The excuses they used helped them explain why they became involved with someone who turned out to be a terrible boyfriend.

I'm Only Attracted to Older Guys

Many teen mothers turned to older boyfriends because the "younger" men they knew (who were, in fact, their same-age peers) were not viewed as an acceptable dating pool. The specific reasons for this perspective varied, but most had to do with the fact that the teen mother felt she was too mature to be attracted to someone her own age. Thus older men were the only desirable dates.

Kerry was eight months' pregnant and fifteen years old when I spoke with her. Her baby's father was eighteen. When asked whether she liked older guys in general, she responded, "All of my boyfriends have been older than me." Her explanation for dating older men was that they were more mature than younger men:

> [I like] somebody I don't always have to babysit. I get tired of being with people that look up to me. Me and my friends were talking about this. You want someone who knows exactly what you need, and a lot of them don't. Someone who can take care of himself and who's not going to look at you like a babysitter, which a lot of them do.

While she touted the virtues of older men, Kerry felt that statutory rape laws were necessary to protect other young women from experiencing the physical abuse she received from her baby's father. When she complained in public about the way he was treating a three-year-old in their care, he dragged her across the room and cut her arms with a knife. Kerry felt that getting involved with this abusive boyfriend was not her fault, however, because she was not attracted to the immature men who were her own age. I spoke informally with Kerry a few months prior to the interview—when she and her boyfriend were still together—and she told me that she was against statutory rape laws because she felt they infringed on her right to make her own decisions. Once the relationship turned sour, however, she changed her account from a justification (consensual sex is not rape) to an excuse, ultimately denying responsibility for her involvement with her abusive boyfriend. This excuse resembles Scott and Lyman's (1968) "appeal to biological drives," wherein people blame their involvement in deviance on something out of their control, such as their sexual drives. For the teen mothers in this study, their sexual attraction to older boyfriends and their own level of maturity were perceived as character traits that were out of their control.

I Need a Father for My Baby

While some teen mothers explained that they were not attracted to younger men, others told me that younger men would not make good fathers for their children. Thus they had to turn to older men. Sixteen-year-old Jennifer, the mother of a one-year-old daughter, offered the following explanation:

> People my age are too immature. And you know, obviously anybody younger than me is not going to be able to deal with

my lifestyle. The people at school, I don't even think about them. You know, I think there's some guys that are cute but that's it. They're cute, but that's as far as it goes. They're immature, and I would not like to support someone else. I want it to be a mutual thing.

When she spoke of younger boys dealing with her "lifestyle," she meant handling the responsibility of dating a woman with a child, and ultimately being a father figure for her child. Sixteen-year-old Staci also told me that the boys at the high school would not be good boyfriends, saying, "They're too immature. I think they'd all have to grow up first before I'd consider them." When I asked her what it was about older boyfriends that appealed to her, she said, "They're not worried about school. If they want to, they can take care of the kid. They're not so much into partying like in high school." These young women, then, felt compelled to date older boyfriends because there was no suitable alternative: the guys their own age were too immature to handle the responsibility of being a father. In using this excuse, the teen mothers conceded the deviance of dating older boyfriends but blamed their involvement with them on something out of their control: the fact that younger men were too immature for them because they could not handle the demands of fatherhood. Statutory rape laws are often thought to limit hedonistic impulses—to make older men think twice before becoming involved with younger women—but these young women said that they turned to older men because the younger men they knew were too irresponsible. Seeking older men was, for them, a responsible, rational thing to do.

I Needed Something That Only He Could Give Me

While some teen mothers spoke of needing older boyfriends, in a general way, others spoke of why they needed to be with a particular older boyfriend. For these young women, the men they dated fulfilled a special role—namely, that of a father figure. Kristina, now age eighteen, explained why she began dating a sixteen-year-old boy when she was twelve:

He and I both had a missing parent, and I think we connected really well because we knew what we wanted that we weren't getting. I was searching for something, and I found it in him. I was out for a father figure, and that's exactly what he was. He was the dad I always wanted. I just wanted somebody to hug me and tell me they loved me and he did it. I was in love with him because he gave me what I needed.

With the benefit of hindsight, Kristina was able to speak more generally about teenagers dating people older than themselves, telling me, "I think girls who date older guys are looking for a father, or just a missing feeling or something that they're not getting from their parents at home. And it can be from a mom or dad, you know?"

Eighteen-year-old Marci only dated older men, including one who was twenty years her senior. Like Kristina, she saw the connection between her choice in men and her desire for a father figure:

I've always been attracted to older men. You know, a lot of people say, "Oh, maybe you're looking for your father or someone to take care of you." I think it does have something to do with being taken care of, but I'm not looking for anyone like my father. I'm pretty sure about that one.

She spoke specifically about her relationship with the thirty-seven-year-old married man that began when she was seventeen:

He was really supportive through my pregnancy, and when my mom kicked me out, was somewhat financially supportive of me . . . until his wife found out! [laughs]. He just felt like, I don't know, like somewhat of a father figure, you know? Not like my dad, but someone who gave me the advice and the caring and everything else. You know, the support that I wasn't getting anywhere else.

For Kristina and Marci, the decision to date an older man was one over which they felt little control. Thus they distanced themselves from blame. Kristina placed the blame on her abusive father, suggesting that his violent treatment drove her to seek an older boyfriend (who also turned out to be violent) as a replacement. Likewise, Marci blamed her father, but she said that his neglect and disinterest were what forced her to seek support elsewhere. This excuse resembles two of Scott and Lyman's (1968) accounts. First, it is similar to the "self-fulfillment" excuse, in that the teen mothers were looking for a relationship they needed to make their lives complete. It also resembles the "scapegoating" excuse, for the young women blame this need for an older man on their own abusive or neglectful fathers.

Conclusion

Scott and Lyman's (1968) accounts are valuable in understanding how teenage mothers view statutory rape. First, accounts allow the researcher to differentiate between people who view certain acts as deviant and those who do not. In the present study, this distinction allowed me to see that the women involved in abusive or unhappy relationships viewed them as deviant because the man was older, whereas women in stable relationships with older men saw nothing wrong with their age difference. Second, they allow the researcher to distinguish between deviants who blame themselves for their wrongdoings and deviants who blame others. Here I noted that women who felt no control over their involvement with older men perceived themselves as victims (and because of this wanted more stringent enforcement of statutory rape laws), while women who claimed responsibility for their behavior felt like equals in their relationships (and thought statutory rape laws were unnecessary). These findings have significant implications for accounts in general because they help us understand who uses excuses and who uses justifications.

The present study suggests that there is more of a difference between excuses and justifications than has been indicated in previous research. Specifically this study shows that the people who rely on the different forms of accounts may be in relationships that are qualitatively different from one another, despite the fact that they are in seemingly similar situations. Teen mothers using justifications felt as though they had as much power in the relationship as their boyfriends, and thus as much responsibility for being involved in the deviance. This group placed as much blame on themselves as they did on anyone else. Teen mothers who relied on excuses, in contrast, felt powerless in their relationships, and thus they did not claim responsibility for the deviance. Indeed, they blamed their deviance on someone else. In more general terms, this study suggests that action and responsibility will be accepted when deviants feel a sense of control over their behavior, while action and responsibility will be rejected when deviants feel as though they have no control over things that happen to them. Persons engaging in the same form of deviance can have dramatically different views about their own agency and the factors that compelled them to engage in that behavior. Whether they blame themselves or others is contingent on this feeling of power or control and influences whether they will use excuses or justifications.

Perhaps the most significant contribution of this study for the accounts literature is that it posits the possibility of a sequential relationship between justifications and excuses that has not been addressed previously. Justifications and excuses may be used independently by deviant actors, but they may also follow in a sequence, as justifications give way to excuses when people become disempowered and disenchanted. In this regard, I have shown that the teen mothers who were still in relationships with older men gave justifications, and those who then broke up with their older boyfriends switched to excuses. The teen mothers demonstrated a tendency to use justifications initially, but they moved on to excuses when the relationships went bad. In essence, they demonstrated a shift from self-blame ("Even if you're thirteen, you know what you're doing") to blaming other factors beyond their control ("Girls who date older guys are looking for a father"). While involved in amicable relationships, they claimed responsibility, but once things turned sour, they placed the blame elsewhere. More generally, one could hypothesize that deviants feeling a sense of power will use justifications, but they will shift to excuses when they become disempowered. Conversely, deviants who become empowered may change their accounts from excuses to justifications. Scott and Lyman (1968) proposed that deviants "phase" their accounts when rationalizing their behavior, suggesting that they go through a series of accounts as they try to negotiate a nondeviant identity with their audience. Rather than shifting accounts in the course of a conversation, as Scott and Lyman suggested, the young women in this study shifted the nature of the account over the course of their relationships, a phasing process that was distinctly sequential in nature.

Individuals engaging in a wide range of deviant behaviors utilize similar aligning actions to rationalize to themselves and others that what they are doing is not wrong, from students cheating on exams (McCabe 1992) to white-collar criminals (Benson 1985). The teenage mothers in the present study were no different, for they also were concerned with preserving a nondeviant identity, both in their minds and in the minds of others. The young women accounting for their involvement with older men are distinct from other groups of deviants, however, for they exercise justifications and excuses in an effort to minimize the damage to their own identities, even though it is their boyfriends who are legally culpable for the crime of statutory rape. In essence, the victims are accounting for the perpetrators' deviance. The fact that the young women do this suggests that while they may not be legally responsible for their involvement with older men, they are receiving messages telling them that they are deviant. They feel deviant because they are aware that they are voluntarily violating several norms at once: the norm of age homogamy in dating partners, the norm of abstaining from sexual relations at a young age, and the norm of delaying parenthood until adulthood. The fact that they are not legally liable for consenting to the sexual relationship has nothing to do with the criminal definition of the act (i.e., it is inherently deviant for the man but not the woman). Rather, it is a law based on the notion that an unmarried woman is her father's property; premarital sex damages the marriage-market value of his property, so he brings suit against the perpetrator (Oberman 1994). Today, however, women blame themselves because they have voluntarily participated in the relationship and because, in our liberated culture, women are viewed as independent actors rather than someone's property. Just as statutory rape laws are beginning to reflect the idea that women are able to give consent by excusing, for the most part, consensual acts of intercourse between minors (Oberman 1994), women have internalized the belief that giving consent means accepting blame, regardless of the circumstances surrounding the consent.

EIGHT

THE STIGMA OF
TEENAGE PARENTING

One of the most prominent themes to emerge from my observations of the young women at the Teen Center was that they felt like motherhood resulted in differential treatment from the public at large. This treatment was overwhelmingly negative, heightening the teens' sense that they were deviant and adding fuel to their efforts to aggressively combat the stigma cast upon them. The teens perceived stigma and negative treatment coming from four sources: social service agencies, students and teachers at school, the general public, and the media. Intentionally or not, each of these groups did things to single out, ostracize, or stigmatize the teen mothers in this study. As a consequence, the young women felt compelled to aggressively combat the stigma cast upon them.

SOCIAL SERVICE AGENCIES

The young women at the Teen Center were involved with several agencies in the community that were designed to help them in some way. While not everyone participated in AFDC/TANF, WIC, or Medicaid, the teens were all required to register for federal child-care support because that money helped defray some of the center's operating costs. Thus to some degree each young woman was involved with at least one agency, and usually several others as well. Social services, the health clinic, the low-income housing agency, and even the Teen Center supposedly had the teens' best interests in mind, but the message conveyed to the young mothers was often quite negative. In many ways, representatives of these different agencies resembled the staff of the GED program for teenage mothers studied by Horowitz (1995), whom she labeled "arbiters." Arbiters treated their teenage clients as subordinates and distinguished between "deserving and undeserving participants," that is, between participants who held jobs and participants who received welfare. The net result of the arbiters' treatment for the teen mothers in Horowitz's study and the young women I observed at the Teen Center was a constant reminder that they had few resources and that others stigmatized them.

Because I often attended social service appointments with the young women or intervened on their behalf over the telephone, I witnessed firsthand much of this negative treatment. My first glimpse of how the local agencies viewed the teen mothers came during my first school year in the setting, when I was pretesting a follow-up survey instrument on some of the teens at the behest of the program coordinator, Helen. Helen had invited representatives of several local social service agencies to contribute questions to her survey, which she asked me to administer. Since so much of the program's success depended on a strong relationship with the city government, Helen asked me to comply with whatever these outside agencies requested. As a result, the questionnaire that was initially designed to assess levels of educational attainment, subsequent pregnancies, and, most of all, an evaluation of the program now included questions on alcohol and drug use, suicide attempts, and child abuse. I asked Katie, a senior, to pretest the survey with these newly included "coping strategies." When she was finished, I asked her what she thought of the additions. She shook her head in disgust and said, "It was really degrading, as if all teen parents have mental problems."

The teens often came to me for advice after negative experiences with social service agencies. For example, eighteen-year-old Sunshine had a terrible toothache during the summer immediately after she graduated from high school. Her Medicaid insurance required that she see a dentist at the local free clinic, who promptly removed the tooth during the office visit. During the procedure, his hand slipped, and his instrument sliced into the back of her throat. She told me she was still crying from the pain when she was leaving the office and asked the dental hygienist what she should do. The hygienist told her that was one of the consequences of "living off the city," and told her that without "real" insurance she would just have to live with the pain. Sunshine came home and immediately called me to see what her options were for receiving care from another provider. A few months earlier, Sunshine ate a handful of peanuts and had a serious allergic reaction. She was home alone with her two-year-old son, so she called 911 and was rushed to the hospital. When she told me the story I asked her what the hospital staff did with her son while she lay on the hospital bed hooked up to an IV. She said, "Oh, you'll love this. The nurse said, 'You made the decision to have a child. That means you have to watch him.' So I was gasping for air, practically dying, and she decided it was a good time to make me feel guilty for being a teen mom. Real nice."

Tracy had an equally bad experience with the local low-income housing authority. When she was seventeen, she was offered an apartment in a public housing complex after being on a wait list for over two years. In early February, the housing agency gave her a move-in date of March 1. Tracy told her mother she would be moving out (her mother had told her earlier that year that she would kick her out when she turned eighteen that summer), and her mother promptly made arrangements to move from the three-bedroom apartment they shared into a one-bedroom apartment on the same day Tracy would be moving. On February 27, when Tracy called the housing agency to confirm the logistics of her move, she was informed that the current occupant had asked for and received a two-week extension on her lease. This same process was repeated four times over the next couple of months—Tracy was given a new move-in date and was only told that things had changed when she called to confirm; no one at the housing agency ever thought to inform her of the change in plans or to offer her assistance in finding temporary accommodations. Because her mother had moved as scheduled, Tracy was homeless for ten weeks, which meant she and her three-year-old son went from couch to couch wherever they were welcome. In the week before she finally moved in—right after it had been postponed again—I ran into her in the program lounge and found her crying and at her wit's end about the entire situation. I asked her if she had told the housing representative that she was homeless, and she said, "Oh yeah, they know. But they think that because we're teen parents that they're doing us a favor. See, the way they look at it, it's our fault for being homeless. So it's like we deserve to be—put at an inconvenience."

Often the young women's views of social services were not based on actual experience but on things they had heard. Usually these negative opinions had to do with the power social services had to take teen parents' children away. For example, when Vanessa first moved to Lakeside, I asked her about her impressions of the Teen Center:

V: The only thing I don't like is being involved with social services. I mean, they think that because you're involved with them they can butt into your business any time. And I don't care because I'm not doing anything wrong, but that doesn't give them the right. I mean, if you get AFDC or food stamps or whatever, they can come knock at your door anytime they want and just look around your house or whatever. They look to see if your house looks . . . if it's trashy, they'll take your kid away. If it's not a good environment for a kid or if they find something they don't like, they can take your kid away. I don't get any of that stuff [AFDC or food stamps], I just get Medicaid. But my sister works for social services in Georgia and that's how they do it. I guess another thing that bothers me is the things you do here that could get you in trouble. Like, you could go outside to smoke a cigarette, and if somebody sees you that works here, they're gonna go tell Helen and then Helen will call social services.

JG: Just for smoking?

V: I think so, yeah. I don't think they'd take your kid away, but I think they'd try to find a way. I think it has to be when you're smoking around your kid that they can take your kid away, and I never do that 'cause I'd feel bad for doing that. But I know people who've gotten their kids taken away because they smoked around them. I just don't like how they butt in like that. They do it because we're younger parents. 'Cause they don't do it with older people. And they just don't think we're mature enough to be parents, I guess. So they try to find something wrong with us.

The perception that adults in the community, especially social service professionals, were trying to find some excuse to take away their children was rampant among Teen Center mothers. This belief that someone was always watching them led them to behave in a way Helen referred to as "parenting on display," meaning they overexaggerated the mainstream parenting skills they learned at the center. This perception only heightened the competitive nature of the culture.

Like Katie, the senior who pretested my survey instrument and thought it was degrading to teen mothers, twenty-year-old Amanda told me she was not happy with the perception that all teen parents were in need of extra mental health support. In particular, she told me she did not like being forced to register for programs or classes as part of her participation at the Teen Center:

The bad thing, I think, is them assuming that you need counseling or parenting classes and all that stuff to help you be a better parent. It's nice that it's there for the people that need it, but it's not nice to make the assumption that everybody needs help. 'Cause not everybody is made to be a mom; there are people with mother instincts and there are people without those instincts who need those classes. But I felt that I didn't need them. I've always been a nurturing person and I don't think I needed the help that they always said I had to have. And having the counselor here, making us go to group every week—I just don't like the assumption that if you're a teen mom you must have these deep emotional problems. I'm not here for that. I'm here to get an education.

As Horowitz (1995) recounted, teen mothers "are often subject to what they experience as humiliating situations and are very sensitive to others' actions that appear not to give them the respect they think they deserve" (185). Forcing teens to participate in mental health sessions with a counselor, reminding them that they are financially dependent, and treating them with great disrespect all served to humiliate the teens. In an ironic twist, the very people who set out to help young mothers were often the source of the greatest stigma and the harshest blow to their self-concepts.

OTHER STUDENTS AND TEACHERS

The Teen Center's location in the basement of Lakeside High School meant the young mothers took classes with other students ("upstairs" students, or students not in the program), forcing the two groups into frequent interaction. Only a few students were friendly to the teen mothers—those who had been good friends with a program mother or who volunteered in the nurseries for home economics credit—but the treatment the teen mothers received from the majority of students ranged from mild castigation to overt criticism.

Sixteen-year-old Angelica brought up the issue of negative treatment from her peers in the context of a story she was telling me about being pregnant: "I loved everything about it except being at school. People would stare at you here at school, but it didn't really bother me. I mean, I knew I was carrying a life, no matter what *they* said." Nineteen-year-old Julie, who was pregnant with her third son when we talked about school, also brought up the other students as being one of her least favorite aspects of school. She told me:

It's definitely a lot different once you have a kid. People, the other students, look at us a lot different I think. They don't necessarily say anything to us, but they'll look at us and you know, they'll think, "Oh, well she must be easy or something," you know? They'll think something like that, especially with having two kids— they're really, they're really picky about it!

I asked her what the most difficult thing was about being a parent at Lakeside. She said:

Probably the worst thing is the criticism, I'd say. From the people upstairs. Even though a lot of the girls up there are having sex, and I know the boys have sex, and they just, they act like, you know, being pregnant and taking care of your responsibilities is just the worst thing in the world to do. They'd rather go get an abortion than actually take care of their responsibility or give it up for adoption. I think the criticism is just the worst thing. Sometimes they say stuff to you, but it's mostly you can see it in the way they look at you, the way they stare at you or whisper when you walk by.

Twenty-year-old Amanda, who had been at the center for three years when we talked, told me that receiving overt criticism from other students was a common experience for members of the Teen Center. She related:

I didn't personally get into any conflicts with people, but I know for other people downstairs that people would say things to them. Like right in front of them in class, "Oh, teen parents are such sluts. There's one right there . . ." and blah, blah, blah. They'd actually *say* stuff and I think that's horrible. Once people know, 'cause in class on the first day they always want you to introduce yourself, and I always say that I have Matthew, you know, that I have a son. And once people know they treat me differently. Like staying away from me, you know? You can just feel the difference in the way they look at you once they know.

Because of my youthful appearance, I often witnessed this treatment myself, because students did not think to alter their behavior around someone they perceived to be a fellow teenager. For example, one afternoon, fifteen-year-old Alicia asked me to walk with her to the bus after school so she could finish telling me a story about her ex-boyfriend's new girlfriend. As we sat on the bench in front of the school, two young men (who I assumed to be ninth graders because they looked so young) sat down with us. They both stared at Alicia's baby, looking back and forth between the two of them as if to discern whether this baby really belonged to this young woman. I recorded the incident in my field notes that night:

> One of the boys asked Alicia how old her baby was. She told them, "Seven weeks," and he said, "So are you a senior?" She nudged me in the side to make sure I heard, mumbled "No," and then turned and faced me with her back to them so they wouldn't be able to say anything more to her. Once they were gone, she told me she was sick of people asking her questions like that, because she felt it was obvious that in asking whether she was a senior they were trying to make her admit how young she really was. Her son had been alive less than two months, yet Alicia had already experienced this scorn so many times that she could predict when it was going to happen and sheltered herself from it as much as she could.

In addition to being treated differently by their fellow students, the teen mothers also spoke of feeling like their teachers treated them differently than their nonparenting peers. Some of the older teen mothers complained that their teachers did not push them hard enough because they had lower expectations for teen moms (whether well intentioned or not), which were not congruent with the image the teens had of themselves as mature, responsible adults. The message sent was one that was deeply disturbing to eighteen-year-old Jessica, an honors student:

> There's a lot of things I don't like about school now. Like, sometimes the way you get treated by teachers. When you're a kid it's OK to be patronized, you're so used to it, but as you get older you don't want to deal with that anymore. And the teachers are sometimes . . . you get a lot more leniency from most teachers because you're a teen mom. That can be good if your baby gets sick and there's nothing you can do about missing class or whatever, but it frustrates me that they don't push as hard, don't expect as much from us.

Amanda expressed a similar opinion, giving the specific example of her gym teacher:

> I don't like the way the teachers look at you, the way they treat you. Like, even when they're trying to be nice, like my gym

teacher. For gym class if you miss a class you have to make it up to get an "A." And every time I missed class because Matthew was sick my teacher was always like, "Oh, I know you're a parent. You don't have to make it up." I mean, I appreciate that nice treatment, appreciate that they acknowledge my circumstances, but it's also kind of degrading for them to think I need extra help. And other teachers on the first day of class when you tell them you're a teen mom, they're always like, "Oh, I know *you're* going to miss class because you're a mom." And I've never used that excuse, ever. When I'm absent I never use Matthew as an excuse. I just come back to class and say, "I missed class and I'm going to make it up. What do I need to do?"

The rude looks, critical comments, and differential treatment were reinforced by a feeling of isolation from the school community. Amanda told me that the school administrators strategically placed the program in the basement to keep the young mothers away from the rest of the students:

I didn't even know about the program when I went to this school, and I went here for a year and a half before I got pregnant. They keep it totally isolated. You're not allowed to have your kids in the halls, you can't bring them to class. The only thing you can do is bring them to the lunchroom where you have to sit in this corner. And then you're isolated together in the basement. They do it on purpose. You're not allowed to go through this school with your kid. They say it's because they don't want the other students to see, because they think it will make them want to have a baby.

Keeping the teen mothers physically isolated from the rest of the students reinforced the message that the school, although providing space for the center, did not advocate early parenting. The young women interpreted this stance as an indelible stamp of disapproval.

THE GENERAL PUBLIC

The teens were confronted on a daily basis by strangers who voiced their opinion—or whose faces conveyed their feelings—about teenage parenting. In their study of teenage mothers in San Diego, Ortiz and Bassoff (1987) found that 41.5 percent of their subjects reported feeling that people look down on teen mothers, and 34 percent reported that people feel sorry for them. In Schofield's (1994) study of teenage mothers in England, a similar theme emerged, with the young women in her study recounting numerous stories of strangers approaching them and criticizing them for having children so young. Things were no different in Lakeside, and every young woman I spoke to at the Teen Center felt like the general public looked down on teenage mothers.

When I interviewed Tracy the summer before her senior year, her son was age three. She felt like the treatment she received from strangers had changed since she first became a mother at age fourteen:

> Lately I think I've been getting treated a little better. Because I'm trying to do most of it on my own and I am older. I think when I first had him, people were totally—people looked like they were disgusted by me because I was so young. Older people, people in their thirties or older. Just people on the bus, around town, whatever. When Kevin was younger I'd be on the bus and people would just think I was babysitting until they heard the word "Mommy" come out of his mouth and I replied. Then they'd go, "Excuse me? What did he say?"

I asked her whether this negative treatment affected her at all.

> The hardest thing I have to do is—I don't like disciplining him in public because I'm always afraid I'm going to get that, "You're abusing your child," when of course I'm not. They're saying it just because I'm younger and they think that any young person can't control their child. I mean, I'm probably discriminating against older people by saying they *all* think the same way, but it definitely enters my mind. I just feel like I have to be extra careful because I don't want him taken away from me. I mean, I know it's really stupid to be scared about that because I don't do anything that could lead to that, but I'm always afraid that there's an extra eye out on me, you know, if they see something or hear something they'll twist words around to make people believe that I'm a bad parent.

When I first met Tracy at the Teen Center, Helen asked me to drive her to the doctor during the school day. Her infant son cried during the entire ride. In my field notes, I recorded that Tracy said, "I'm so sorry, honestly, I'm not a bad mother, he just doesn't like the car. . . . I don't want you to think I'm a bad mother. I hate riding in the car with people because he always cries and I'm always afraid it makes me look like a bad mother." At that point in time I was one of those strangers Tracy perceived as a possible threat.

Linda, the former cheerleader, told me that most of the teen mothers she knew parented differently in public than they did in the privacy of their own homes for the same reasons Tracy gave me:

> 'Cause you know, they're afraid they're gonna get their kids taken away. I would do a lot of things differently—you know, dye my hair like my sister does or get an eyebrow ring—except I'm afraid that they would take Lili away. 'Cause I think the system basically finds anything to pick at, and if they want, they can just really screw your life if they want to. They can take your child away. And it scares me quite a bit, because, you know, all I can think of is if our country got away with killing our president and covering the whole thing up, then why wouldn't they screw me over too. It would be very easy to do and I wouldn't be able to fight it. So I basically tread very slowly and carefully. But maybe when she's grown I'll do my hair in different stripes of color! I think a lot of girls here worry about getting their kids taken away just for being too young.

Eighteen-year-old Andrea told me the criticism was so much a part of her daily life that she even dreamt about it at night:

> I had this dream that I was at a concert or something and I told this guy, "Well I need a ticket and I need one for my son," and he was talking like, "Oh teen mothers, you're all welfare mothers, you'll all amount to nothing. Oh, but I have nothing against *you*." And I think that's kind of an idea that some people get, that all of them are on welfare. But I work very hard to take care of my son. So I think that a lot of the criticism that teen parents get is unfair because some teen parents do work hard to keep their kids and they take care of them. There are those who don't, too, but for those who do there's too much criticism. And I think it's like a myth or something that you're not grown up, you're just a kid having a kid. But it's not as much that as you're just having your kids *younger*. It's like, that's how people used to be a long time ago, they used to have kids when they were thirteen or fourteen. But now it's just like, you're a teen, you have a baby, that's wrong.

When she came to speak to my university class about her experiences as a teen mother, Amanda provided another example of this negative treatment. She told my class that strangers on the city bus constantly made comments about her being too young to be a parent—that it happened so frequently that she had come to accept it as an unavoidable consequence of using public transportation. She told my class that she did not let two-year-old Matthew sit on her lap anymore because she was afraid that he would squirm around and "accidentally touch her somewhere inappropriate," which could make people think she was molesting him and might lead to having him taken away from her.

THE MEDIA

The mothers at the Teen Center were acutely aware of the media's depiction of teenage parenthood. Whether the source was a nationally syndicated television talk show or an article in the local newspaper, the message was perceived to be the same: teenagers are bad, irresponsible mothers. The young women made constant reference to these ideas, which they unanimously regarded as inaccurate.

The Teen Center received considerable attention from the local press, and at least once a year a reporter from the local newspaper came to take pictures of the facilities, the babies, and the mothers themselves. These articles were typically sympathetic—highlighting the mothers' success in school, for example—but the readers' responses were anything but. Like clockwork, an article on the Teen Center elicited a flurry of letters to the editor. One such article came out shortly before twenty-year-old Amanda was assigned to write a persuasive speech for her communications class. She chose as her topic the media coverage of teen parenting, exploring the perception the media led the public to hold. When I asked her what the perception was, she instantly replied:

> Being a bad parent. Being a slut. Giving their kids to their parents to raise. Being irresponsible. Not being able to give love or teach love, which is totally not true. That's what the lady said in that letter to the editor of the *Lakeside Times*. She'd read about the Teen Center and wrote in a letter saying all these terrible things. I don't think I've ever been as angry as I was when I read that letter. I was so mad. I think every stereotype that people have about teen parents is wrong, and it makes me mad because they treat us like the stereotypes are *true*. I think that the negative stuff may be true in a lot of cases, but that's no matter what age the mom is. And people should look at the Teen Center and see that every mom there is trying. They're in school, you know, they're trying to make a better life for their

kid. And you can look at the kids too. You can see the joy on their faces when we walk in the nursery at the end of the day, and that doesn't come from being a bad parent.

Another regular source of media attention came in the form of the television talk shows the young women watched after school. During my four years at the Teen Center, I heard numerous reports of shows with topics including teenage daughters who wanted to get pregnant and teen mothers who did not know who their baby's father was. The day after such shows aired, the young women analyzed each episode and the show's guests, typically putting them down and discussing how they—the Teen Center moms—differed from the guests on the show. Occasionally, the young women felt sympathetic toward the teen mothers they saw on television, recognizing their shared experiences as victims of an undeserved stigma. Their response to these talk shows was so passionate that one year a group of seniors worked together to write a letter to one of the talk show hosts, urging him to visit the Teen Center if he wanted to see what teenage mothers were really like. They referred to this collective action frequently in the months that followed, beaming about their effort to change one element of the system that stigmatized them.

NINE

TRANSFORMED SELVES, TRANSFORMED RELATIONSHIPS

The Consequences of Teenage Parenting

The consequences of adolescent childbearing are the focus of considerable scholarly research and political debate. This issue is usually construed in terms of "costs"—costs incurred by the teens themselves, by their children, and by society at large. In recent years, however, researchers have presented findings that have resulted in a shift in the way many people view these consequences. For example, Upchurch and McCarthy (1990) presented compelling evidence suggesting that adolescent childbearing does not necessarily lead to a truncated education, as had been assumed for so many years; in fact, it may provide some young women with the motivation they need to finish school. Furstenberg (1991) found that early parenting provides direction for young women who feel no sense of purpose before becoming parents. As Dellman-Jenkins, Sattler, and Richardson (1993) asserted, "Further research on adolescent parents . . . is needed in light of recent suggestions that adolescents' positive responses to the challenges of parenthood are often overlooked, whereas the negatives of the adolescent parenting situation are overstated" (591).

What these recent studies are suggesting is that teenage parenting may not result in tragedy for the young women involved as much as it leads to transformation (Thompson 1995). In her qualitative study of adolescent women, Thompson recounts stories of young women going "from here to there"—from unhappy, dysfunctional childhoods to the

139

unconditional love and sense of purpose that come with motherhood. The longitudinal nature of my study was ideally suited for an examination of how motherhood changed the young women. I witnessed these changes firsthand as I watched the teens progress through high school and beyond, and as I compared interview transcriptions from different points in their lives.

In this chapter, I explore the transformations the young women underwent as a result of becoming mothers. Specifically, I examine how parenthood transformed their self-identities and their relationships with significant others in the months and years following the birth of their children.

TRANSFORMATIONS OF SELF

The most profound and, in large measure, the most positive changes the young women talked about were transformations of self. The teens described themselves as better people for having become parents. This was reflected in increased feelings of self-worth as they found themselves succeeding at something and being unconditionally loved by someone, a newfound sense of purpose in life, heightened educational and career plans, and healthier ways of living. These positive sentiments contrasted with the negative conceptions they had of themselves and the potentially destructive behavior they were engaging in before they became parents.

A NEW IDENTITY

Research by Zongker (1977) revealed that pregnant adolescents have lower self-esteem than other teenage women, that they have "pervasive feelings of being 'bad,' dissatisfaction with their own behavior, intense doubts about their identity, and only nominal feelings of self-worth" (488). My research suggests that these feelings are short-lived. Motherhood gave the young women at the Teen Center a new identity and a high level of self-worth. Thus while they may have doubted themselves when they were pregnant, it did not take long for the new identity of motherhood to give the young women a different perspective of themselves. When I asked the young women how they felt about motherhood, the overwhelming response was positive, and often reflected back on this notion that they now had a new definition of themselves and, as a result, a new purpose in life.

Many of the young women talked about motherhood giving them a positive identity that they would have forever. For example, LaNiece, the African American teen with a two-year-old son, told me, "I like it. I mean, sometimes I get frustrated when he's upset about something and I don't know what he wants, but I don't see myself as being anything else. Like, no matter what I do I'll always be a mom." Sixteen-year-old Angelica also viewed motherhood as providing her with a positive new identity, telling me, "I love it. Everything. Just everything about it. I mean, seeing him grow up, being there for him. It's the best thing I've ever done." Angelica's comments reflect not only her new sense of maturity and responsibility ("being there for him") but also the fact that she viewed motherhood as a personal accomplishment ("it's the best thing I've ever done"). Motherhood gave both LaNiece and Angelica a positive identity, something they had never experienced before. LaNiece told me she was a "great big nerd" in her special classes for gifted students, but she always felt like an impostor because her parents and brothers made her feel like she was stupid. Angelica also had a negative sense of self before she became a mother, telling me she was teased by everyone at school because she wore thick glasses and inexpensive, unstylish clothes. Motherhood gave both of these young women an identity that they, their families, and the larger society valorized.

Being a mother allowed other teens to experience things they never experienced as children or young adolescents. Sunshine provides a good example of this pattern. She was raised by her abusive grandparents who were so strict that she could not have friends over after school or speak to them on the phone. She described her childhood as being incredibly lonely and "not really like childhood at all" because she spent all of her time doing chores, going to church (they went five times a week), and trying not to upset her grandmother. Motherhood, ironically, gave her the childhood she always wanted. When she was eighteen, she told me, "I like being a mom. I like it because it's like I've got a little playmate and I can be a kid now." She went on to explain how she liked "little things" like making funny faces to make her son laugh, watching *Sesame Street*, and playing outside without worrying about getting dirty. Motherhood provided Sunshine with the identity of someone who could be happy and carefree, which stood in sharp contrast to the view of herself she had growing up.

Tracy also made references to motherhood giving her something she'd never had before: a reason for living. Tracy grew up the only child of divorced parents. Her mother drank heavily and was hardly ever home when Tracy was a pre-adolescent, and her father rarely spent time with her despite living only thirty miles away. Both parents bombarded her with comments about her inability to achieve in school and their beliefs that she would never amount to anything in life. I talked to Tracy about motherhood in the summer before her senior year, when she was eighteen and her son was three years old. She said the following:

> My life is a lot more fulfilling now. It's harder, but at least I know where I'm going in life because I want to make a life for him. I don't think I would be satisfied with my life if I didn't have him. Before I had him, you know, I never knew why I was on this earth. I mean, I know now that my role in life is to be his mom. And for the rest of my life I'll have that. I was so suicidal before I had him that my mom and dad both told me they didn't know if I was actually going to allow myself to live. So in a way he kind of saved my life. He turned it around because he gave me something to live for.

Furstenberg (1991) analyzed several studies on teenage childbearing and concluded that "childbearing sometimes provided direction and purpose to youth who were uncertain about their chances of rising out of poverty" (133). Although Tracy and the other working-class adolescents at the Teen Center were not concerned about rising out of poverty, they *were* concerned about having a purpose in life. Motherhood gave the young women at the center the direction they were missing, the chance to do something well and change their view of self from someone who failed at everything to someone who succeeded.

EDUCATION AND CAREER PLANS

Along with a new identity as a mother and a new purpose in life came a renewed interest in school, something many of the teens had not felt since they were young children. When sixteen-year-old Angelica said, "I'm doing it for my son," she voiced a common sentiment: having a child provided motivation to go to school and succeed. Other qualitative researchers have noted similar patterns, finding that the new purpose of taking responsibility for their children provides the incentive for many young mothers to complete school (Jacobs 1994) because adolescent mothers recognize "the value of education as a means for ensuring a 'better' life" (Farber 1989, 524). Like their peers in other school-based parenting programs, the young women at the Teen Center internalized the mainstream view of education as being the ticket to a better life, and they were practically unanimous in their aspirations to complete high school as part of taking responsibility for their children.

Most of the teens told me they did not like school before they became parents. In fact, a large number of the young women were having so much difficulty in school that they dropped out—or tried to drop out—prior to becoming pregnant. This pattern is similar to findings described by Zongker (1977), who noted that the teen mothers in his study experienced less success in school prior to becoming parents than did their nonparenting peers. More recently, Rauch-Elnekave (1994) found significant evidence of learning disabilities among the majority of teenage mothers in her study, disabilities so severe that the young women would have qualified for special education classes had they been tested for them. Nineteen-year-old Julie, a Teen Center mother, exemplifies this pattern of difficulty in school before becoming a parent. Julie, the mother of three sons, dropped out of school two months before she became pregnant with her first child at age sixteen. She had no plans to ever return to school, telling me, "I just didn't like it," and "I was never good at it anyway." When Julie became pregnant with her first son, her baby's father deserted her. Despite her early frustrations in school, she enrolled at Lakeside and joined the Teen Center because she realized she could not support her son without an education. For Julie, becoming a mother was sufficient motivation to return to school.

Sunshine also dropped out of school before getting pregnant. Like Julie, she described academic difficulties as leading to her eventual decision to drop out of school:

> I started liking school less, except to socialize. And then my junior year I started ditching. It was just getting too hard. Well, not all my classes. But math was hard. Algebra was a breeze, but then I got to geometry and it seemed like my brain was just . . . stopped. You know, I couldn't learn anymore. It was over my head. See I never failed any classes until I took geometry and that started me—made me like school less. Because I tried, I tried so hard, and no matter what I did I kept getting "E, E, E," which means "fail, fail, fail." And so after a couple of times it was like, well even if I get an "A" next time I'm not going to pass, so why bother. So I finished that school year and then I just didn't go back the next year.

She went on to tell me that she never envisioned going back to school because she had decided that she just could not learn anymore. It was not until a year-long road trip and an unexpected pregnancy landed her in

Lakeside City that she changed her mind. She did not know which of two men was her baby's father, but neither accepted responsibility for it. Sunshine decided she needed to get at least a high school education if she was going to survive as a single parent.

Seventeen-year-old Andrea told a similar story of dropping out, getting pregnant, and then returning to school:

> I dropped out of school in February of my sophomore year. I dropped out, and then two months later is when I got pregnant with Gary. I was just tired of the classes and the people there. The people were all jerks, and I was having trouble in my classes. I've just never been much of a school person. A few months after I found out I was pregnant, I decided to go back. I knew I had to. 'Cause I didn't know if Charlie was going to stick around. 'Cause we didn't really, we only knew each other for like six weeks and we were dating for like three weeks before I got pregnant, and I didn't know if he was going to stick around so I decided I better do something just in case I was going to be raising Gary all by myself. I thought I'd better do something so I could support us.

When she was fifteen, Tracy told me the only reason she did not drop out of school before she became pregnant was because her mother prevented her from doing so:

> When I was younger, you know, elementary school or whatever, I thought I'd graduate. But when I got into middle school I thought if I can just hang on until I'm sixteen then I can quit. I tried to quit several times before that, but my mom wouldn't let me. You know, I'd try staying home from school or ditching or whatever but she always found me and made me go.

Three years after that interview I spoke with Tracy again, in the summer before her senior year. At age eighteen and with a three-year-old son, Tracy was clearly a different person, and her views about school had changed dramatically:

> School is not a social event anymore, definitely, and that's all it used to be for me. Now it's learning skills I'll need to get through life. Before I had him, I wasn't very good in school, and I never imagined myself graduating. Now I'm just what, eight months away? And I'm going to be the first person in my family

to ever graduate from high school. Having Kevin changed everything, because I knew I wasn't going to get anywhere in life if I didn't finish. I knew I couldn't support him if I didn't get an education.

These four women's stories are similar in many ways. First, all of these young women experienced frustration in school before becoming mothers—frustration so significant that they dropped out (or in Tracy's case, tried to drop out) of school. Second, having a child was the motivation for them to return to school and complete their high school education. Third, they all mentioned that they came back to school to support their child; they assumed from the beginning that they would be (or might be) raising the child alone, and they did not think they would be receiving financial support from anyone else (the baby's father, their parents, social services). Thus going back to school was not just in preparation for parenthood but for *single* parenthood. Finally, they construed motherhood as involving supporting someone; when they used this term, they referred to providing monetary support for their children, not emotional support, representing an ideological shift in the way motherhood is defined for women.

In addition to an increased motivation to complete high school, many of the teens spoke of parenthood as giving them incentive to complete postsecondary education in preparation for specific careers. Because of the center's partnership with the local community college, many of the young women enrolled in vocational certification programs as part of their participation in the Teen Center. The most popular courses were in professions involving caregiving, particularly veterinary assistance and medical assistance programs. Teens who had never before considered working in retirement homes or as emergency medical technicians suddenly found themselves wanting to know first aid and basic medical knowledge for their personal gain, and wanting a career doing something they discovered they loved: nurturing and taking care of other people.

Some of the teens saw these programs as providing skills they would need for temporary jobs while they got on their feet. Brooke, for example, planned on getting her certificate in medical assistance, working for a few years, and then going to the university to get her BS in nursing once her son entered kindergarten. Others saw their high school career training programs as providing all the training they would need for their future work. Dana and Janell worked as nursing assistants in a retirement home, a job they both said they would stay in "forever." Sunshine and Vanessa took the veterinary assistance classes necessary to become certified assistants. After high school, Sunshine found immediate employment at a local veterinary office. The expectations the young women had for their careers were mainstream—doing something gender appropriate (caregiving) and moderately prestigious (in the medical field). But like the adolescent mothers in Farber's (1989) study, their understanding of what it would take to reach these goals was not always realistic. For example, seventeen-year-old Blair told me she wanted to be a pediatrician. When I asked her how she would accomplish that goal, she told me she would first get her medical assistant certificate and then go on to nursing school. The young women at the Teen Center adopted mainstream career aspirations, but they had a limited ability to conceptualize how these plans could be realized. Like Farber (1989), I found this to be especially true for the young women like Blair who were from lower-class backgrounds. The other teens had a better idea of the steps involved to enter into these professions because their family members and friends had careers in these fields.

DRUG AND ALCOHOL USE

Another change in the way the teens lived their lives was in their consumption of and attitudes toward drug and alcohol use. Codega, Pasley, and Kreutzer (1990) found substance use to be quite frequent in their study of adolescent mothers. In fact, when they asked teen mothers which types of coping strategies they used when they were dealing with problems, the most common response was "Using drugs not prescribed by a doctor." The response "Drinking beer, wine, or liquor" was not far behind, ranking sixth out of fifty-four possible strategies. In summarizing their respondents' behaviors, the researchers posited, "Substance abuse, considered by some to be a typical adolescent behavior, is not a behavior that reflects movement toward responsible parenting . . ." (1990, 45). The mothers at the Teen Center concurred with this sentiment—and contrasted from the aforementioned group of teen mothers—by viewing drug and alcohol use as inconsistent with responsible motherhood. As Jacobs (1994) found in her study of adolescent mothers, parenthood allows young women the chance to nurture someone the way they wished they had been nurtured themselves. As part of that nurturing, many young mothers take responsibility by eliminating from their lives violence, drugs, and alcohol. Jacobs reported that motherhood allowed the young women in her study the chance to "save themselves" from destructive behaviors. The young women at the Teen Center exemplified a similar pattern, using their new identity as mothers to reinvent themselves.

Before becoming parents, most of the teens told me they experimented with drugs and alcohol, a finding that is consistent with Mott and Haurin's (1988) conclusion that early sexual activity is linked to early experimentation with drugs and alcohol, especially among teenage women. The Teen Center mothers' consumption ranged from minor experimentation to addiction, but in general the teens were heavy users. Once they became pregnant, though, things changed. Fifteen-year-old Vanessa explained to me how motherhood changed her identity from troublemaker to responsible parent, and how she changed her lifestyle accordingly:

> I like being a mom. I don't want things to go back the way they were before I had her. 'Cause I would have been in so much trouble. I mean, she's changed my life totally. 'Cause if I didn't have her, I'd probably be in jail or something like that right now. I was running with gangs and I was doing drugs, drinking. So when I had her, I changed. You don't have time to do that stuff anymore, and I wouldn't want to anyway. I mean, when you have a kid you don't have time to think about drugs and alcohol. It's your kid that comes first. I mean, if you're drunk and there's something wrong with your kid, you're not gonna know 'cause you're over there drunk. And that's just not being a good parent.

Vanessa, who became pregnant toward the end of her ninth-grade year, had just begun drinking and smoking pot a few months earlier. She told me her older boyfriend, Marcus, introduced her to getting drunk and high, and that he and his friends supplied her with alcohol and marijuana. By the spring of her freshman year, she was drinking every weekend and a few days a week before school. Motherhood transformed her from a heavy user of both substances to someone who completely abstained, and she was proud of this change.

Eighteen-year-old Linda, the former cheerleader who told her father she was pregnant after her baby was born, told me she used drugs frequently before she became a mother. She started smoking pot in seventh grade, although it was not until she was in high school that she began smoking it daily. She explained:

> Well I started doing it on a regular basis towards the end of my sophomore year. I used to do it everyday. I mean, *every* day. I'd go to cheerleading practice and then I'd get high. And none of the other cheerleaders ever knew! It was like my little secret.

Sunshine's exposure to drugs and alcohol came at a very early age, as did her addiction. She told me that her father had regained custody from her abusive grandparents for a short period and was living with a woman named Betty:

> I smoked pot when I was four. While my dad was at work during the day, Betty would be there, and she would invite her friends over, and I remember they were all like hipped-out looking, and they would smoke pot, but I didn't know what it was. And one day, I was watching them and they were all laughing and acting silly, and one of her friends said, "Let's make her smoke it," and I didn't even know what smoking was. And so they gave it to me and I just put it to my lips but I didn't inhale, but they kept making me do it until I learned to inhale. And I just coughed and coughed and my eyes watered and I was like, "Well why do they like that?" And Betty used to always get my dad really shit-faced drunk, and then give us beer. I don't know what her pleasure in doing these things was! And I didn't think it was wrong because my dad was letting me, so I was like, "yahoo!"

After her early experimentation with marijuana, Sunshine began to take interest in her father's cigarettes, although she didn't start smoking them until she was six years old. By age eight, she was smoking several cigarettes a day and getting drunk before school. She explained to me that her grandfather was a closet alcoholic, which made her binge drinking easy:

> My grandmother didn't want him to drink, so he had hiding places—he had liquor stashed everywhere. And I knew where all of his stash was. And so I'd wait until everyone was out of the house and I'd raid it. Junior high got to be the worst, because I was the last one out of the house. Both grandparents had jobs, and my brother's bus came first. So everyone was out of the house, and I had to lock up. And so I'd raid the stashes. I had an old Mello-Yello bottle, so first I'd drink some out of each bottle, and then I'd pour some from each bottle into my Mello-Yello bottle, and have like a big splash mixture. I'd take it with me and it would last for the school day. Well I just started getting carried away so that I was almost drunk before I got to school. One day, in seventh grade, I was drunk before I got to school, and that was my first blackout. I got thrown out of school for it. I actually stopped drinking for like seven months, and I didn't smoke either for like seven months. I didn't do anything for

seven months. But then things were the same at home and getting worse, so I went back to it.

Alcohol and cigarettes were Sunshine's escape from an abusive and unhappy childhood. Having her son was the ticket out of that situation, and a reason to stop using both substances—she quit cold turkey when she learned she was pregnant, and with the exception of a glass of beer someone bought her on her twenty-first birthday, she did not touch either substance in the three years I knew her.

The exception to the pervasive anti-drug sentiment among Teen Center mothers was tobacco. The vast majority of teen mothers smoked cigarettes, and it was a widely acceptable practice. The ethos of responsibility influenced their consumption, however, as it was considered a major transgression to smoke while pregnant or in the presence of babies or young children. Adolescent mothers who smoked when they were pregnant were publicly castigated by other teens and by the program staff, and those who did so around their infant or toddler-age children were treated only slightly better.

TRANSFORMED PRIMARY RELATIONSHIPS

The young women at the Teen Center spoke of their relationships with peers and family as being significantly altered by their transition to parenthood. Most of the teens spoke of improved peer relations, but there were varied outcomes for their relationships with family.

Peers

Most studies of teenage mothers report a similar pattern with respect to their social lives: they find adolescents report a sharply curtailed social life after becoming mothers (de Anda and Becerra 1984; Richardson, Barbour, and Bubenzer 1991; Thompson 1995). Researchers have found that this is not usually considered a negative consequence by young mothers, however, because they view their friends as being too immature to play much of a role in their mature parenting lifestyle (de Anda, Becerra, and Fielder 1988). At the Teen Center, the young women who had active social lives before becoming parents replaced their pre-parenting friends with "role-specific" friends (Richardson, Barbour, and Bubenzer 1991), that is, with friends who were also mothers. Most of the young women reported these friendships as being the most significant of their lives.

One of the things that many of the teen mothers had in common was a lonely childhood characterized by few, if any, friends. In fact, during the first three interviews I conducted the young women all used the word "loner" to describe themselves before they had their children. For example, when I asked Angelica about her social life before becoming a mother, she told me:

> I didn't really have any . . . I never really had any . . . I considered myself a loner. Because I really, all I ever did was go to school and do my homework. I mean, I never went out and hung out at the mall or went to movies, stuff like that. I just stayed home and did my homework. I had friends that I talked to at school, but that's it.

Similarly, Kristina told me she had few friends before she became a mother. About two months after she enrolled in the Teen Center, I interviewed her about her past experiences in school. She told me her experiences had been terrible—so bad, in fact, that she dropped out when she was a sophomore. When I asked her what she did not like about school, she told me this:

> The other kids. I'm—I'm really shy, I'm unsocial. Just—I've always been a loner because—well, that's how people quote you when you like school, you're just kind of a loner, and that's the way everybody has always seen me. You know, cause I always just—I had very, very few friends. I feel a lot different than everybody else. I've always been older, always had home problems, always kept to myself, thinking, you know, I always thought I was the only one who was shy and had an—an abusive family.

I asked her if things were any different now that she was at the Teen Center: "You know, I'm slowly realizing that I'm not the only one who's had bad experiences. It's the first time I've ever talked about it with other people who have been through the same thing." Like Angelica, who invited everyone from the center to her son's first birthday party and who regularly talked on the phone with two of the other teen mothers, motherhood and the Teen Center gave Kristina a social life unlike anything she had ever experienced.

Over time, the teens bonded over their shared experiences. Self-proclaimed "loners" like Angelica and Kristina found friends for the first time ever, while other teens abandoned previous friends for their parenting peers. Tracy and Robyn exemplify the latter pattern, as both young women had active social lives before becoming parents. The two teens met at a summer picnic hosted by the program nurse. I was sitting with fifteen-year-old Tracy and her two-month-old son Kevin when Robyn, who was five months' pregnant at the time and whom neither one of us had ever met, joined us on the grass. I recorded the following in my field notes:

> The pace of friendship development is really accelerated. This new girl, Robyn, sat with Tracy and I at the picnic and within five minutes (and scarcely any conversation other than, "How old is your baby?," "When are you due?," and "How old are you?") said to Tracy, "We should do something sometime." I thought for sure that Tracy would blow her off or at least look at her strangely for being so forward, but she did not seem the least bit put off by it. She simply said, "That would be cool" and started searching for a pen so they could exchange phone numbers.

That fall, when Robyn joined the center, she and Tracy were already best friends. In the four years I spent at the Teen Center, I witnessed several other teens forge immediate friendships. The adolescent mothers were desperate for companionship, because their early parenting put them in a position of receiving a tremendous amount of public denouncement, and because many of them were dealing with similar past experiences in abusive families, lonely childhoods, or failures in school. Friendship with other mothers was thus highly desirable, especially because other teen parents were viewed as being more mature and responsible than nonparenting peers, which was keeping in line with the new identity they were carving out for themselves.

The teens who had friends before becoming mothers usually spent less time with them in favor of their Teen Center peers. Jen and Alice, who were from two different cliques in their pre-parenting days at Lakeside, exemplified this pattern. At the beginning of the year, they were friendly to each other—they chatted when they were in the nursery at the same time, but each went her separate way during free periods or at lunch, choosing to sit with old friends. By springtime, they were inseparable. Alice asked Jen to be her maid of honor in her upcoming wedding, and Jen referred to Alice as her daughter's "Auntie Alice." Like the loners who hit it off with other mothers, the once-popular teens found friendship with other adolescent mothers to be desirable, for parenting peers can better relate to their mature lifestyles.

Several teens spoke of having a more active social life before parenting, but a better social life afterward. When I first interviewed fifteen-year-old Tracy, her son was five months' old and she was feeling depressed about the effects of parenting on her social life. For example, when I asked about her friends' reactions to her pregnancy, she said:

> What friends? They dropped me as soon as I got pregnant. I think it's because they know I can't go out anymore, and that's the only kind of friendship they know how to have. I don't get to do anything anymore. Go to the movies, go to a party. Like Halloween. I want to go to a Halloween party, but I can't. I can't even take a simple bath without Kevin coming in with me. And being with friends, blasting my music—all the stuff I used to do.

Three years later, when she was eighteen and her son was three, I asked her about her social life:

> Well, I don't have much of a social life. The few friends I have are all moms! They're all in the same situation that I am. Trying to do exactly the same things for their kids that I'm trying to do for him. I used to be really social with a big group of friends, but it was like, we'd go out every night, go to the mall, go to the dance club, get drunk. And none of that seems very fun anymore. Now, I have two or three really close friends who are going through the same things as I am, you know, being a teen parent, raising a kid, going to school, and all that. So I don't have much of a social life now, but when I compare it to the way it was before I had Kevin, I'd have to say it's a *better* social life. That these are better friends.

Vanessa, too, remarked on Teen Center friends being better friends than she'd had before: "Well, I had friends before, it's not like I was a loner, but I've made *good* friends here. People I can relate with, finally. People here know your problems, they understand your problems." Sunshine said, "One of my favorite things about school is socializing with the other teen parents. Because these are people of my understanding. People I can relate to."

Although Sunshine felt like she made better friends since she became a mother, she was one of the few teens who remained upset about the loss in social activity several months after her son was born. The rest of the teens, like Tracy, got over it. Sunshine's case may have been different, though, because she became pregnant right after she experienced an active social life for the first time in her life. She told me that she never really had friends when she was younger because her grandmother would not allow it:

> In elementary school, I wasn't allowed to have friends of what was called the "Old World." That means I couldn't be friends with anyone who wasn't in Jehovah's Witness. And all of the people in Jehovah's Witness were dorks and geeks, and they wouldn't befriend me anyway, although I tried. And then when I actually made a friend in Jehovah's Witness I tried to tell her that my grandmother was abusing my brother and I. And she ended up spilling everything I said to her mom, and her mom was like, "No way. She couldn't be this way." And she told my grandmother, which made things totally worse. And I was like, if I can't trust a friend, well then why have one. And then I had a friend in the sixth grade and my grandmother let me be her friend but, like, I never really got to do anything with her. She called me on the phone a few times but I wasn't allowed to call her. So the only thing I could really do was talk to her at school, but at least that was something.

After she was removed from her grandparents' abusive home, Sunshine began to have an active social life. She told me before her son was born she was "with people twenty-four hours a day." Although she thought the people at the center were people with whom she could become very close, she became depressed thinking about the fact that she rarely did anything outside of school with anyone because everyone was too busy, too tired, or could not find a babysitter.

Eighteen-year-old Jessica was another teen who felt like her social life had changed for the worse after she became a mother, but unlike Sunshine, who wished she could go back to the way things were when she was beginning to have friends for the first time, Jessica no longer viewed her old friends in a positive light. She explained to me how she and her boyfriend Patrick viewed their old friends:

> It's like, our friends aren't dumb or anything, but there are a lot of people who are kind of—under you. They want to go have childish, immature fun, and we can't really do that anymore. We don't really *want* to do that anymore. We can have moments like that, when we're playing laser tag or whatever, but that's it, then it's back to real life. And you know how you have acquaintance friends and friend-friends? All of our acquaintance friends are

long gone. So if we see them we can say, "Hi," but we don't have much to say beyond that. It's like, we don't have anything in common with them anymore.

Not only did they have too little time to invest in maintaining their old friendships, they had little interest in being with the friends with whom they used to be so close because their old friends were too immature, too childish. Although Jessica described being sad about her less active social life, she would not have wanted it any other way—her old lifestyle was not congruent with her new identity as a mature, responsible mother.

Parents

Like their relationships with peers, most of the teens spoke of improved relationships with their mothers since becoming mothers themselves. The young women at the Teen Center described being closer with their mothers because they had something in common and because their mothers now treated them like adults, a pattern identified by Jacobs (1994) in her research with teen mothers. For example, fifteen-year-old Vanessa, who told me the reason she became pregnant was because her mother never talked with her about birth control, said, "We're closer now that I'm a mother too." She went on to tell me that being a mother brought them closer as they discussed the changes in her body during her pregnancy and the daily back-and-forth dialogue they engaged in regarding her daughter's needs and accomplishments. Blair discussed a similar change:

> I think me and her are closer now, because we didn't used to be that close and now we're like best friends. Me and my mom never really got along before. My parents were divorced and I was always like the favorite of my dad, daddy's little girl. So we always fought and we just weren't close. But now it's different. It's like, since I'm a mother now too we have that in common. It's like, our thing.

Jill also referred to her mother as her closest friend: "Now she's my best friend, we're like best friends, I love her." Pregnancy brought women closer to their mothers, who were the only people they knew who could relate to what they were going through, and parenthood helped them forge an even tighter bond, because they wanted their mothers' advice, and their mothers were eager to participate in the lives of their grandchildren.

Julie is another teen who told me motherhood changed her relationship with her mother for the better. She had a tremendous amount of resentment for her mother for the way she treated Julie and her sister when they were younger. She explained:

> My parents divorced when I was six months old, so it was just my mom and my sister and me. My mom was an alcoholic and by the time I was ten she was pretty much choosing her boyfriend over taking care of us. She got child support and AFDC and all kinds of funding from the state, and me and my sister never saw any of it. When I was eleven, my mom's boyfriend held a gun to my head one night, threatening to kill me, and I decided that, you know, I didn't want to get killed. And I ended up jumping out of my bedroom window and I ran over to the 7-11 by my house and called the cops and told them what happened, and my mom covered up for him. The cops brought me back to the house and she said I made it up. I think it was about 2 o'clock in the morning and my mom just said, "I can't handle her anymore. Just get her out of here. I don't want to see her again." And then we went to court and they told her that they were going to take away all of the funding if she didn't have custody of us. All she could say was, "Well how am *I* gonna survive?" It was then that me and my sister were like, "All she cares about is money."

Both sisters were placed in foster homes and had only sporadic contact with their mother. When Julie became pregnant three years later, she gave her mother a second chance. By the time she had her third child, her mother was back in her life:

> Well, I try to be exactly the opposite with my kids as my mom was with us—so it's not like I've changed my mind and now I think she's the greatest mother ever. I still think she was a terrible mother when we were growing up. But she was just out here visiting and we actually get along. I tolerate her now. It's something different now that I have the boys. As [she is] a grandmother [now], I can get along with her.

She went on to tell me that she wanted to get along with her mother because, regardless of the way her mother had treated her growing up, she thought it was important for her boys to know their grandmother.

Several young women told me their relationships with their mothers were better in the sense that they at least communicated on a regular basis—because there was always something related to the baby that they could discuss— but that their relationships were nonetheless strained. For example, Tracy explained to me that her mother's shortcomings as a parent were now clearer to her because she was doing things so much differently with her own son:

> I don't have much respect for my mom now. 'Cause she never really was a parent, she was always trying to be more of a friend. I don't know, it's always a situation where I love her because she's my mom, but now that I'm a parent I see a lot of ways that she could have raised me differently. So being a parent has maybe brought us a little farther apart because of my resentment towards her.

Kristina was in a constant battle with her parents over their efforts to influence her parenting and her perception that they loved her baby Lea more than her. I recorded the following excerpt in my field notes:

> Kristina invited me to her birthday dinner at her parents' house last night and I jumped at the chance to finally meet them in person. She was very chilly towards them. The day before, they had given Kristina her birthday gift, the video "Pete's Dragon" ("You mean you gave it to Lea?" she said when they told me about the gift at dinner). When Kristina read the card her parents gave her after dinner she mumbled, "What a surprise, something about Lea." I got the impression that she was tired of getting her parents' approval/love/attention only with respect to Lea and was glad that I made no mention of the baby in my card (something I debated for a while).

Although their relationship was strained, they did at least talk to each other. Before Lea was born, Kristina ran away from home and did not contact her parents for two years, vowing never to return to the home where she was physically and verbally abused. Once the baby was born, however, she decided it was important to renew contact with them for her sake.

Eighteen-year-old Linda also had a strained relationship with her mother. One afternoon, when the children were asleep in the nursery, she told me that she had visited one of the other teen moms in the hospital the day before (the teen's baby was seriously ill) and that her mother was furious with her for spending forty-five minutes inside, telling her she was selfish for keeping her waiting outside so long even though she had volunteered to go with her to the hospital. When she was done telling the story, Linda said, "My mom has never once said that she was proud of me." I could tell that she had thought about it before and that it saddened her tremendously. Like Kristina and some of the other teens, Linda was angry about the way her mother treated her, but that did not stop her from wanting a loving relationship with her. With the exception of Tracy, the teens were very forgiving of their mothers, whose love and approval meant the world to them.

Sunshine is one of the few teens who spoke of an improved relationship with her father, but that may be because he had full custody of her and her brother after her parents were divorced—before he relinquished them to her abusive grandparents, that is. Because Sunshine was convinced that her father must have known about the abuse (because she suspected that he probably experienced it too), she harbored a great deal of resentment toward him. In fact, when she first arrived at the Teen Center she wrote a poem in her English class expressing her feelings toward him, a poem the teen mothers voted to put in the program yearbook:

Father, please love me. That is all I want. Do not play games,
     Father.
Please love me. Do not taunt me, leaving my heart to be
     smeared upon the floor underneath the shoe of hatred.
Do you care? Your eyes are blinded, always unseeing that my
     love is there.

As it did for many of her peers and their mothers, parenthood brought Sunshine and her father closer together. After Sunshine's son was born, her father quit his job and moved to Lakeside from another state, explaining to her that he wanted to "do it right" the second time around. After his first year in Lakeside I asked her whether she noticed any changes in their relationship: "Well, in the past he never talked about anything. I mean, nothing personal—nothing about my grandparents and how they treated him when he was young, nothing emotional. He's just started opening up this past year." Six months later, I attended Sunshine's high school graduation with her father and son, and he repeatedly told me how proud of her he was. In the next few weeks, he bought her a car and a washing machine, the first gifts he had ever purchased for her. A month later, he moved in with her and her son so he could be there every day to help her out and watch his grandson grow. The following year, Sunshine moved to Alabama to reunite with her son's father. Her dad quit his job and moved with them, telling her he did not want to lose her now that they had reconnected. Sunshine was delighted to have her father back in her life and beamed when she told people about it, but she told me she was skeptical about how permanent his newfound interest in her would be.

Oz and Fine (1991) and Landy et al. (1983) noted that the improved relationships adolescent mothers report having with their own mothers stand in sharp contrast to the negative relationships teen mothers talk of having with their fathers—both before and after they become parents. This was the case at the Teen Center as well. In many cases, the young women's fathers were still angry with them for becoming pregnant in the first place; in other instances, the teens distanced themselves from their fathers because they resented them for being absent or abusive during their childhood. Regardless of the reason, Sunshine was the only teen to speak of her father when I asked the young women how their relationships with their parents had changed since they became mothers. For the rest of the teens, pregnancy and parenthood were women's business, and their own fathers were scarcely mentioned.

The teens regard their personal transformations since becoming parents as mostly positive, which helps support their contention that they did the right thing by having and raising these children. Successfully pulling off early parenting—feeling good about themselves and their new identities—proves that they are old enough, mature enough, and competent enough to be parents. As Kirkman et al. (2001) found in their research with teenage mothers in Australia, the Teen Center mothers were aware that they were stigmatized, and as a result, they framed their personal parenting experiences in a way that contradicted the widely held perception that teen mothers' lives are difficult and unhappy. The way other people treat them is more difficult to cast in a positive light. Because the responses they received were mixed, if not overwhelmingly negative, the teen mothers reacted by emphasizing their personal transformations and their successes as parents.

TEN

CONCLUSION

Participation in the Teen Center immersed teenage mothers in a culture with a unique cultural toolkit (Swidler 1986): one containing a set of symbols, beliefs, worldviews, ideologies, and stories. The dominant characteristic of the teen parents' culture was a pervasive effort to prove that they had made a successful transition to adulthood, despite the non-normative timing of their entry into parenthood. These efforts to prove their maturity permeated all aspects of their lives. In the preceding chapters I discussed how the teens' decisions to keep and rear their children were framed as responsible, mature choices, how they competed with one another and with older parents to demonstrate that they were fit parents, how they defended their relationships with their significantly older boyfriends on the grounds that they were competent when choosing their own mates, and how they cast a positive light on the personal consequences of their early parenting. Membership in the culture thus influenced their experiences as parents and their reactions to the stigma that was cast upon them. The teen mothers' age, gender, social class, and race shaped the nature of their culture.

AGE

The adolescent mothers' age influenced their collective culture in four ways. First, their young age and the stigma associated with early parenting influenced the teens' reactions to their pregnancies. Casting their decisions to keep and rear their babies as the only responsible choice deflected the stigma onto another group—the irresponsible adolescents who have abortions or relinquish their babies for adoption. Regardless of whether the pregnancy was planned or unplanned, the teens' descriptions of their decision-making processes revealed their efforts to persuade people that they made the right choice, the mature choice, and the responsible choice. Given the position they were in, doing anything *other* than becoming a teenage mother was construed as deviant. In this way, they effectively deflected the stigma cast upon them because of their age.

The stigma associated with their age was also a key factor in fueling the teenage parents' competitive culture. Stigmatized persons are often thought to have a range of other undesirable attributes, a set of auxiliary traits associated with a given form of deviance (Goffman 1963; Hughes 1945). The auxiliary traits associated with early childbearing include being welfare-dependent (Adams, Adams-Taylor, and Pittman 1989), abusive (Baumrind 1994), and generally incompetent parents (Roosa and Vaughan 1984). The mothers at the Teen Center worked hard to prove these images wrong, both to persuade others and to convince themselves that they were not deviant. To fight the deviant label applied by others (and their own internalization of this label), they pointed out the negative qualities of other parents, such as the rigid and strict parenting styles of older parents, and they emphasized the positive qualities of their own parenting, such as their unconditional love for their children or their ability to weed out the good child-rearing advice from the bad. In doing so, the teen mothers also relied on disidentifiers (Goffman 1963) to recast their behavior in a positive (nondeviant) light by bragging about their affluence or their children's developmental successes or by presenting their relationship with their child as ideal—all with the intent of distracting people from their deviant reality of being teen parents. Each teen tried to outparent other parents to prove that she was nothing like the stereotype of the incompetent teenage mother. This stigma management occurred primarily at an individual level; teen mothers contrasted themselves to other mothers in an effort to make themselves look good, rather than fighting the stigma of all teen mothers in the form of identity politics, where they might seek to change societal conceptions of teenage mothers. However, some teen mothers strove to fight the negative image of all teen parents. Brooke, for example, staged a letter-writing campaign to talk show hosts, Kristen wrote a letter to the editor of the local paper, and Amanda presented a speech in her communications class on myths surrounding teenage mothers.

The second way the teen mothers' age was influential was through the school setting in which their age placed them. The setting enhanced the competitive nature of the group, as schools generate competitiveness in many ways. Competitiveness was imbued in them academically, because this is a place where people are sorted into those who will go on to college and those who will not, where standardized tests are administered to stratify students nationally, and where students are stratified and ranked in their classes by grades. The school setting also fosters extreme social competition, because students are sorted into cliques with different amounts of status or popularity (Kinney 1993). Bringing together the teen parents in a school setting that is competitive both academically and socially enhances the competitive nature of their culture. In addition to fueling their competition, the school setting also increased teen parents' feelings of alienation; the other students publicly outcast them, the teachers often patronized them, and the center's location in the school basement isolated them. The negative treatment they received "upstairs" served to heighten the aggressive stigma management that occurred in the basement. Being in a school also exposed them to adult influence, and the mainstream parenting norms and values of the Teen Center staff trickled into their cultural ideas about "good" mothering. From a dramaturgical perspective (Goffman 1959), the school setting can be understood as providing a backstage and a front stage. The teens' cultural norms and values surrounding pregnancy and parenting can be viewed as front-stage behavior, insofar as they intentionally performed in many ways that helped them deflect the stigma associated with early childbearing; at times, however, the front stage shifted to a backstage region in the Teen Center basement—when the young women let down their guards and together lamented over the challenges they faced on the front stage.

Third, as teenagers, the mothers were caught at an age that juxtaposes dependence and independence. Adolescents are dependent; they have limited economic resources, excessive legal constraints, and restricted access to certain activities (Pearl 1981), such as drinking, voting, driving, marrying, or working full time. Adolescence is also a time of emotional independence and maturity, of breaking away from parents and striving to act like and be treated as an adult (Smith 1962), as well as reaching physical and sexual maturity. The teen mothers were caught in this ambiguous social status between child and adult, which surfaced in the way they parented. They worked hard to demonstrate that they were competent parents to prove that they had successfully made an early transition to adulthood. This may explain why so many of the mothers at the Teen Center rejected their own parents' advice. A crucial characteristic of adolescence involves gaining autonomy from one's parents by distancing oneself from the behaviors and attitudes of parents in favor of those demonstrated by peers (Fasick 1984). By rejecting their parents' advice about child rearing in favor of advice that they sought out them-selves, the teen mothers demonstrated a quest for autonomy like most adolescents. When their own mothers stepped in, the teenage mothers felt insecure about their transition to adulthood, and this led them to both doubt their own competency as parents and resent their mothers' interference (Buchholz and Korn-Bursztyn 1993). The younger parents were not as concerned about proving their independence from their parents because the idea of autonomy was not as important to them as it was to the mothers in their late teens. For the younger mothers, there was no question about their dependency (Shapiro and Mangelsdorf 1994). Adolescence is a time of "unsettledness" (Swidler 1986), when the cultural toolkits of adulthood and childhood are present, and the net result is a culture that simultaneously draws on and is at odds with features of both (Fine 2004).

The developmental tasks associated with adolescence also explain why the teens rationalized their relationships with their significantly older boyfriends. The attitude among most members of the Teen Center was that dating older boyfriends was not deviant. In large measure, this may be because identifying the act as nondeviant makes their consent meaningful. If their consent makes the relationships acceptable, then their judgment is valued and their moral independence is not questioned. On the other hand, calling the relationships deviant insults them and their ability to make decisions that affect their lives. Being able to give consent is crucial if one wants to be thought of as a mature adult, which can explain why so many teens, including those not involved with older men themselves, did not cast the relationships as deviant. The teen mothers wanted to make responsible choices (in choosing older men because of their potential to be responsible fathers), and they strove to be viewed as mature (in wanting their consent to be meaningful). For them, dating older boyfriends was the grown-up, mature thing to do. When these older men did not live up to their expectations for the father role they envisioned them filling, the young women did not despair; they either broke up with these boyfriends, because their ultimate objective was to find the most responsible father for their children (in keeping in line with their own identity), or they assumed full responsibility for parenting their children themselves. The impression they worked to convey was that they could be single parents because they were mature and competent; if they were not single, then they would have boyfriends who were equally mature and responsible.

The fourth way in which age was influential in shaping the culture of teenage parents was through several elements of American youth culture. Studies of teens have illustrated that two important elements of youth culture are competition (Coleman 1961) and materialism (White 1993). Coleman (1961) posited that adolescents compete not for grades or teachers' attention but for the respect and recognition of their peers. They compete with each other for status. One way in which this competition for status is carried out is through a comparison of material possessions; the adolescent with the best car, the most CDs, or the nicest clothes is afforded the most status (Coleman 1961; White 1993). Thus the competition to be good parents and to have the most material possessions may be a reflection of youth culture in general, rather than a characteristic of teen parents alone. Like their nonparenting peers, the teen mothers competed with one another for status, but instead of showing off their own clothes or cars, they competed to have the best-dressed baby with the most toys.

GENDER

It is difficult to isolate the effects of age from the effects of gender in shaping the teens' collective culture, because gender interacts with age in shaping the way young women carve out identities for themselves. Gilligan (1990) noted that although autonomy and individuation are important goals of adolescence, these are not the only processes at play for teenage women. Women in general also desire a connection to others. Thus according to Gilligan, adolescent women simultaneously strive to achieve two paradoxical identities. On the one hand, they experience the pulls for autonomy and independence described earlier—developing an adult identity that is distinct from their parents. At the same time, however, they experience a "crisis of connection," wherein they desire intimate relationships with others and seek to identify themselves in relation to others. These seemingly contradictory identities are not so much at odds with one another as they may sound. At the Teen Center, the young women demonstrated a desire for an autonomous identity when they initiated sexual relationships, rejected adults' advice, and deflected the stigma cast upon them for having children as teens. They demonstrated a wish to connect with others in their desire to have the unconditional love of a baby, their continual efforts to gain their parents' (especially their mothers') approval, and the immediate and intense friendships they formed with one another. From a psychological perspective, their behaviors make perfect sense—motherhood was an ideal vehicle for the teens to meet these two seemingly contradictory objectives.

As Tolman (1994) reported, however, adolescent women find themselves physically and psychologically experiencing this desire for connection but unable to locate their desire in an existing cultural script for adolescent women's sexuality. Lacking cultural norms telling them how they should handle their emerging desires, they are left to invent this script themselves. Swidler's (1986) notion of an "unsettled" cultural toolkit is once again useful, for it sheds light on the fact that the teen parents grappled with norms of childhood sexual innocence in tension with their burgeoning adult desires. The findings presented here regarding the teenage mothers' initiation into sexuality suggest that this script was often constructed with the help of their older boyfriends, who told them that sexual desires should be acted on through sexual intercourse, and that the best way to express desires was without birth control.

A second influence of gender can be gleaned from sociological research on gender socialization. American women are socialized to believe that loving, nurturing, and caring for children are positively valued female traits (Broverman et al. 1972), and that motherhood is the ultimate identity. The "motherhood mandate," as Russo (1976) referred to it, teaches young girls that their destiny is to become a mother, that motherhood is one of the few identities for women that is valued by our culture, and that motherhood is key for women to be considered adults. The teens who intentionally became pregnant, and the others who welcomed an unplanned pregnancy, were merely doing what they had been taught to expect of themselves all along: having children. My findings come from a sample comprised primarily of white teenage mothers, but Ladner's (1972) study of African American adolescent mothers revealed that motherhood is also viewed as a transition to adulthood among black teenagers. Dating older boyfriends may have been one way for the white, black, and Latina mothers at the Teen Center to make this transition to an acceptable adult gender role. As Leahy (1994) contended, many girls prefer relationships with older boyfriends, because these serious relationships allow them to practice the nurturing skills that they know are valued in women and, for many girls, provide them with the first person in their lives who can "authoritatively" validate their transition to adulthood.

The young women were not only doing what they had been taught, they were also reacting to structural constraints. Thus a third influence of gender was that it dictated what the young women could and could *not* do. As Fischman contended, "Within the milieu of poverty and inadequate education, childbearing may be sought deliberately because it is one of the few acceptable roles available to teenage women who feel unable to achieve success in the competitive social world" (1975, 222). For the young women at the Teen Center, having a child was a visible sign of achievement. As the chapter on transformations illustrated, many of the young women experienced failure and frustration at school, both academically and socially, and as a result, they perceived few future options. Their gender and social class made motherhood one of the only options the working-class teens saw available to them for achieving autonomy, adulthood, and success.

A fourth way in which gender sheds explanatory light on the experiences of Teen Center mothers is through studies of male gender socialization. Fathers may not participate in their children's upbringing to the extent that adolescent mothers do because of their gender. The male sex role calls for a parental role that is characterized by such instrumental activities as providing financially for the family rather than the expressive activities of nurturing and caring for emotions that the female sex role entails (Marsiglio and Menaghan 1990; Teti and Lamb 1986). On a day-to-day basis, then, the young mother is expected to do the nurturing and caregiving, while the father is expected to provide a paycheck. Research by Teti and Lamb (1986) revealed that adolescent males think the breadwinner role is the most important feature of a masculine identity, finding that when adolescent males cannot provide for their children, they see no need to participate in any other way. Quantitative research on the fathers of children born to teen mothers has revealed that these men are likely to have attained only low levels of schooling and have poor employment histories, explaining why they have trouble meeting the demands of the provider role (Hardy et al. 1989; Marsiglio 1987). This explanation can also be applied to the older fathers (those who are not teenagers) of Teen Center babies, most of whom worked in low-paying jobs, if they worked at all. Teen Center fathers who were universally regarded as "good dads" were from middle- and upper-middle-class backgrounds, which makes sense, given their definition of fatherhood: if they had the money to be involved, they were. In this way, the influence of gender is confounded with social class, for those men who were from more affluent class backgrounds were able to fulfill their expected gender role, while those from less privileged backgrounds were not. As Anderson (1989) noted, the male adolescent's peer group is extremely influential; adolescent boys are given status for having sex with a number of girls but committing to no one. The peer group devalues domestic life and ostracizes the young man who seems more interested in "playing house" than in hanging out with his friends (Anderson 1989). Thus adolescent women are often left with messages telling them that they should be full-time parents, and with boyfriends who are not interested in contributing, leaving them with no other option (realistically or idealistically) than single parenthood.

CLASS

A third sociological variable with tremendous implications for the culture of teenage mothers is social class. An analysis of social class can provide insight into the working-class and lower-middle-class teens' decisions to become parents at an early age. Poor teenage women are both more likely to consider single, early parenthood and are more likely to actually become young, single parents (Abrahamse, Morrison, and Waite 1988). Many of the young women at the Teen Center considered early parenting an option because it was one of the few avenues for success open to them—they saw no reason to delay childbearing until after high school or college, because they knew they were not going to college, and they were unsure about even finishing high school. The jobs they imagined themselves having one day were working-class jobs like their parents had. Their decisions to keep and rear their children make sense when they are compared to the group of adolescents who are more likely to relinquish their babies through adoption or to terminate their pregnancies through abortion—adolescent women who aspire to white-collar, professional careers and their requisite educational investments (Brazzell and Acock 1988).

Although the competitive nature of the teen parenting culture was driven in large measure by the teens' age as adolescents, the manner in which these competitions were carried out was shaped in different ways by the social class of the teen mothers. The work of Kohn in the 1960s (Kohn 1963, 1969) identified distinct parenting styles of working-class (blue-collar) and middle-class (white-collar) parents, and most research on class and parenting styles since then has replicated his findings (see, e.g., Gecas and Nye 1974; Luster, Rhoades, and Haas 1989; Wright and Wright 1976). At the Teen Center, the majority of parents came from lower-middle-class and working-class backgrounds, yet the values they held for their children clearly reflect what Kohn and others have described as a middle-class ideology. The attitudes of these teen parents can be viewed as part of a historical shift, whereby mothers of all social classes have come to value self-direction and autonomy more than conformity and obedience, thus moving closer to middle-class values (Alwin 1988; Wright and Wright 1976). For example, most teen mothers espoused the values of middle-class parents when they explained that their only expectations for their children were that they be happy and self-fulfilled, and when they asserted that they planned to be more permissive and lenient than their own parents had been. Similarly, the majority of teens, exhibiting the influence of middle-class ideology, accepted the advice of doctors, books, and other nonfamilial experts rather than turning to their kin (Kohn 1963). This shift has been explained as a widespread diffusion of middle-class parenting ideals and values due to mass media and its transmission of middle-class images of ideal parents (LeMasters and DeFrain 1983; Wright and Wright 1976). The culture at the center also reflects the parenting culture of the surrounding community: the middle-class students, staff, and faculty of the university.

Finally, social class can shed light on the teens' partnering with men who do not measure up to their ideal expectations. The teens may have tolerated substandard boyfriends because that was the best they could get; they did not have enough value in the mate selection market to command higher-status boyfriends or fathers for their children (i.e., employed, educated, not incarcerated). More than 80 percent of teen mothers live in poverty or near poverty *before* they become mothers, and their economic condition rarely improves with the arrival of a child (Luker 1996; Jaffee 2002). Coming from lower socioeconomic statuses, a young age group, and having attained relatively little education, they were not valuable enough to command greater power in romantic relationships that would yield them the kind of boyfriends and fathers for their children that they ideally wanted. Because of their difficult family situations, they were desperate for a man to comfort them and fill the void left by their absent fathers (Zongker 1977), so they settled for what their resources would allow them to attain. In many cases, this meant men with low education and employment histories (Hardy et al. 1989) who had run into problems with the law (Elster et al. 1987).

RACE

The Teen Center was racially homogenous, precluding much of a discussion of the discrete effects of different racial or ethnic backgrounds on the teens' shared culture. However, a few patterns are worth mentioning. First, the differences in the teens' motivations to become pregnant and their descriptions of these motivations may be partly explained by their racial backgrounds. The Latina teens I interviewed were more likely than the white teens to report becoming pregnant intentionally; indeed, few white teens admitted to getting pregnant on purpose. It is difficult to assess whether Latina and white adolescents have different motivations to become pregnant, or if the cultural norms surrounding motherhood made it easier for the Latina teens to tell the truth. Mexican American cultural norms proscribing motherhood as a more significant female identity than education or outside employment may have motivated the Latina teens to become mothers (Segura 1984; Segura and Pierce 1993).

Anglo norms may have made motherhood less appealing for the white mothers who have felt the influence of the women's movement and have been taught that they should take advantage of economic and educational opportunities now available for women. It is also possible, however, that these same cultural norms may have influenced the way the teens describe their pregnancies. Thus cultural differences may have made it easier for the Latina teens to admit that they wanted to become mothers, while the white mothers may have felt pressure to retrospectively reinterpret their motivation to have children by framing their pregnancies as accidental.

Race was also influential in creating some of the diversity within the teen parenting culture with respect to parenting styles. Literature on Mexican American culture describes familial values as distinctly different from those in Anglo and African American cultures (Mindel 1980; Rothman, Grant, and Hnat 1985). Studies have suggested that Mexican American families have more interaction with their kin and with a greater level of intensity than Anglo and African Americans, and that the nature of their familial relations is qualitatively different. Specifically, Mexican American culture emphasizes reliance on extended families for support and advice, as well as expectations that elders in the family will be obeyed. Emotional security is centered around family life, and for Mexican American women, status is earned through mothering—by performing domestic tasks, socializing and nurturing children, and, as they grow older, serving as ministers of important knowledge on how to raise children (Mirande 1977; Segura and Pierce 1993). The Mexican American parents at the Teen Center and in other studies as well (see, e.g., Codega, Pasley, and Kreutzer 1990) readily took the advice of their mothers and other family members while rejecting the advice of professional experts. The behavior of these parents can be viewed as a reflection of their culture, for it was expected that they would turn to their kin for support. Segura and Pierce (1993) reported that this behavior is based on a cultural belief of Chicanos that outsiders should not be trusted with intimate information, a pattern they trace to survival and resistance in the face of racism and domination.

Anglo parents place less emphasis on the family as a source of support than Mexican Americans. Instead, they turn to friends and others outside the family network (Mindel 1980). Mindel has suggested that the cultural differences in support relationships may boil down to socioeconomic status and available avenues of support. Perhaps by virtue of their economic position, white parents are more able to utilize resources such as doctors, magazines, classes, and books about parenting, and Mexican American families have had fewer options. Mindel's argument helps explain why the white mothers at the Teen Center turned to credentialed experts they believed knew what was best for their children, and the Mexican American mothers sought advice from their families.

The race and ethnicity of Teen Center participants were also significant in shaping their relationships with program staff. With the exception of one Asian American program coordinator, the remainder of the adult staff members with whom the teen mothers interacted on a daily basis were middle-class, middle-age, white women. The staff had a diffi-cult time bridging the age difference between themselves and all of the teenage mothers, and a particularly hard time bridging the cultural differences between themselves and the Latina teen mothers, whose culture they knew little about. This cultural difference may explain why the Latina teenagers were less willing than the white teenagers to accept advice from staff members, and why they may have had more intermittent patterns of participation in the program. Lacking role models they could relate to and forced to participate in Anglo-centered parenting activities, the Latina teen mothers often felt very little connection to the center and the women who ran it.

Finally, the racial background of the Teen Center participants illuminates the nature of the stigma cast upon them. The young women at the center were accused of making personal transgressions against norms of premarital sexuality and nonmarital births; they were not assumed to have been led to these norm violations because of their Anglo culture but, rather, because of a personal failure on their part or through some fault of their family of orientation. As Solinger (1992) noted in her research on nonmarital births, white women have historically been shamed for unwed pregnancies, whereas black women have been blamed. Solinger posited that this difference has meant that white women have been allowed the opportunity for personal redemption through relinquishing their children, whereas black women, who have been blamed for becoming parents because of the norms and values of their culture, have been provided with no such similar opportunity. According to Solinger, personal mistakes are seen as correctable; cultural inferiority is viewed as irreparable. This may explain why the white teenage mothers felt such pronounced public castigation, for they turned down an opportunity for redemption when they chose to bear and raise their children themselves.

Consequences of the Teen Parenting Culture

The net result of teenage motherhood and participation in the Teen Center's unique culture was a transformed personal identity, something most of the participants viewed as a positive change. The transformation happened on four different levels.

First, early motherhood left no doubt as to the young women's transition from adolescent to young adult. Having a child was a surefire way of proving one was an adult; indeed, Rossi (1968) suggested that motherhood has been unanimously defined as being essential for a woman to attain full adult status in our society. Adult status was highly coveted by the young women—responsible, competent parenting helped prove that they had achieved this status, which became one of the most salient parts of their personal identity.

The second change in the adolescents' personal identity was from a dependent person to an independent person. Prior to motherhood and participation in the Teen Center, the teens were dependent on others. They were dependent on their parents financially, and on their parents and boyfriends for emotional nurturance, attention, and affection. Parenthood changed that. Although participation in programs such as AFDC and WIC only shifted their financial dependence from family to strangers, the change was important. The teens received regular checks and managed their own money, and they did not have to account for their expenses to their parents or boyfriends—it was their money to use as they saw fit. Becoming a mother meant someone was dependent on them, a change that was incongruent with them still being dependents themselves. Having a child also meant that they were no longer dependent on the sporadic love and attention they received from their families, boyfriends, and sometimes friends. Their babies were constant sources of affection and love. Together these shifts enabled them to break away from the dependent relationships they had with others and the dependent images they had of themselves.

The third personal identity transformation was from an incompetent to a competent person. As the preceding chapters illustrated, most of the young women at the Teen Center had never experienced success in their school or social lives—they perceived themselves as being academically and socially incompetent. Motherhood allowed the teens to demonstrate competency in an area that was recognized by others as important. Motherhood thus changed their negative self-concepts as the teens found themselves capable of succeeding at something.

The fourth personal identity transformation was from a person unworthy of receiving love to a person deserving unconditional love. The Teen Center mothers reported abusive and absent fathers and emotionally distant mothers. The perception they were left with was that something about themselves made them "unlovable." Some researchers have posited that teens have children in an effort to make up for what they did not get as children, wanting boyfriends and children of their own to compensate for these perceived losses of affection and love (Zongker 1977). Regardless of their motivation for becoming parents, the outcome of early motherhood was that the teens had someone to love who loved them back, resulting in a profound transformation of personal identity.

POLICY IMPLICATIONS

The teen parenting culture was characterized by competition to be a good parent and an obsession for each teen mother to prove that she could parent effectively. The findings have important implications for scholars and policy makers interested in teen parenting. First, the data suggest some potentially negative consequences of the competitive culture. For example, some teen mothers were not willing to ask for advice when they had questions, because they did not want to seem ignorant, and other mothers ignored the advice of program staff to save face in their peer group. Additionally, the competitive parenting culture overshadowed the fact that these mothers were young, inexperienced, and dependent on support and advice from others. To successfully compete with their peers, the mothers had to deny this dependency and act as though they did not need any help. The program staff intervened in any way they could to give the teens support and information without offending them, but in most cases even subtle suggestions were deemed meddlesome.

Despite these negative consequences, the findings suggest that the teen mothers' child-rearing culture had a largely positive effect on their parenting. The overall goal of being a good parent ameliorated the feelings of antagonism among the teens and the expressions of belligerence toward authority that a competitive adolescent culture might otherwise breed. Instead, it led them to distinguish themselves from the negative image of teen mothers they saw in the mass media and pushed them toward a mainstream model of child rearing. In striving for this mainstream image, the teen mothers actively pursued a positive model of parenting, one that was characterized by efforts to advance their children's development, to provide them with quality toys and clothes, and to know the facts about child rearing and child development. The group, and its location in a school in a middle- and an upper-middle-class university community, pushed its members toward a normative, family-based, middle-class child-rearing model. These factors, as well as the combination of age, gender, class, and race influences, discussed earlier, pushed the teens to be better mothers. In most cases, the teen mothers did not have the resources to support the family structure and lifestyle they would have liked to have, which was a source of embarrassment for them. This embarrassment pushed them to self-sacrifice for the sake of their children and to try to hide their poverty from their peers—to do otherwise would mean a potential loss in status in the teen parent culture.

These findings suggest that school-based parenting programs have a largely positive influence on teen parenting. Although some of the positive consequences are, no doubt, related to the group being lodged in a middle- and an upper-middle-class community, a further benefit of such school-based programs is to keep the teen mothers on a mainstream path. It keeps them in school, prepares them for legitimate ways of making a living, and provides them with normative ways of thinking about parenting and dealing with the difficulties of having and raising a child at a young age. By providing them with a peer group to serve as a constant source of comparison, the programs also function to keep their parenting behaviors in check. With other parents watching their (and their children's) every move, the teens are constantly on stage, requiring them to abide by the conventional model of parenting if they want to maintain status in the group.

The findings on statutory rape also have important implications for policy. The chapter on statutory rape explains some of the reasons some young women see nothing wrong with dating older men, which helps shed light on the question of whether or not current statutory rape laws are effective deterrents. This research suggests that existing laws do not deter young women from getting romantically involved with older men because the teen culture has adopted a set of justifications making the relationships legitimate—and because their boyfriends apparently see nothing wrong with the relationship either. The teen mothers in this study do not view themselves as being incapable of voluntarily consenting to sex, as being their fathers' property, or as being tainted by having relations with older men—the rationales underlying statutory rape laws (Oberman 1994). Thus for the teenagers currently involved with older boyfriends, statutory rape laws were viewed as something of an anachronism; the teens do not see the necessity for these laws, do not feel that they will be caught and/or punished for violating them, and thus do not feel the need to abide by them. These findings suggest that statutory rape laws need to be modified in one of two ways. One alternative is to prevent the crime of statutory rape by enforcing existing laws (to modify the normative component that "everyone does it and nobody minds"). A move in this direction would coincide with the strengthening of sexual harassment regulations and would further emphasize the important influence of power in sexual relations, in this case, the relative power that older men hold over younger women—despite the fact that the young women do not always recognize the power imbalance.

The move toward enforcing statutory rape laws would also reflect a notion that sexual relations between people of unequal ages are socially intolerable and detrimental. The other alternative would be to eliminate statutory rape laws altogether. Doing so would reflect the idea that these laws are inherently unequal and unfair (in criminalizing men and not women). Their removal would further liberate young women from their historically disadvantaged position, the position of needing protection from their own irrational desires. Policy makers concerned with the negative consequences of such a move (e.g., that more teenagers might become pregnant by older men) might choose to focus energy and money on sex education and contraception for adolescents rather than on enforcing ineffective laws. Both policy modifications suggested here — either enforcing or eliminating existing laws—can result in positive consequences for women, for they transform women from being someone's property to being rational actors in command of their own lives, a legal move that reflects a greater egalitarianism between men and women in all spheres of social life, especially a change in the status and power of young women.

Finally, the findings regarding the positive transformations of self that the young women reported can be used to inform policy. The young women at the Teen Center considered motherhood the best thing that ever happened to them. Despite the hardship resulting from the stigma associated with early childbearing, the financial difficulties of being young, mostly single parents, and the time constraints of being student parents, motherhood was viewed positively. It made them more responsible and more mature, gave them a means for demonstrating their competency, and provided them with someone to love. What this suggests is that any efforts to reduce teenage pregnancy and parenting will need to encompass compelling reasons for teens to prevent pregnancy. With few available alternatives for achieving success, early parenting is a logical response for some young women; for prevention efforts to be effective, teens must be convinced that delaying pregnancy and parenthood is in their best interest. To accomplish this goal, teens must be provided with other means of achieving the desirable ends of maturity, competency, and love. For teens with limited life options to be sufficiently motivated to delay childbearing, prevention efforts must therefore simultaneously focus on strengthening their academic skills and access to higher education, providing them with opportunities to learn about and have rewarding careers, improving their access to emotional support systems, and providing them with an increased capacity to prevent pregnancy.

Of course, none of these suggestions will do anything for the young women who have already chosen—or will choose—early motherhood. My research suggests that the obstacles that make it difficult for teenage mothers to complete high school and to be good parents should be removed, so that young mothers may dedicate themselves to achieving both of these goals. The identity they desperately want to embrace— being mature, competent, capable mothers—is difficult to achieve in the face of poverty, time and energy constraints, and public castigation. The existence of school-based programs with on-site day care, such as the Teen Center, is an example of such a program that would facilitate their positive transformations of self by allowing the necessary emotional and practical support to complete their educations. A second implication involves changing the way social service agency representatives view and interact with teenage mothers. Social service programs such as WIC and low-income housing agencies were designed to alleviate some of the hardship of poverty so parents can focus on family and work. As my data showed, however, the young women at the Teen Center viewed their interactions with these agencies as difficult, stressful, and humiliating. The existence of programs that young mothers are afraid, embarrassed, or wary of using runs counter to the fundamental purposes of these programs and poses a formidable obstacle to the teens' internalization of their transformed identities.

The homogenous sample of teen mothers in this study is both its greatest strength and most significant limitation. I intentionally studied a population of white teen mothers because they are so infrequently included in the teen parenting literature, despite constituting the largest racial/ethnic group of adolescent mothers (Hamilton, Martin, and Ventura 2007). But this sample—a self-selecting group of teens who participated in a school-based program located in a middle-class university town—is clearly not representative of all teenage mothers. I did not study teens who had abortions or relinquished their children for adoption, teens who became pregnant and reared them outside of a school setting, or groups of black and Latino teens in a racially or an ethnically diverse community. My argument throughout this book has been that the unique set of circumstances among Teen Center participants—their stigmatized early parenthood, their age as adolescents, their socioeconomic position, their school-based social world—is what makes this culture distinct.

Because the stigma of teenage parenting cuts across racial lines and socioeconomic categories, it would be fascinating to see how the cultural toolkit (Swidler 1986) of other groups of adolescent mothers compares to that of the Teen Center parents.

REFERENCES

Abrahamse, Allan F., Peter A. Morrison, and Linda J. Waite. 1988. *Beyond Stereotypes: Who Becomes a Single Teenage Mother?* Santa Monica, CA: Rand Corporation.

Adams, Gina, Sharon Adams-Taylor, and Karen Pittman. 1989. "Adolescent Pregnancy and Parenthood: A Review of the Problem, Solutions, and Resources." *Family Relations* 38: 223–29.

Adler, Patricia A., and Peter Adler. 1987. *Membership Roles in Field Research*. Newbury Park, CA: Sage.

Adler, Patricia A., and Peter Adler. 1996. "Preadolescent Clique Stratification and the Hierarchy of Identity." *Sociological Inquiry* 66:2: 111–42.

Albert, Bill. 2007. *With One Voice 2007: America's Adults and Teens Sound Off about Teenage Pregnancy*. Washington, DC: National Campaign to Prevent Teen Pregnancy.

Alwin, Duane F. 1988. "From Obedience to Autonomy: Changes in Traits Desired in Children, 1924–1978." *Public Opinion Quarterly* 52: 33–52.

Ambert, Anne-Marie, Patricia A. Adler, Peter Adler, and Daniel F. Detzner. 1995. "Understanding and Evaluating Qualitative Research." *Journal of Marriage and the Family* 57: 879–93.

Anderson, Elijah. 1989. "Sex Codes and Family Life among Poor Inner-City Youths." *Annals of the American Academy for Political and Social Science* 501: 59–78.

Astone, Nan Marie, and Dawn M. Upchurch. 1994. "Forming a Family, Leaving School Early, and Earning a GED: A Racial and Cohort Comparison." *Journal of Marriage and the Family* 56: 759–71.

Atkinson, Maxine P., and Becky L. Glass. 1985. "Marital Age Heterogamy and Homogamy, 1900 to 1980." *Journal of Marriage and the Family* 47: 685–91.

Baldwin, Wendy. 1983. "Trends in Adolescent Contraception, Pregnancy, and Childbearing." In *Premature Adolescent Pregnancy and Parenthood*, ed. Elizabeth R. McAnalney, 3–19. New York: Gruen and Stratton.

Barratt, Marguerite Stevenson, Mary A. Roach, and Karen K. Colbert. 1991. "Single Mothers and Their Infants: Factors Associated with Optimal Parenting." *Family Relations* 40: 448–54.

Barret, Robert L., and Bryan E. Robinson. 1982. "A Descriptive Study of Teenage Expectant Fathers." *Family Relations* 31: 349–52.

Barth, Richard P. 1987. "Adolescent Mothers' Beliefs about Open Adoption." *Social Casework* 68: 323–31.

Baumrind, Diana. 1994. "The Social Context of Child Maltreatment." *Family Relations* 43: 360–68.

Benson, Michael L. 1985. "Denying the Guilty Mind: Accounting for Involvement in a WhiteCollar Crime." *Criminology* 23: 583–607.

Blumer, Herbert. 1969. *Symbolic Interactionism:Perspective and Method*. Englewood Cliffs, NJ: Prentice Hall.

Boyle, Maureen. 1989. "Spending Patterns and Income of Single and Married Parents." *Monthly Labor Review* 112: 37–41.

Bracken, Michael B., Lorraine V. Klerman, and Maryann Bracken. 1978. "Abortion, Adoption, or Motherhood: An Empirical Study of Decision-Making during Pregnancy." *American Journal of Obstetrics and Gynecology* 130: 251–62.

Bralock, Anita R., and Deborah Koniak-Griffin. 2007. "Relationship, Power, and Other Influences on Self-Protective Sexual Behaviors of African American Female Adolescents." *Health Care for Women International* 28: 247–67.

Brazzell, Jan F., and Alan C. Acock. 1988. "Influence of Attitudes, Significant Others, and Aspirations on How Adolescents Intend to Resolve a Premarital Pregnancy." *Journal of Marriage and the Family* 50: 413–25.

Brooks-Gunn, J., and Frank F. Furstenberg. 1986. "The Children of Adolescent Mothers: Physical, Academic, and Psychological Outcomes." *Developmental Review* 6: 224–51.

Broverman, Inge K., Susan Raymond Vogel, Donald M. Broverman, Frank E. Clarkson, and Paul S. Rosencrantz. 1972. "Sex-Role Stereotypes: A Current Appraisal." *Journal of Social Issues* 28: 59–79.

Buchholz, Ester S., and Carol Korn-Bursztyn. 1993. "Children of Adolescent Mothers: Are They at Risk for Abuse?" *Adolescence* 28: 361–82.

Burt, Martha R., and Rochelle S. Albin. 1981. "Rape Myths, Rape Definitions, and Probability of Conviction." *Journal of Applied Social Psychology* 11: 212–30.

Carlip, Hillary. 1995. *Girl Power: Young Women Speak Out*. New York: Time Warner.

Cervera, Neil J. 1993. "Decision Making for Pregnant Adolescents: Applying Reasoned Action Theory to Research and Treatment." *Families in Society* 74: 355–65.

Chandra, Anjani, Joyce Abma, Penelope Maza, and Christine Bachrach. 1999. "Adoption, Adoption Seeking, and Relinquishment for Adoption in the United States." *Vital and Health Statistics of the Centers for Disease Control and Prevention* 306. Hyattsville, MD: National Center for Health Statistics.

Chedraui, Peter. 2008. "Pregnancy among Young Adolescents: Trends, Risk Factors, and Maternal-Perinatal Outcome." *Journal of Perinatal Medicine* 36(3): 256–59.

Christian-Smith, Linda K. 1995. "Young Women and Their Dream Lovers." In *Sexual Cultures and the Construction of Adolescent Identities*, ed. Janice M. Irvine, 206–27.Philadelphia, PA: Temple University Press.

Cocozzelli, Carmelo. 1989. "Predicting the Decision of Biological Mothers to Retain or Relinquish Their Babies for Adoption: Implications for Open Placement." *Child Welfare* 68: 33–44.

Codega, Susan A., B. Kay Pasley, and Jill Kreutzer. 1990. "Coping Behaviors of Adolescent Mothers: An Exploratory Study and Comparison of Mexican-Americans and Anglos." *Journal of Adolescent Research* 5: 34–53.

Coleman, James Samuel. 1961. The Adolescent Society: The Social Life of the Teenager and Its Impact on Education. New York: The Free Press.

Coleman, Priscilla K. 2005. "Resolution of Unwanted Pregnancy during Adolescence through Abortion versus Childbirth: Individual and Family Predictors and Psychological Consequences." *Journal of Youth and Adolescence* 35: 903–11.

D'Emilio, John, and Estelle Freedman. 1988. *Intimate Matters: A History of Sexuality in America*. New York: Harper and Row.

Dangal, Ganesh. 2006. "An Update on Teenage Pregnancy." *Internet Journal of Gynecology & Obstetrics* 5(1): 3.

de Anda, Diane, and Rosina M. Becerra. 1984. "Social Networks for Adolescent Mothers." *Social Casework: The Journal of Contemporary Social Work* 65: 172–81.

de Anda, Diane, Rosina M. Becerra, and Eve P. Fielder. 1988. "Sexuality, Pregnancy, and Motherhood among Mexican-American Adolescents." *Journal of Adolescent Research* 3: 403–11.

Dellman-Jenkins, Mary, Susan Hagey Sattler, and Rhonda A. Richardson. 1993. "Adolescent Parenting: A Positive, Intergenerational Approach." *Families in Society* 74: 590–601.

Denzin, Norman K. 1973. *Children and Their Caretakers*. New Brunswick, NJ: Transaction Books.

Denzin, Norman K, and Yvonna S. Lincoln. 1994. "Introduction: Entering the Field of Qualitative Research." In *Handbook of Qualitative Research*, ed. Norman K. Denzin and Yvonna S. Lincoln, 1–18. Thousand Oaks, CA: Sage.

Eder, Donna. 1985. "The Cycle of Popularity: Interpersonal Relations among Female Adolescents." *Sociology of Education* 58: 154–65.

Elster, Arthur B., Michael E. Lamb, Laura Peters, James Kahn, and Jane Tavare. 1987. "Judicial Involvement and Conduct Problems of Fathers of Infants Born to Adolescent Mothers." *Pediatrics* 79: 230–34.

Emerson, Robert M., ed. 1988. *Contemporary Field Research: A Collection of Readings*. Prospect Heights, IL: Waveland Press.

Farber, Naomi. 1989. "The Significance of Aspirations among Unmarried Adolescent Mothers." *The Social Service Review* 63:4: 518–32.

Farber, Naomi. 1991. "The Process of Pregnancy Resolution among Adolescent Mothers." *Adolescence* 26: 697–716.

Fasick, Frank. A. 1984. "Parents, Peers, Youth Culture, and Autonomy in Adolescence." *Adolescence* 19: 143–57.

Fergusson, David M., and Lianne J. Woodward. 2000. Teenage Pregnancy and Female Educational Underachievement: A Prospective Study of a New Zealand Birth Cohort. *Journal of Marriage and the Family* 62: 147–61.

Field, Tiffany, Susan M. Widmayer, Sharon Stringer, and Edward Ignatoff. 1980. "Teenage, Lower-Class Black Mothers and Their Preterm Infants: An Intervention and Developmental Follow-Up." *Child Development* 51: 426–36.

Fields, Jessica. 2005. "'Children Having Children': Race, Innocence, and Sexuality Education." *Social Problems* 52(4): 549–71.

Fine, Gary Alan. 2004. "Adolescence as Cultural Toolkit: High School Debate and the Repertoires of Childhood and Adulthood." *The Sociological Quarterly* 45(1): 1–20.

Fischman, Susan H. 1975. "The Pregnancy-Resolution Decisions of Unwed Adolescents." *The Nursing Clinics of North America* 10: 217–27.

Furstenberg, Frank F. 2007a. *Destinies of the Disadvantaged: The Politics of Teen Childbearing*. New York: Russell Sage Foundation.

Furstenberg, Frank F. 2007b. "Teenage Mothers in Later Life (and the Researchers Who Study Them)." *Contexts* 6(3): 78–79.

Furstenberg, Frank F., J. Brooks-Gunn, and S. Philip Morgan. 1987a. *Adolescent Mothers in Later Life*. New York: Cambridge University Press.

Furstenberg, Frank F., J. Brooks-Gunn, and S. Philip Morgan. 1987b. "Adolescent Mothers and Their Children in Later Life." *Family Planning Perspectives* 19: 142–51.

Furstenberg Jr., Frank F. 1988. "Good Dads-Bad Dads: Two Faces of Fatherhood." In *The Changing American Family and Public Policy*, ed. Andrew J. Cherlin, 193–218. Washington, DC: Urban Institute Press.

Furstenberg Jr., Frank F. 1991. "As the Pendulum Swings: Teenage Childbearing and Social Concern." *Family Relations* 40: 127–38.

Garcia-Coll, Cynthia, Janet L. Surrey, and Kaethe Weingarten. 1998. *Mothering against the Odds: Diverse Voices of Contemporary Mothers*. New York: The Guilford Press.

Gecas, Viktor, and F. Ivan Nye. 1974. "Sex and Class Differences in Parent-Child Interaction: A Test of Kohn's Hypothesis." *Journal of Marriage and the Family* 36: 742–49.

Geronimous, Arlene T. 1987. "On Teenage Childbearing and Neonatal Mortality in the United States." *Population and Development Review* 13: 245–79.

Geronimous, Arlene T., and Sanders Korenman. 1992. "The Socioeconomic Consequences of Teen Childbearing Reconsidered." *Quarterly Journal of Economics* 107: 1187–1214.

Gershenson, Harold P. 1983. "Redefining Fatherhood in Families with White Adolescent Mothers." *Journal of Marriage and the Family* 45: 591–99.

Gilligan, Carol. 1990. "Teaching Shakespeare's Sister: Notes from the Underground of Female Adolescence." In *Making Connections: The Relational Worlds of Adolescent Girls at Emma Willard School*, ed. Carol Gilligan, Nona P. Lyons, and Trudy J. Hanner, 6–29. Cambridge, MA: Harvard University Press.

Glaser, Barney, and Anselm Strauss. 1967. *The Discovery of Grounded Theory*. Chicago, IL: Aldine.

Glesne, Corrine, and Alan Peshkin. 1992. *Becoming Qualitative Researchers: An Introduction*. White Plains, NY: Longman.

Goffman, Erving. 1959. *The Presentation of Self in Everday Life*. New York: Anchor Books.

Goffman, Erving. 1963. *Stigma: Notes on the Management of Spoiled Identity*. Englewood Cliffs, NJ: Prentice Hall.

Gold, Raymond L. 1969. "Roles in Sociological Field Observation." In *Issues in Participant Observation*, ed. George J. McCall and Jerry L. Simmons, 30–39. Reading, MA: Addison-Wesley.

Guba, Egon G., and Yvonna S. Lincoln. 1994. "Competing Paradigms in Qualitative Research." In *Handbook of Qualitative Research*, ed. Norman K. Denzin and Yvonna S. Lincoln, 105–17. Thousand Oaks, CA: Sage.

Hamilton, Brady E., Joyce A. Martin, and Stephanie J. Ventura. 2007. "Births: Preliminary Data for 2006." *National Vital Statistics Report, Centers for Disease Control and Prevention* 56:7. Hyattsville, MD: National Center for Health Statistics.

Hamilton, Brady E., Arialdi M. Miniño, Joyce A. Martin, Kenneth D. Kochanek, Donna M. Strobino, and Bernard Guyer. 2008. "Annual Summary of Vital Statistics: 2005." *Pediatrics* 119: 345–60.

Hansen, Laura B., and Elizabeth Jacob. 1992. "Intergenerational Support during the Transition to Parenthood: Issues for New Parents and Grandparents." *Families in Society* 73: 471–79.

Hardy, Janet B., Anne K. Duggan, Katya Masnyk, and Carol Pearson. 1989. "Fathers of Children Born to Young Urban Mothers." *Family Planning Perspectives* 21: 159–63.

Henshaw, Stanley K. 1997. "Teenage Abortion and Pregnancy Statistics by State, 1992." *Family Planning Perspectives* 29: 115–22.

Henshaw, Stanley K. 1998. "Unintended Pregnancy in the United States." *Family Planning Perspectives* 30: 24–29, 46.

Hochschild, Arlie. 1989. *The Second Shift*. New York: Avon Books.

Hofferth, Sandra L. 1987. "The Children of Teenage Childbearers." In *Risking the Future: Adolescent Sexuality, Pregnancy, and Childbearing*, vol. 2, ed. S. L. Hofferth and C. D. Haynes, 174–206. Washington, DC: National Academy Press.

Hofferth, Sandra L., and Kristin A. Moore. 1979. "Early Childbearing and Later Economic Well-Being." *American Sociological Review* 44: 784–815.

Hofferth, Sandra L., Lori Reid, and Frank L. Mott. 2001. The Effects of Early Childbearing on Schooling over Time. *Family Planning Perspectives* 33: 259–67.

Hoffman, Samuel D., E. Michael Foster, and Frank F. Furstenberg. 1993. "Reevaluating the Costs of Teenage Childbearing." *Demography* 30: 1–13.

Horowitz, Ruth. 1986. "Remaining an Outsider: Membership as a Threat to Research Rapport." *Urban Life* 14: 409–430.

Horowitz, Ruth. 1995. *Teen Mothers: Citizens or Dependents?* Chicago, IL: University of ChicagoPress.

Hoyt, Helina H., and Betty L. Broom. 2002. "School-Based Teen Pregnancy Prevention Programs: A Review of the Literature." *Journal of School Nursing* 18(1): 11–17.

Hughes, Everett. 1945. "Dilemmas and Contradictions of Status." *American Journal of Sociology* 50: 353–59.

Jacobs, Janet. 1994. "Gender, Race, Class, and the Trend toward Early Motherhood: A Feminist Analysis of Teen Mothers in Contemporary Society." *Journal of Contemporary Ethnography* 22: 442–62.

Jaffee, Sara R. 2002. "Pathways to Adversity in Young Adulthood among Early Childbearers." *Journal of Family Psychology* 16(1): 38–49.

Jones, Rachel K., Mia R. S. Zolda, Stanley K. Henshaw, and Lawrence B. Finer. 2008. "Abortion in the United States: Incidence and Access to Services, 2005." *Perspectives on Sexual and Reproductive Health* 40(1): 6–16.

Jorgensen, Danny L. 1989. *Participant Observation: A Methodology for Human Studies.* Newbury Park, CA: Sage.

Kahn, Janet. 1994. "Speaking across Cultures within Your Own Family." In *Sexual Cultures and the Construction of Adolescent Identities*, ed. Janice M. Irvine, 285–309. Philadelphia, PA: Temple University Press.

Kalab, Kathleen A. 1987. "Student Vocabularies of Motive: Accounts for Absence." *Symbolic Interaction* 10: 71–83.

Kaplan, Elaine Bell. 1997. *Not Our Kind of Girl: Unraveling the Myths of Black Teenage Motherhood.* Berkeley: University of California Press.

Kelly, Deirde M. 1998. "Teacher Discourses about a Young Parents Program: The Many Meanings of 'Good' Choices." *Education and Urban Society* 30(2): 224–41.

Kinney, David A. 1993. "From Nerds to Normals: The Recovery of Identity among Adolescents from Middle School to High School." *Sociology of Education* 66: 21–40.

Kirby, Richard, and Jay Corzine. 1981. "The Contagion of Stigma: Fieldwork among Deviants." *Qualitative Sociology* 4: 3–20.

Kirkman, Maggie, Lyn Harrison, Lynne Hillier, and Priscilla Pyett. 2001. "'I Know I'm Doing a Good Job': Canonical and Autobiographical Narratives of Teenage Mothers." *Culture, Health, & Sexuality* 3(3): 279–94.

Kisker, Ellen Eliason, Rebecca A. Maynard, Anu Rangarajan, and Kimberly Boller. 1998. *Moving Teenage Parents into Self-Sufficiency: Lessons from Recent Demonstrations   Final Report* Princeton, NJ: Mathematica Policy Research.

Kohn, Melvin L. 1963. "Social Class and Parent-Child Relationships: An Interpretation." *The American Journal of Sociology* 48: 471–80.

Kohn, Melvin L. 1969. *Class and Conformity: A Study in Values*. Homewood, IL: Dorsey.

Montgomery. 1983. "Teenage Pregnancy: Family Syndrome?" *Adolescence* 18: 679–94.

Ladner, Joyce A. 1972. *Tomorrow's Tomorrow: The Black Woman*. New York: Anchor Books.

Landy, Sarah, Jacquelin S. Montgomery, Josef Schubert, John F. Cleland, and Camilla Clark. 1983. "Mother-infant interaction of teenage mothers and the effect of experience in the observational sessions on the development of their infants." *Early Child Development and Care*, Volume 10 (Issue 2–3): 165–86.

Lauer, Rebecca J. 1981. "Fourteenth Amendment—Statutory Rape: Protection of Minor Female and Prosecution of Minor Male." *The Journal of Criminal Law and Criminology* 72: 1374–92.

Leahy, Terry. 1994. "Taking Up a Position: Discourses of Femininity and Adolescence in the Context of Man/Girl Relationships." *Gender & Society* 8: 48–72.

Leigh, Barbara C., Diane M. Morrison, Karen Trocki, and Mark T. Temple. 1994. "Sexual Behavior of American Adolescents: Results from a U.S. National Survey." *Journal of Adolescent Health* 15: 117–25.

LeMasters, E. E., and John DeFrain. 1983. *Parents in Contemporary America: A Sympathetic View*. Homewood, IL: Dorsey.

Lemay, Celeste A., Dianne S. Elfenbeing, Suzanne B. Cashman, and Marianne E. Felice. 2008. "The Body Mass Index of Teen Mothers and Their Toddler Children." *Maternal and Child Health Journal* 12(1): 112–19.

Lofland, John, and Lyn Lofland. 1995. *Analyzing Social Settings*. 3rd ed. Belmont, CA: Wadsworth.

Luker, Kristin. 1975. *Taking Chances: Abortion and the Decision Not to Contracept*. Berkeley: University of California Press.

Luker, Kristin. 1996. *Dubious Conceptions: The Politics of Teenage Pregnancy*. Cambridge, MA: Harvard University Press.

Luster, Tom, Kelly Rhoades, and Bruce Haas. 1989. "The Relation between Parental Values and Parenting Behavior: A Test of the Kohn Hypothesis." *Journal of Marriage and the Family* 51: 139–47.

Mandell, Nancy. 1988. "The Least-Adult Role in Studying Children." *Journal of Contemporary Ethnography* 16: 433–67.

Manlove, Jennifer. 1998. "The Influence of High School Dropout and School Disengagement on the Risk of SchoolAge Pregnancy." *Jour-*

nal of Research on Adolescence 8: 187–220.

Manlove, Jennifer, Cassandra Logan, Kristin A. Moore, and Erum Ikramullah. 2008. "Pathways from Family Religiosity to Adolescent Sexual Activity and Contraceptive Use." *Perspectives on Sexual and Reproductive Health* 40(2): 105–17.

Marini, Margaret Mooney. 1984. "Women's Educational Attainment and the Timing of Entry into Parenthood." *American Sociological Review* 49: 491–511.

Marsiglio, William. 1987. "Adolescent Fathers in the United States: Their Initial Living Arrangements, Marital Experience, and Educational Outcomes." *Family Planning Perspectives* 19: 240–51.

Marsiglio, William, and Elizabeth G. Menaghan. 1990. "Pregnancy Resolution and Family Formation: Understanding Gender Differences in Adolescents' Preferences and Beliefs." *Journal of Family Issues* 11: 313–33.

Martin, Joyce A., Brady E. Hamilton, Paul D. Sutton, Stephanie J. Ventura, Fay Menacker, Sharon Kirmeyer, and Martha L. Munson. 2007. *Births: Final Data for 2005*. National Vital Statistics Reports 56:6. Hyattsville, MD: National Center for Health Statistics.

Maynard, Rebecca, ed. 1996. *Kids Having Kids: A Robin Hood Foundation Special Report on the Costs of Adolescent Childbearing*. New York: Robin Hood Foundation.

McCabe, Donald L. 1992. "The Influence of Situational Ethics on Cheating among College Students." *Sociological Inquiry* 62: 365–74.

Miller, Brent C., and Kristen A. Moore. 1990. "Adolescent Sexual Behavior, Pregnancy, and Parenting: Research through the 1980s." *Journal of Marriage and the Family* 52: 1025–44.

Mills, C. Wright. 1940. "Situated Actions and Vocabularies of Motive." *American Sociological Review* 5: 904–13.

Mindel, Charles H. 1980. "Extended Familialism among Urban Mexican Americans, Anglos, and Blacks." *Hispanic Journal of Social Sciences* 2: 21–34.

Mirande, Alfredo. 1977. "The Chicano Family: A Reanalysis of Conflicting Views. *Journal of Marriage and the Family* 39: 747–56.

Monmouth University/Gannet New Jersey Poll. 2008. *Jersey Views on Teen Pregnancy and Sex Ed*. West Long Beach, NJ: Monmouth University Polling Institute.

Moore, Kristin A. 1990. *Facts at a Glance 1990*. Washington, DC: Child Trends.

Mott, Frank L., and R. Jean Haurin. 1988. "Linkages between Sexual Activity and Alcohol and Drug Use among American Adolescents." *Family Planning Perspectives* 20: 128–36.

Nathanson, Constance A. 1991. *Dangerous Passage: The Social Control of Sexuality in Women's Adolescence*. Philadelphia, PA: Temple University Press.

Newcomer, Susan F., and Richard Udry. 1985. "Parent-Child Communication and Adolescent Sexual Behavior." *Family Planning Perspectives* 17: 169–74.

Oberman, Michelle. 1994. "Turning Girls into Women: Re-Evaluating Modern Statutory Rape Law." *The Journal of Criminal Law and Criminology* 85: 15–79.

Odem, Mary E. 1995. "Statutory Rape and Prosecutions in California." In *Delinquent Daughters: Protecting and Policing Adolescent Female Sexuality in the United States, 1885–1920*, ed. Mary E. Odem, 63–81. Chapel Hill: University of North Carolina Press.

Ortiz, Elizabeth Thompson, and Betty Z. Bassoff. 1987. "Adolescent Welfare Mothers: Lost Optimism and Lowered Expectations." *Social Casework* 68: 400–405.

Oz, Sheri, and Marshall Fine. 1991. "Family Relationship Patterns: Perceptions of Teenage Mothers and Their NonMother Peers." *Journal of Adolescence* 14: 293–304.

Paasch, Kathleen M., and Jay D. Teachman. 1991. "Gender of Children and Receipt of Assistance from Absent Fathers." *Journal of Family Issues* 12: 450–66.

Pearl, Arthur. 1981. "A Phenomenological Cost-Benefit Analysis Approach to Adolescence." In *Parent-Child Interaction: Theory, Research, and Prospects*, ed. R. W. Henderson, 293–323. San Francisco: Academic Press.

Phipps, Maureen G., Cynthia Rosengard, Sherry Weitzen, Ann Meers, and Zoe Billinkoff. 2008. "Age Group Differences among Pregnant Adolescents: Sexual Behavior, Health Habits, and Contraceptive Use." *Journal of Pediatric & Adolescent Gynecology* 21:1: 9–15.

Phoenix, Ann. 1991. *Young Mothers?* Oxford: Polity Press.

Polit, D. F. 1989. "Effects of a Comprehensive Program for Teenage Mothers: Five Years after Project Redirection." *Family Planning Perspectives* 21: 169–87.

Punch, Maurice. 1994. "Politics and Ethics in Qualitative Research." In *Handbook of Qualitative Research*, ed. Norman K. Denzin and Yvonna S. Lincoln, 83–98. Thousand Oaks, CA: Sage.

Rauch-Elnekave, Helen. 1994. "Teenage Motherhood: Its Relationship to Undetected Learning Problems." *Adolescence* 29: 91–103.

Ray, Melvin C., and Ronald L. Simons. 1987. "Convicted Murderers' Accounts of Their Crime: A Study of Homicide in Small Communities." *Symbolic Interaction* 10: 57–70.

Reis, Janet S., and Elicia J. Herz. 1987. "Correlates of Adolescent Parenting." *Adolescence* 22: 599–609.

Rhode, Deborah R. 1993–1994. "Adolescent Pregnancy and Public Policy." *Political Science Quarterly* 108(4): 635–69.

Richardson, Rhonda A., Nancy Benham Barbour, and Donald L. Bubenzer. 1991. "Bittersweet Connections: Informal Social Networks as Sources of Support and Interference for Adolescent Mothers." *Family Relations* 40: 430–34.

Rindfuss, Ronald R., Larry Bumpass, and Craig St. John. 1980. "Education and Fertility: Implications for the Roles Women Occupy." *American Sociological Review* 45: 431–47.

Robinson, Bryan E. 1988. *Teenage Fathers*. Lexington, MA: D.C. Heath and Company.

Rolfe, Alison. 2008. "'You've Got to Grow Up When You've Got a Kid': Marginalized Young Women's Accounts of Motherhood." *Journal of Community and Applied Social Psychology* 18: 299–314.

Roosa, Mark W. 1986. "Adolescent Mothers, School Drop-Outs, and School-Based Intervention Programs." *Family Relations* 35: 313–17.

Roosa, Mark W. 1991. "Adolescent Pregnancy Programs Collection: An Introduction." *Family Relations* 40: 370–72.

Roosa, Mark W., and Linda Vaughan. 1984. "A Comparison of Teenage and Older Mothers with Preschool-Age Children." *Family Relations* 33: 259–65.

Rossi, Alice S. 1968. "Transition to Parenthood." *Journal of Marriage and the Family* 30: 26–39.

Rothman, Jack, Larry M. Grant, and Stephen A. Hnat. 1985. "Mexican-American FamilyCulture." *Social Service Review* 59: 197–215.

Rubin, Valerie, and Patricia L. East. 2008. "Adolescents' Pregnancy Intentions: Relations to Life Situations and Caretaking Behaviors Prenatally and 2 Years Postpartum." *Journal of Adolescent Health* 24: 313–20.

Ruddick, Sara. 1993. "Procreative Choice for Adolescent Women." In *The Politics of Pregnancy: Adolescent Sexuality and Public Policy*, ed. Annette Lawson and Deborah L. Rhode, 126–43. New Haven, CT: Yale University Press.

Russo, Nancy. 1976. "The Motherhood Mandate." *The Journal of Social Issues* 32: 143–53.

Sangalang, Bernadette B. 2006. "Teenage Mothers in Parenting Programs: Exploring Welfare Outcomes during Early Transition to Parenthood." *Families in Society* 87(1): 105–11.

Santelli, John S., Joyce Abma, Stephanie Ventura, Laura Lindberg, Brian Morrow, John E. Anderson, Sheryl Lyss, and Brady E. Hamilton.

2004. "Can Changes in Sexual Behaviors mong High School Students Explain the Decline in Teen Pregnancy Rates in the 1990s?" *Journal of Adolescent Health* 35: 80–90.

Schamess, Stephanie. 1993. "The Search for Love: Unmarried Adolescent Mothers' Views of, and Relationships with, Men." *Adolescence* 28: 425–38.

Schofield, Gillian. 1994. *The Youngest Mothers*. Brookfield, VT: Ashgate.

Scott, Marvin B., and Stanford M. Lyman. 1968. "Accounts." *American Sociological Review* 33: 46–62.

Scully, Diana, and Joseph Marolla. 1984. "Convicted Rapists' Vocabulary of Motives: Excuses and Justifications." *Social Problems* 31: 530–44.

Segura, Denise. 1984. "Labor Market Stratification: The Chicana Experience." *Berkeley Journal of Sociology* 29: 57–91.

Segura, Denise A., and Jennifer L. Pierce. 1993. "Chicana/o Family Structure and Gender Personality: Chodorow, Familism, and Psychoanalytic Sociology Revisited." *Signs* 19: 62–91.

Shapiro, Janet R., and Sarah C. Mangelsdorf. 1994. "The Determinants of Parenting Competence in Adolescent Mothers." *Journal of Youth and Adolescence* 23: 621–41.

Smith, Ernest A. 1962. *American Youth Culture: Group Life in Teenage Society*. New York: The Free Press.

SmithBattle, Lee. 2007. "Legacies of Advantage and Disadvantage: The Case of Teen Mothers." *Public Health Nursing* 24: 409–20.

Solinger, Rickie. 1992. *Wake Up Little Susie: Single Pregnancy and Race before Roe v. Wade*. New York: Routledge.

Sorensen, Elaine. 1997. "A National Profile of Nonresident Fathers and Their Ability to Pay Child Support." *Journal of Marriage and the Family* 59: 785–97.

South, Scott J. 1991. "Sociodemographic Differentials in Mate Selection Preferences." *Journal of Marriage and the Family* 53: 928–40.

Stokes, Randall, and John P. Hewitt. 1976. "Aligning Actions." *American Sociological Review* 41: 839–49.

Stone, Rebecca, and Cynthia Waszak. 1992. "Adolescent Knowledge and Attitudes about Abortion." *Family Planning Perspectives* 24: 52–57.

Studer, Marlena, and Arland Thornton. 1987. "Adolescent Religiosity and Contraceptive Usage." *Journal of Marriage and the Family* 49: 117–28.

Sullivan, Mercer L. 1989. "Absent Fathers in the Inner City." *Annals of the American Academy for Political and Social Science* 501: 48–58.

Sung, Kyu-taik and Dorothy Rothrock. 1980. "An Alternate School for Pregnant Teenagers and Teenage Mothers." *Child Welfare* 59:7: 427–36.

Swanson, Nancy. 1988. "Infant Feeding Patterns of Teenage Mothers in a Small New England Town." *International Journal of Sociology of the Family* 18: 249–82.

Swenson, Ingrid, Deanne Erickson, Edward Ehlinger, Gertrude Carlson, and Sheldon Swaney. 1989. "Fertility, Menstrual Characteristics, and Contraceptive Practices among White, Black, and Southeast Asian Refugee Adolescents." *Adolescence* 24: 647–54.

Swidler, Ann. 1986. "Culture in Action: Symbols and Strategies." *American Sociological Review* 51: 273–86.

Sykes, Gresham M., and David Matza. 1957. "Techniques of Neutralization: A Theory of Delinquency." *American Sociological Review* 22: 664–70.

Teti, Douglas M., and Michael E. Lamb. 1986. "Sex-Role Learning and Adolescent Fatherhood." In *Adolescent Fatherhood*, ed. Arthur B. Elster and Michael E. Lamb, ch. 2. Hillsdale, NJ: Lawrence Erlbaum.

Teti, Douglas M., and Michael E. Lamb. 1989. "Socioeconomic and Marital Outcomes of Adolescent Marriage, Adolescent Childbirth, and Their Co-occurrence." *Journal of Marriage & Family* 51:1: 203–12.

Thompson, Maxine Seaborn. 1986. "The Influence of Supportive Relations on the Psychological Well-Being of Teenage Mothers." *Social Forces* 64: 1006–22.

Thompson, Sharon. 1995. *Going All the Way: Teenage Girls' Tales of Sex, Romance, and Pregnancy.* New York: Hill and Wang.

Thornberry, Terence P., Carolyn A. Smith, and Gregory J. Howard. 1997. "Risk Factors for Teenage Fatherhood." *Journal of Marriage and the Family* 59: 505–22.

Tolman, Deborah L. 1994. "Doing Desire: Adolescent Girls' Struggles for/with Sexuality." *Gender & Society* 8: 324–42.

Trent, Katherine, and Kyle Crowder. 1997. "Adolescent Birth Intentions, Social Disadvantage, and Behavioral Outcomes." *Journal of Marriage and the Family* 59: 523–35.

Trussell, James, and Kathryn Kost. 1987. "Contraceptive Failure in the United States: A Critical Review of the Literature." *Studies in Family Planning* 18:5: 237–83.

Upchurch, Dawn M., and James M. McCarthy. 1990. "The Timing of a First Birth and High School Completion." *American Sociological Review* 55: 224–34.

Van Maanen, John. 1992. "The Moral Fix: On the Ethics of Fieldwork." In *Contemporary Field Research: A Collection of Readings*, ed. Robert M. Emerson, 269–87. Prospect Heights, IL: Waveland Press.

Vaz, Rosalind, Paul Smolen, and Charlene Miller. 1983. "Adolescent

Pregnancy: Involvement of the Male Partner." *Journal of Adolescent Health Care* 4: 246–50.

Vulkelich, Carol, and Deborah S. Kliman. 1985. "Mature and Teenage Mothers' Infant Growth Expectations and Use of Child Development Information Sources." *Family Relations* 34: 189–96.

Wax, Rosalie. 1979. "Gender and Age in Fieldwork and Fieldwork Education: No Good Thing Is Done By Any Man Alone." *Social Problems* 26: 509–22.

Weinman, Maxine, Maralyn Robinson, Jane T. Simmons, Nelda B. Schreiber, and Ben Stafford. 1989. "Pregnant Teens: Differential Pregnancy Resolution and Treatment Implications." *Child Welfare* 68: 45–55.

Wharton, Carol S. 1991. "Why Can't We Be Friends? Expectations versus Experiences in the Volunteer Role." *Journal of Contemporary Ethnography* 20: 79–106.

White, Merry I. 1993. *The Material Child: Coming of Age in Japan and America*. New York: The Free Press.

Wright, James D., and Sonia R. Wright. 1976. "Social Class and Parental Values for Children: A Partial Replication and Extension of the Kohn Hypothesis." *American Sociological Review* 41: 527–37.

Zabin, Laurie Schwab, Nan Marie Astone, and Mark R. Emerson. 1993. "Do Adolescents Want Babies? The Relationship between Attitudes and Behavior." *Journal of Research on Adolescence* 3: 67–86.

Zongker, Calvin E. 1977. "The Self-Concept of Pregnant Adolescent Girls." *Adolescence* 12: 477–88.

INDEX

Abortion
    Pressure from parents to have,
      66–67
    Teen mothers' perceptions of, 65
    Trends, 1, 70
Accounts, 105–107
    Sequential relationship between jus-
    tifications and excuses, 123–124
Acock, Alan, 58, 72, 166
Adams, Gina, 2, 160
Adams-Taylor, Sharon, 2, 160
Adoption
    Changing mind about, 70
    Pressure from parents to relinquish,
      66–67
    Teen mothers' perceptions of, 65
    Trends, 1, 70
Age
    Influences on Teen Center culture,
      159–163
    Pregnancy resolution decisions,
      72–73
    Reaction to pregnancy, 50
    Teens' feeling of superiority over
      older mothers, 85–87
    Use of contraception, 41
Albin, Rochelle, 112
Anderson, Elijah, 165
Astone, Nan Marie, 3, 49

Barbour, Nancy, 149
Barret, Robert, 89, 100
Barth, Richard, 1, 65
Bassoff, Betty, 76, 134
Becerra, Rosina, 47, 149
Blumer, Herbert, 8, 9, 30
Boyfriends. *See also* Fathers of teens'
    children
    Contraceptive use, 43–44, 50
    Reaction to pregnancy, 68–69
    Romantic script, 46
    Statutory rape, 4
Bracken, Maryann, 59, 65
Bracken, Michael, 59, 65
Bralock, Anita, 44
Brazzell, Jan, 58, 72, 166
Brooks-Gunn, J. 3, 4, 7
Bubenzer, Donald, 149
Bumpass, Larry, 3, 53
Burt, Martha, 112

Carlip, Hillary, 86, 87
Cervera, Neil, 70, 72
Children of teenage parents
    Life outcomes, 4
    Seen as reflecting teenage mothers'
      successful parenting, 76–82
Christian-Smith, Linda, 110
Clark, Camilla, 90, 158

191

Cleland, John, 90, 158
Codega, Susan, 146, 168
Coleman, James, 163
Contraception
    Access to, 41–43
    Accounts for use, 45
    Age, 41
    Boyfriends' influence on use, 43–44, 50
    Communication with parents about, 41
    Embarrassment in using, 41–42
    Failure of methods, 39, 44–46
    Intentional avoidance of, 46, 49, 52
    Irregular use, 40
    Lack of knowledge about, 41–42
    Obstacles to use, 40–44
    Religion and, 42
    Risk-taking, 40, 45–46
    Trends in adolescent use of, 40–41
Crowder, Kyle, 39, 40
Culture, 8
    Age influences on, 159–163
    Anti-abortion, anti-choice stance, 65–67
    Attitudes toward drug, alcohol, and tobacco, 149
    Competitive nature of Teen Center culture, 75
    Consequences of Teen Center culture, 169–171
Cultural toolkit, 8, 49
    Gender influences on, 163–167
    Race/ethnicity influences on, 167–169

de Anda, Diane, 47, 149
Dellman-Jenkins, Mary, 139
Denzin, Norman, 16, 30, 80
Drug and alcohol use
    Among teen mothers, 146–149
    Among teens before parenthood, 147–149

East, Patricia, 47

Education
    Difficulties in school prior to pregnancy, 53
    Dropping out, 3, 10, 53
    High school graduation rates for teenage mothers, 10
    Outcomes for pregnant/parenting teens, 2–3, 139, 142–146
    School-based programs for pregnant/parenting teens, 6–7
    Title IX, 3
Emerson, Mark, 49
Emerson, Robert, 15, 16
Employment
    Career plans of teen parents, 145–146

Family of origin
    Fear of sharing news of pregnancy with, 57–61
    Influence in pregnancy resolution decision, 72
    Reactions to pregnancy, 58–65
    Relationships with fathers, 157–158
    Relationships with fathers vs. mothers, 59–61, 64–65, 90, 96, 101
    Relationships with mothers, 154–158
Farber, Naomi, 57, 58, 65, 67, 68, 72, 73, 142, 146
Fathers of teen's children. See also Boyfriends
    Age relative to teen mother, 89
    Disciplining children, 101–103
    Disinterest in fatherhood, 92–95
    Enthusiasm about fatherhood, 90–92, 96–97
    Providing financial support, 99–101
Fielder, Eve, 47, 149
Fine, Gary, 162
Fine, Marshall, 90, 158
Fischman, Susan, 52, 70, 164
Friends
    Before vs. after parenthood, 149–154

Friendship
    Among Teen Center participants,
        150–154
Furstenberg, Frank, 2, 3, 4, 7, 10, 39,
    68, 90, 139, 142

Gender
    Influence on Teen Center culture,
        163–167
Gershenson, Harold, 93, 103
Gilligan, Carol, 163
Glaser, Barney, 30, 31, 36

Harrison, Lyn, 158
Haurin, R. Jean, 147
Hillier, Lynne, 158
Hochschild, Arlie, 98
Horowitz, Ruth, 7, 18, 76, 77, 78, 79,
    81, 83, 86, 128, 131

Identity shifts, 140–142

Jacobs, Janet, 39, 142, 146, 154
Jaffee, Sara, 4, 5, 167
Jorgensen, Danny, 23, 25, 27

Kahn, Janet, 41, 58
Kalab, Kathleen, 106
Kaplan, Elaine, 5
Kelly, Deirde, 7
Kirkman, Maggie, 158
Klerman, Lorraine, 59, 65
Kliman, Deborah, 80
Kohn, Melvin, 166
Koniak-Griffin, Deborah, 44
Kreutzer, Jill, 146, 168

Ladner, Joyce, 164
Lamb, Michael, 3, 92, 165
Landy, Sarah, 90, 158
Leahy, Terry, 164
Luker, Kristin, 1, 2, 3, 4, 40, 41, 42,
    43, 45, 48, 49, 167
Lyman, Stanford, 42, 106, 111, 113,
    123, 124

Mandell, Nancy, 25
Marolla, Joseph, 106
Matza, David, 105
McCarthy, James, 3, 10, 53, 139
Miller, Brent, 40, 41, 45, 48, 76, 90
Mills, C. Wright, 105
Mindel, Charles, 168
Montgomery, Jacquelin, 90
Moore, Kristin, 3, 4, 40, 41, 45, 48,
    76
Morgan, S. Philip, 3, 4, 7
Motherhood as positive status, 53
Mott, Frank, 3, 10, 147

Nathanson, Constance, 1, 4, 5, 40
Newcomer, Susan, 41

Ortiz, Elizabeth, 76, 134
Oz, Sheri, 90, 158

Parenting styles (teens')
    Advice, accepting or rejecting, 82–85
    Competitive, 75–87
    Demonstrating financial independ-
        ence, 76–79
    Emphasizing child's development,
        80–82
    Proving competence, 75
    "Spoiling" children, 77–78
Pasley, B. Kay, 146, 168
Pierce, Jennifer, 167, 168
Pittman, Karen, 2, 160
Policy implications
    For pregnancy prevention pro-
        grams, 173–174
    For school-based parenting pro-
        grams, 172, 174
    For statutory rape laws, 172–173
    Of teen parenting culture, 171–172
Pregnancy. See Teenage Pregnancy
Punch, Maurice, 26
Pyett, Priscilla, 158

Qualitative research methods. See
    Research

Race/ethnicity
  Contraceptive use, 48
  Influence on Teen Center culture,
    167–169
  Pregnancy intentionality, 47–48
  Pregnancy resolution decisions, 67
  Teen Center participants, 9–10
  Teenage motherhood, 10
  Telling parents about pregnancy, 58
Rauch-Elnekave, Helen, 143
Ray, Melvin, 106
Religion
  Contraceptive use, 42
  Pregnancy resolution decision, 68
Research
  Challenges of studying teenagers,
    31–36
  Data analysis, 30–31
  Data gathering, 29–31
  Data gathering challenges, 31–34
  Establishing rapport with teens,
    18–27
  Ethical issues, 34–36
  Gaining access to the Teen Center,
    16–17
  Interviews, 29
  Key informants, 21–23
  Least-adult role, 25–26
  Leaving the setting, 36–37
  Longitudinal contact with partici-
    pants, 16, 30
  Marginal members of setting, 24
  Participant-observation, 18
  Qualitative research paradigm, 7–9,
    15–16
  Relations with Teen Center staff, 19
  Relations with teens' families and
    significant others, 27–29
  Roles in setting, 18–20, 25
  Teen Center setting, 9–10, 17–18
Rhode, Deborah, 5
Richardson, Rhonda, 139, 149
Rindfuss, Ronald, 3, 53
Robinson, Bryan, 89, 100
Romantic script, 46

Roosa, Mark, 6, 160
Rossi, Alice, 179
Rubin, Valerie, 47
Ruddick, Sara, 40
Russo, Nancy, 164

Sattler, Susan, 139
Schamess, Stephanie, 90, 93, 96
Schofield, Gillian, 51, 57, 58, 61, 86,
  91, 94, 95, 135
School. *See* Education
Schubert, Josef, 90, 158
Scott, Marvin, 42, 106, 111, 113, 123,
  124
Scully, Diana, 106
Segura, Denise, 167, 168
Simons, Ronald, 106
Smolen, Paul, 90
Social marginalization, 4–5
Socioeconomic status
  Relationship to teenage pregnancy
    and parenting, 3, 10
  Teen Center Participants, 10
Solinger, Rickie, 65, 169
Sorensen, Elaine, 100
St. John, Craig, 3, 53
Standards of "good" mothering, 5
Statutory rape, 4
  Laws, 105
  Teens' excuses for, 119–122
  Teens' justifications for, 107–113
  Teens' perceptions of deviance of,
    113–119
Stigma management, 160
  Circumstances of pregnancy and
    parenthood, 73
  Contraceptive failure accounts, 40
  Critiquing older mothers, 85–88
  Deflecting stigma onto abortion
    and adoption, 73
  Deflecting stigma onto baby's
    father, 103
  Excusing and justifying statutory
    rape victimization, 124–125
  Through parenting, 75, 77, 83

Stigmatizing teenage motherhood. *See also* Stigma Management
  General public, 134–137, 160
  Media, 137–138
  Social service agencies, 127–131
  Students and teachers, 131–134
  Welfare dependency, 76
Strauss, Anselm, 30, 31, 36
Studer, Marlena, 42
Sullivan, Mercer, 89, 90, 95
Swanson, Nancy, 79, 81, 83, 84, 85
Swidler, Ann, 8, 49, 159, 162, 164, 175
Sykes, Gresham, 105
Symbolic interactionism, 8–9

Teen Center. *See* Research
Teenage pregnancy
  Accounts provided by teens, 39, 42
  Birthrates, 1
  Consequences for children born to teenage parents, 4
  Consequences for teen mothers, 2, 139–158
  Financial costs, 4
  Intentional vs. Unintentional, 39, 46–49
  Intervention, 6
  Prevention, 6
  Public concern over, 1–5
  Rates, 1

Reactions by parents, 58–65
Reactions by teens, 50–55, 57
Resolution decisions, 1, 57
Telling parents, 51–52, 54, 57–65
Teti, Douglas, 3, 92, 165
Thompson, Sharon 46, 57, 58, 66, 67, 139, 149
Thornton, Arland, 42
Tolman, Deborah, 163
Trent, Katherine, 39, 40

Udry, Richard, 41
Ultrasound, importance of, 71–72
Upchurch, Dawn, 3, 10, 53, 139

Vaz, Rosalind, 90
Vulkelich, Carol, 80

Wax, Rosalie, 26
Welfare
  AFDC, 3
  TANF, 3
  Teenage mothers use of, 76–77, 127
  Teens' perceptions of, 76–77
Wharton, Carol, 6, 7, 22

Zabin, Laurie, 49
Zongker, Calvin, 90, 140, 143, 167, 171